CUT TO THE CHASE

CUT
to the
CHASE

WRITING FEATURE FILMS with the
PROS at **UCLA EXTENSION**
WRITERS' PROGRAM

Edited by Linda Venis, Director, UCLA Extension
Department of the Arts and Writers' Program

GOTHAM BOOKS

GOTHAM BOOKS
Published by the Penguin Group
Penguin Group (USA) Inc., 375 Hudson Street,
New York, New York 10014, USA

USA | Canada | UK | Ireland | Australia | New Zealand | India | South Africa | China
Penguin Books Ltd, Registered Offices: 80 Strand, London WC2R 0RL, England
For more information about the Penguin Group visit penguin.com.

LIBRARY OF CONGRESS CATALOGING-IN-PUBLICATION DATA
has been applied for.

ISBN 978-1-592-40810-8

Printed in the United States of America
1 3 5 7 9 10 8 6 4 2

Set in Adobe Garamond
Designed by Spring Hoteling

CONTENTS

SECTION II
Writing Your First Draft Feature Screenplay

SECTION III
Rewriting Your Feature Screenplay

SECTION IV
Being a Professional in the Movie Business

To Gary

ACKNOWLEDGMENTS

Cut to the Chase: Writing Feature Films with the Pros at UCLA Extension Writers' Program and its companion book, *Inside the Room: Writing Television with the Pros at UCLA Extension Writers' Program,* grew out of creating and refining Writers' Program's film- and television-writing curriculum, in close collaboration with its instructors and staff, for more than two decades. My sincere hope is that these books appropriately thank and honor the expertise, generosity, and contributions of all of the program's screenwriting and creative-writing teachers and staff members—past, present, and future. I have assigned all royalties over to UCLA Extension Writers' Program.

Foremost gratitude goes to Cindy Lieberman, program manager of the Writers' Program, my right-hand person, colleague, and friend who has been *Cut to the Chase* and *Inside the Room*'s most meticulous and dedicated reader. Special appreciation goes to Program Representative in Screenwriting Chae Ko for his helpful comments on every chapter; to Assistant to the Director Carla Janas for her abiding support; and to UCLA Extension Interim Dean Michelle Stiles, whose work on the highest administrative level of this project helped bring it to fruition.

I am indebted to and in awe of four screenwriters whom I call, for lack of a more elegant term, the books' "core authors": Writers' Program instructors Cindy Davis, David Isaacs (now at USC), Steve Mazur, and Billy Mernit. This dream team provided invaluable feedback on the books' content and organization, contributed spectacular sample chapters, and maintained a steadfast commitment to this project that is humbling. My gratitude also goes to the Editorial Board, whose constructive advice and insights, generously rendered, made every chapter better.

Thank you to my agent, Betsy Amster (Betsy Amster Literary Enterprises); Gotham Books/Penguin Group (USA) Executive Editor Lauren Marino; and Emily D. Wunderlich, Susan M. Barnes, and Aja Pollock of Penguin Group for their belief in and support of *Cut to the Chase* and *Inside the Room*. That my name would appear on the same page as the Penguin logo is amazing to me.

To my precious late parents, Grace Bullock Miller and Ashton and Dona Venis; to my "I'm so lucky I married into it" family Leona Berg Town, Alec Berg, and Maggie Trinh; to my dear friends David Bushnell and Karla Klarin; to my talented, kind, and lovely-inside-and-out daughter, Laura Berg; and to my husband, Gary Berg, whom I always love at all times and without whom *Cut to the Chase* and *Inside the Room* would not exist: thank you.

INTRODUCTION

by Linda Venis

Welcome to *Cut to the Chase: Writing Feature Films with the Pros at UCLA Extension Writers' Program*—a truly unprecedented, comprehensive (and entertaining!) guide to writing feature-length screenplays and understanding what it takes to have a successful career as a screenwriter. Whether you dream of writing a screenplay but don't how to begin or you're already writing your script but need some targeted advice, you've opened the right book!

The title, *Cut to the Chase,* comes from the days of silent films, when a chase scene would be inserted to move the plot along, excise anything extraneous, and raise the action to a climactic peak. Taking a cue from those early filmmakers, I'll get right to the point and tell you all the ways this book is a one-of-a-kind resource to screenwriters at all levels.

Real Screenwriters Teach You to Write (and Think!) Like a Pro

Let's start with the three most basic and yet absolutely unique reasons that *Cut to the Chase* stands apart from any other book on screenwriting.

First, it is based on UCLA Extension Writers' Program's screenwriting curriculum, which is the largest and most in-depth in the nation. As screenwriter-director and former student Stuart Beattie (*Pirates of the Caribbean: The Curse of the Black Pearl; Collateral*) describes it: "Writers' Program courses at UCLA Extension offer the best of both worlds: academic excellence and the real-world experience of accomplished screenwriters."

Second, just like the curriculum upon which it is based, *Cut to the Chase* is *process-oriented*. As you work through its lessons, do its exercises, and apply its strategies, you will develop a methodology for thinking and working like a professional screenwriter. While the book is packed with practical, usable advice that guides you to finish your screenplay, you won't be given a simple formula that results in a quick product. Writing a screenplay, as chapter 2 author Jon Bernstein says, is "a journey, not a race. It takes a while, and it's supposed to, so try to learn to embrace and enjoy the process."

Third, *Cut to the Chase* is written by pros whose collective level of professional experience has never before been available in a single volume. They have nearly two dozen produced feature films to their credit, including *Liar Liar, Heartbreakers, Journey to the Center of the Earth, Meet the Robinsons, Asylum,* and the Oscar-winning *Spirited Away,* and have sold projects to Pixar, Working Title, Miramax, Disney, 20th Century Fox, MGM, Warner Bros., and Sony, among many others. Important as well, they are seasoned Writers' Program instructors who have trained thousands of aspiring screenwriters just like you.

Customized Screenwriting Education to Meet Your Goals

Cut to the Chase is designed to reflect the "screenwriting à la carte" nature of the Writers' Program's curriculum, which allows students to customize their own screenwriting education. You can work your way through *Cut to the Chase* linearly and build your skills incrementally, from first idea to final draft. Alternately, you can jump into the book where it best suits your writing goals and needs, as each chapter stands alone.

In addition, *Cut to the Chase* welcomes you back again and again as you continue to develop and refine your craft. The chapters cumulatively embody a layering of knowledge; they are a prism through which craft issues and film examples are examined and reexamined, from different points of view, at different points in the screenwriting process, and with new meaning accruing each time as you grow and refine your own skills.

Your "Bible of Best Practices"

The verb *cut* in *cut to the chase* literally refers to the process—pre-digitally—of cutting and splicing strips of celluloid together to change scenes, locations, or points of view. That's what *Cut to the Chase* does: The chapters *cut* into the complex art and craft of writing a feature film with multiple points of view on the nuts, bolts, subtleties, and nuances of how to do it. "Cut" together, its fifteen chapters capture the fact that the process of writing feature films is dynamic and diverse; there is no "one right way," in the world of professional screenwriting, to come up with a great premise, to map out a plot, or to construct a scene.

Consider one of the most common of screenwriting topics: the three-act structure. Most of *Cut to the Chase*'s authors (and most people who write and sell movies) agree that acts 1, 2, and 3 provide a "ready-made armature," as Billy Mernit calls it in chapter 5, for constructing feature-length stories. You'll read a lot about its many uses in this book—for example, how the protagonist's growth is charted over three acts, and how scene choice and placement within three acts create dramatic movement. That said, you'll also encounter alternate "takes." Dan Vining says, "I think of screenplay structure (and teach it) not in terms of acts, but in the looser terms of the beginning, the middle, and the end." Juliet Aires Gi-glio prefers to divide act 2 in half, making a four-act structure, because ". . . the middle, or the midpoint, is often just as important as the other act breaks."

In this way, *Cut to the Chase* gives you different ways to envision such important feature film writing topics and to sample the complexity of the screenwriting process—all the while knowing, as Cindy Davis says, that "screenwriting tips aren't rules for you to obey; they're tools for you to try." What ultimately emerges is a collection of sophisticated, useful, rooted-in-deep-experience best practices—a bible of best practices.

You Join a Community of Writers

Many people take UCLA Extension courses on-site in Los Angeles, and increasingly, from all points of the globe online—not only to learn how to write screenplays, but to gain a community of like-minded peers to help them along the way. If you are using *Cut to the Chase* in the context of a workshop or writers' group, that's great—you have an instant circle of feedback and support.

But even if you are writing on your own, you're not taking this journey alone. There is a worldwide community of people just like you, yearning to get ideas out of their heads and onto the page. Throughout *Cut to the Chase*, you will feel the authors' *empathy* as they guide you through the process. Describing it as a "marathon," Quinton Peeples assures you that "no one laces up a pair of Nikes on the day of a marathon and decides to run for the first time. We build up to it. We start small and make our way forward, and somehow, some way, we end up crossing the finish line. You can do this. You have everything you need. Now write."

To inspire you, take a look at the community of former Writers' Program students turned professional screenwriters you'll be joining as you seek to combine your talent and perseverance with the training that *Cut to the Chase* provides:

Lee Eisenberg (*Bad Teacher, Year One*); Al Gough and Miles Millar (*Spider-Man 2, Shanghai Knights*); Peter and David Griffiths (*The Hunted, Collateral Damage*); Carol Heikkinen (*Center Stage*); Gavin Hood (*Tsotsi,* Academy Award winner, Best Foreign Language Film); Mark Steven Johnson (*Grumpy Old Men, Daredevil, Ghost Rider*); Melissa Rosenberg (*Twilight*); Randi Mayem Singer (*Mrs. Doubtfire*); David Self (*The Wolfman; The Haunting*); Earl W. Wallace (*Witness,* Academy Award winner, Best Original Screenplay); Kevin Williamson (*Scream*); and Iris Yamashita

(*Letters from Iwo Jima,* Academy Award nominee, Best Original Screenplay), who says, "Before I started taking [Writers' Program] classes, I didn't know a lot about the structure and mechanics of screenwriting. Extension has given me a solid grounding in these skills."

How the Book Is Organized and a Chapter-by-Chapter Road Map

Just like UCLA Extension Writers' Program's feature film writing curriculum, *Cut to the Chase* is divided into "beginning level" chapters ("Section 1: From Idea to Outline: Preparing to Write Your Feature Screenplay"), "intermediate level" chapters ("Section 2: Writing Your First Draft Feature Screenplay"), "advanced level" chapters ("Section 3: Rewriting Your Feature Screenplay"), and "business" chapters ("Section 4: Being a Professional in the Movie Business"). Here's a glimpse into the book's treasure trove of information and insight.

Section 1: From Idea to Outline: Preparing to Write Your Feature Screenplay

In chapter 1 ("Hollywood Storytelling: Its Enduring Appeal and Universal Principles"), **Billy Mernit** introduces aspiring screenwriters who burn "with a passion to tell their own stories" to all the storytelling elements that make up a great Hollywood movie. **Jon Bernstein** (chapter 2, "Jump-starting the Screenplay") launches you on the journey of writing a screenplay by showing you how to generate story ideas; understand the key craft issues of premise, genre, world, tone, and theme; and banish the inner critic.

To tackle screenplay structure, **Andy Guerdat** (chapter 3, "'What Happens Next?' Structuring the Screenplay") gives you a wealth of techniques for organizing your "seemingly random bits of story" and shaping them into three compelling acts that will keep agents, producers, actors, and directors asking, "What happens next?" as they read it.

Delving into the world of characters, **Cindy Davis** (chapter 4, "Building Characters") arms you with eight major ways to create big, juicy, riveting characters, including how to define their broad stroke, give them signature traits, and make them "actor bait." In chapter 5 ("Deepening Characters and Defining Their Arcs"), **Billy Mernit** covers how to imbue your characters with purpose, credibility, and empathy, and how to invent active journeys for them in which what they discover and decide makes up their character arc.

Before diving into the actual writing process, you need to create the all-important "blueprint": a four-to-five-page outline of your movie. **Juliet Aires Giglio** (chapter 6, "Outlining the Screenplay") guides you through this key step and shows you how to take your story and turn it into "a feature-length movie with characters whose problems, conflicts, and ultimate transformation will grab . . . viewers from beginning to end."

Section 2: Writing Your First Draft Feature Screenplay

Now the *writing* begins, and the first-draft phase is the place to "*explore* and *discover*" the possibilities of your script's premise, theme, plot, main characters, story line, and heart. **Steve Mazur** (chapter 7, "Writing Through the First Draft") coaches you to "cut loose" and plow through a complete first draft with advice like "Don't feel tethered to your outline" and "keep moving forward!"

The first-draft phase is a great time to focus on the subject of chapter 8, "the who, what, where, when, why (and how!) of writing a scene." In this chapter, **Dan Vining** teaches you all the basic elements of how to write tight, compelling scenes, including how to start scenes late and end them early and infuse them with humanity. You further develop scene work with **Chrysanthy Balis** (chapter 9, "Pictures in Motion: Scenes and the Movement They Create") as you learn to think of your screenplay as "a selection of scenes that involve your reader emotionally, that continuously reveal moments of dramatic tension in the lives of your characters, and that push your story along its arc."

Section 3: Rewriting Your Feature Screenplay

Every professional screenwriter will tell you that "writing is rewriting," and this section provides the tools you need to make your script viable in the marketplace. Before you start rewriting, throw yourself "a First-Draft Fiesta," says **Quinton Peeples** (chapter 10, "Taking the Script to the Next Level: The Rewrite Process Begins"). Then buckle down and commit to revising your script, adhering to the chapter's surefire, step-by-step rewrite process.

The revision phase is also where you hone your script's dialogue and visual power. **Karl Iglesias** (chapter 11, "The Art and Craft of Dialogue Writing") shows you how to shape a character's unique voice, fashion subtext and authentic language, and amp up each scene's tension with what's said and left unsaid. In chapter 12 ("'Show, Don't Tell': Visual Screenwriting"), **Philip Eisner** provides unique insight on topics such as how to maximize a screenplay's visual quality, emotional impact, and relevance, and how to make choices that ensure your story translates to the screen visually.

And then . . . you take the last step: turning a good revised script into a great polished one under the tutelage of **Michael Weiss** (chapter 13, "Polish Workshop: Making Your Best Even Better"). You learn to know when you're done with a script; take a final pass at tone and theme; put the finishing touches on scenes, dialogue, and style; and edit for length—in short, make your script a "professional calling card," ready for managers, agents, producers, and contests.

Section 4: Being a Professional in the Movie Business

"Screenwriting is a *career*; it's not a one-shot affair," says **Laurence Rosenthal** (chapter 14, "Demystifying the Business of Feature Film Writing"), who then lays out how the movie industry operates: the power of branding; various routes a script can take to be seen, represented, and sold; what roles readers, agents, managers, attorneys, and producers play; and the importance of building relationships.

Cut to the Chase concludes with chapter 15 ("Launching and Sustaining a Feature Film Writing Career") by **Deborah Dean Davis,** who offers practical (and sometimes eye-popping!) advice on how to market yourself; draw up a career to-do list; take meetings ("the meeting is the plasma that keeps our industry alive"); pitch stories under duress; and make healthy choices that help to ensure a long, prosperous career.

CUT TO: Time to Tell Your Story!

Like a great screenplay, *Cut to the Chase* has a story to tell, an emotional through-line, main themes, a clear structure, plenty of conflict and passion, and it presents the world of the art and craft of screenwriting in a vivid, fresh way. My greatest hope for *Cut to the Chase* is that it helps you discover your story and your voice, and that you find genuine value in what the extraordinary community of UCLA Extension Writers' Program, distilled in this book, has to offer.

SECTION I

From Idea to Outline:
Preparing to Write Your Feature Screenplay

CHAPTER 1

Hollywood Storytelling:
Its Enduring Appeal and Universal Principles

by Billy Mernit

I don't know if your fantasy life is particularly rich, but check out mine:

I have fought a tyrannical emperor in a Roman coliseum. I've been marooned on an island with only a volleyball for companionship and been captive on an island overrun by malevolent dinosaurs. I was a white Southern housewife who adopted an African-American NFL draft pick. I was a male Wyoming ranch hand who fell in love with a rodeo cowboy. I've been a masked superhero with the skill set of an insect. I've matched wits with a super-shrewd serial killer who had a taste for fine wines. I successfully hid from the Nazis for the whole of World War II. I survived the wreck of the *Titanic*. I've set sail with pirates who were really ghosts, and I've *been* a ghost who thought he was alive. I had my memory erased and restored again. I've lived life backward.

I owe all of these incredible, mind-altering, and heart-grabbing experiences to one powerful, even magical entity: the Hollywood movie.

No other storytelling medium can make you feel so intensely what it's like to be inside of another human being's world, so it's no wonder that writers who burn with a passion to tell their own stories are drawn to it.

For the past twenty years, I've been a student of this tradition. I'm a screenwriter, author (*Writing the Romantic Comedy*), novelist (*Imagine Me and You*), teacher at UCLA Extension Writers' Program, previously a reader for Sony and Paramount, and currently a studio story analyst at Universal. As a story analyst, in addition to reading hordes of screenplays submitted to studio executives and recommending that they "Consider" or "Pass" on them, I also write notes on projects that the studio has bought and put into development.

This combination of professional experience has put me in a unique position to study the screenwriting craft from both the writing and the production sides, and I've developed the ability to identify *objectively* the elements that lead to getting movies made, finding an audience, and being deemed successful. (To show you what I mean about putting personal taste aside: When I gave notes on an early draft of J. Michael Straczynski's *Changeling,* long before director Clint Eastwood's involvement, I thought the script had some major problems. But I could also see that its lead role would be star bait—the subsequently Oscar-nominated Angelina Jolie gulped it right up—and therefore gave it a "Consider.")

Despite the huge variety of Hollywood movies that strike a chord with the mainstream audience—from the sophisticated family fun of *Toy Story* to the simplistic scares of *The Exorcist*—certain elements consistently bubble to the top. Moreover, I've found, over the years, that this checklist roughly corresponds to the more subliminal responses I have had to movies I've seen in theaters.

In this chapter, I share my checklist of these "universal principles," or elements of a successful Hollywood screenplay: a strong story concept, characters, structure, theme, dialogue, imagery, world, and genre—all driven by the writer's passion for his creation. Think of it as a "wide shot"—a panoramic view of what you will learn in the ensuing chapters.

Let's start by taking a quick look at just why the Hollywood movie has captured moviegoers for more than one hundred years and then move on to defining the elements that continue to make it tick.

The Enduring Appeal of Hollywood Storytelling

The cinematic master Alfred Hitchcock once said that film is life "with all the dull bits cut out," but the Hollywood movie is more than that. It is distinguished by a passionate emotional intensity that pilots its storytelling, an often ruthless speed and compression of narrative, the presence of larger-than-life personalities observed with up-close-and-personal intimacy, and the kind of superior production values that can most vividly realize a given world.

In addition, the Hollywood movie represents a uniquely American kind of idealism: It often shows life as it should be, as opposed to as it actually is, with the tacit intent to inspire our better selves. When you hear the phrase *Hollywood ending,* it refers to a happy one, in which justice prevails, good vanquishes evil, and boy does get girl by the fade out. Such cinematic resolutions do not tend to mirror what often happens in real life, of course; that's the point. Hollywood movies show humanity in all its infinite variety, while often celebrating love and decency as the bedrock positive values we all aspire to uphold.

This inspirational feat is achieved using state-of-the-art technology and the kind of collaborative creative effort that once yielded cathedrals. Herein lies a deeper aspect of the Hollywood movie's enduring appeal: We're transported, for a couple of hours, into a realm where we feel a part of something greater than our individual selves. As an aspiring screenwriter, you have been repeatedly transformed by the mind-rocking, gut-tugging effect of a great Hollywood movie, one that prompted you to think, *How do I do that?*

It all begins with words on a page.

The Universal Principles of Hollywood Storytelling

What's first and foremost among the factors a good screenplay must possess? The answer is easy to spot but can be complicated to achieve, because it rests in the heart of the screenwriter.

The Writer's Passion

I've come to believe that the most fundamental element of an effective screenplay is a *core emotional passion* that drives a movie and comes from the storyteller who first conceived it. As viewers, we accept all kinds of approaches to telling a story, but nothing draws us so magnetically to a movie, on a basic, instinctual level, as the beating heart and propulsive energy of a story that *must be told.*

Consider the case of British screenwriter David Seidler. Traumatized in his childhood by the battles and bombings in the early days of World War II, Seidler developed a stutter and thus was fascinated to learn that King George VI was similarly afflicted yet managed to talk to his subjects on national radio broadcasts as they continued to fight against the Nazis. The king's bravery stayed with Seidler well into his adult career as a screenwriter, and in the late 1980s, he began researching the life of Lionel Logue, the speech therapist who helped the king conquer his stutter. Turning the story into a movie entailed getting permission from the Queen Mother herself, who requested that the writer not go public with the fruits of his archival research until after her death.

Out of respect for the Queen Mother's wishes and nearly thirty years later, Seidler adapted the story of King George and Logue into a script, then a stage play, and ultimately, dozens of rewrites later, saw his labor-of-love movie *The King's Speech* made and released to Oscar acclaim . . . when he was seventy-three years old.

Knowing none of this backstory, I read the script as a writing sample, well before its release, and gave a "Writer Recommended" to Seidler. Why? Because along with the screenwriter's impeccable craftsmanship and an admirable ability to make a distant historical epoch come alive, his love for his subject and personal investment in the story was palpable in the draft. The eventual success of this "story that must be told" only seemed inevitable.

Seidler's commitment was born of a profound personal experience, but you can feel that kind of passionate intensity in a seemingly lightweight escapist adventure like *Raiders of the Lost Ark.* No one who's ever seen this George Lucas–Steven Spielberg collaboration will ever forget its first five minutes, featuring Indiana Jones pursued by a giant rolling boulder. Lucas and Spielberg had been wowed by such cliffhanger excitement in the old Saturday-morning serials and Hollywood movies they'd seen in their youth, and you can feel their "Watch us top that last one!" enthusiasm throughout the whole of *Raiders,* a movie that moves like greased lightning and delights in piling impossible thrill upon thrill.

Such passion and enthusiasm are contagious. When you take your screenplay into the marketplace, you're asking for the support of first one, then a few, and finally what may be thousands of people, and the investment of what could be millions of dollars. That massive commitment only arises from an emotional involvement on the writer's part that packs palpable heat. If you're not writing a story that you're truly passionate about, and fully invested in on a personal level, why should we care about your movie?

For this reason, I ask my screenwriting students, early on in any given class, why they're writing what they're writing. I say, "What made you want to tell this story?" Maybe it started with a character that fascinated them, a real-life experience that transformed them, or an issue that pissed them off. If the seed for your screenplay is something that matters to you, your enthusiasm is more likely to sustain the long writing process that leads to a completed screenplay.

The Story Concept

Once you discover a project that you are passionate about, the next step is to translate your emotional intensity into a working blueprint for a cinematic cathedral. This is one hefty undertaking. So after the feeling and the passion . . . then what?

Industry insiders acknowledge that it's a strong story idea that is generally the basis for getting a movie made. The *story idea*—also referred to in the industry (as well as in this book) as the *story concept* or the *premise*—refers to the basic idea of a movie: It expresses what the movie is about, in its simplest terms. Ask your average Hollywood player what exactly makes a story concept strong—what he or she wants in a story— and the most honest response will probably be "The same, but different." In other words, Hollywood looks to what's already proven popular . . . but seeks to come at it from a fresh enough angle to make reapproaching such a subject worthwhile.

Ideas for movies sometimes bubble up out of our collective unconscious, and different writers snatch these notions from the ether at roughly the same time (one reason why lawsuits fought over supposed plagiarism in Hollywood generally come to naught). Some years ago, over the same six-month period, I read at least four different spec screenplays entitled *Always a Bridesmaid*. The plight of "the woman who never gets to be the bride" was clearly a movie that wanted to get made.

The one that actually did get produced was Aline Brosh McKenna's savvy *27 Dresses*. Why? Because it had the quirkiest, smartest angle. Its heroine is the ultimate bridesmaid, a woman who lives and breathes other people's weddings . . . and gets unwittingly involved with the very guy who writes her favorite wedding column. When her older sister snatches the man of our heroine's dreams, her always-a-bridesmaid dilemma is replicated. McKenna's idea was familiar at its core but surprising in how it took this idea to its most extreme and amusing conclusions.

Why go see a movie about a guy who's scared to meet his fiancée's parents? Well, what if his prospective father-in-law is an ex–CIA agent with lie-detector equipment in his basement . . . and our hero is a nurse? Casting Robert De Niro was the coup, of course, but *Meet the Parents* had its distinctive take already there on the screenplay page.

Similarly, I can't count how many "bunch of guys go to Vegas and high jinks ensue" specs I've read over the years. But "guys wake up after a wild night's bachelor party in Vegas with no idea what happened to them or where the groom is"? I've only read one of those, and you know what became of it. *The Hangover* was a monstrous hit because it was driven by a *mystery*. Yes, it had good guy gags. But its writers' choice of story concept—"leaving out last night"—is what made the difference.

No hero sounds more same-old than Sherlock Holmes. But 2009's writing team of Johnson-Peckham-Kinberg found a viable concept by making both Holmes (Robert Downey Jr.) and Watson (Jude Law) action-comedy heroes who were closer to *Lethal Weapon*'s Murtaugh and Riggs. No story is more commonplace than boy meets girl, yet romantic comedy specs sell every year. Sometimes it's the story concept alone (boy meets girl at the end of the movie, as in *Sleepless in Seattle*); sometimes it's how the concept is spun in execution (*Four Weddings and a Funeral*). It's familiar—but something we haven't quite seen before must be put into the mix.

One prominent studio head, when asked what he looks for in a project, said he'd only green-light a picture if it could be pitched to him in thirty seconds or less. While this may sound flippant and reductive, it also makes sense. A strong story concept immediately conveys the essential interest and appeal of your movie. And having a firm grip on the essence of what your story is about is the key to keeping that story on track, in the writing of it. That's why I require my students to distill the thrust of their story into one or two dynamic sentences and, once they've achieved this task, submit it to the acid test: What's the unique factor? What will make someone hearing such a pitch ask, "What happens next?"

When you begin to develop your movie, think about what tweaks you'll add to the equation. What will make the same thing different and get it to the screen?

The Main Character (Otherwise Known as the Protagonist or Hero/Heroine)

When Sandra Bullock won her Oscar for *The Blind Side* in 2010, pundits had a field day analyzing this star's appeal, delighting in her unlikely trajectory toward such an honor, but I was absolutely unsurprised by her win. That's because when I read John Lee Hancock's screenplay, the character of tough yet big-hearted Texas housewife Leigh Anne Tuohy brought me to tears—on the page.

I'm not saying that *any* actress playing that part would've ended up thanking the Academy, but the role as written was that good. And Jeff Bridges, Bullock's fellow Best Actor award winner that year, made a point of thanking writer-director Scott Cooper for giving him the gift of Bad Blake, the memorably on-the-skids country singer who made *Crazy Heart* worth watching. Savvy actors understand the value of good characterization work, and shrewd screenwriters understand the tacit agenda behind any screenplay that goes to market: One primary purpose of any script is to allow anyone in power who reads it to identify and empathize with the story's protagonist, so that they'll want nothing more than to be with that character from fade in to fade out.

Flip through any roll call of Hollywood's most beloved movies, and you will find that a number of them are named after their protagonists: from *Spartacus* to *Capote,* from *Annie Hall* to *Erin Brockovich* (another movie that practically yelled "*Star!*" in its early drafts, long before Julia Roberts got her Academy certification). The ability to write credible, complex, compelling people has been the not-so-hidden power at the core of so many screenwriters' successful careers—it's the skill that most often attracts the star power that gets a movie made and makes that movie memorable.

This vital storytelling element of *characterization* is discussed at length in chapters 4 and 5, but in the spirit of a Hollywood movie's "cut to the chase" sensibility, here's a quick exercise that helps my students get their main character defined and into focus.

Exercise: Four Basic Questions to Ask of Your Hero or Heroine

What Does Your Character Want?

The more specific and personal the character's purpose is, the stronger the story. In the beginning of the movie that bears her name, Erin Brockovich wants to earn a salary, but as she takes on the larger goal of defending a damaged community against a heedlessly corrupt corporation, we realize Erin really wants to prove her worth as a human being to the world.

Why Do We Believe in Your Character?

What convinces us that this hero or heroine might be capable of achieving his or her goal? We see the fierce devotion of Erin-as-mom early on in *Erin Brockovich* and experience the force of her willpower when she brazens her way into a job at her accident-attorney's office. This is a female David just waiting for a Goliath to knock off.

What's Standing in Your Character's Way?

The surest path to making an audience identify with a character is to show us what kind of formidable obstacle is coming between her and her fervent desire. We've all had the experience of desperately wanting something and being denied it, so we empathize with someone who's up against the odds. A huge corporation's battery of attorneys makes a formidable antagonist for Erin. How will she prove her worth when her own company benches her before the final fight?

> ## What Makes Your Character Memorable?
>
> None of us are all one thing, and what delights and fascinates us in a person is most often her complexity. Be it a flaw or a strength, what's the quality that makes the heroine exceptional? Erin's worst enemy is actually Erin: Her in-your-face sensuality comes second only to her utter lack of impulse control in alienating people. This complexity makes us love Erin. Her defensive mistrust of her fellow humans is as exasperating as it is vastly entertaining when she lets it rip.

Purpose, credibility, empathy, complexity: The best Hollywood movies boast memorable characters built on this time-honored, foursquare foundation. Will the protagonist of your screenplay embody answers to all the questions posed here?

The Plot and Structure

While character is key, any story is only as good as the predicament its protagonist is in. It's when your character is between a powerful rock and an equally formidable hard place that an audience sits up and takes notice.

When novelist Vikas Swarup wanted to tell the story of what it was like to grow up dirt-poor in one of the world's most infamous slums, he had any number of ways to bring readers into that world. He could have started with his hero's birth. He could have begun with his hero as a child, showing us how brutal and dangerous a place Mumbai was and the extreme lengths to which one had to go to survive there. He could have introduced his hero on the verge of adulthood, facing the challenge of getting out of that slum. Instead, he began his novel with a provocative pair of sentences: *I have been arrested. For winning a quiz show.*

Screenwriter Simon Beaufoy, faced with the challenge of adapting *Slumdog Millionaire,* seized upon this point of entry, recognizing its potential. The movie kicks off on an adventure with the kind of propulsive energy endemic to the Hollywood movie: Jeopardy begins with the first sentence, and high stakes follow in the second. How could a reader resist reading on? How could a viewer turn away from such an opening, when realized on the big screen?

Let's follow Swarup and Beaufoy's logic.

I'd like to tell you the story of what it's like to grow up dirt-poor in Mumbai. Here's where I was born, here are my parents, here's the kids I used to play with, and . . . *Bo-ring!*

How about instead, I put you in the epicenter of the most important moment of my life, when I'm poised on the brink of either becoming a millionaire (live on national TV) or leaving as poor as I've always been? *Now you've got our attention.*

By the way, in between quiz show questions, I'm getting strung up and having electrical wires attached to my privates . . . and may get thrown in prison for the rest of my days, if I can't prove I'm innocent of cheating to get this far. *We're listening.*

Actually, I knew the answer to the first question I got right on this show because of something I went through when I was a kid. It was a pretty awful experience. *Go on.*

How about, via each how-I-learned-an-answer tale, you meet my best friend the gangster and learn how the beautiful girl I fell in love with came between us . . . and I spin this decades-spanning tale (it's got guns, betrayal, and the Taj Mahal in it) up to the present moment, where all three of us hang in the balance of: What happens next?

Dude! Where's it playing and what time's the next show?

If story is the heart of a movie, plot is its head. And through structure, a deft manipulation of intriguing complications, and ever-escalating conflict, a plot is maximally organized to sustain the audience's interest. What beats at the heart of *Slumdog Millionaire* is the visceral experience of what it's like to grow up poor in India, but we wouldn't go on the ride if it weren't for how artfully Beaufoy adapted Swarup's novel, keeping us on tenterhooks for every twist and turn in young Jamal's journey. A well-structured plot that's both convincing and surprising, whether it be conventional (e.g., *The Lion King*) or anything but (e.g., *Adaptation*), is another essential component of good storytelling.

For this reason, once my students have defined their story concept and identified what's distinctive about its trajectory, I invariably ask them, "How do you propose to tell it? From what point of entry, and from what point of view?" Sometimes a writer starts at the climax and puts us inside the hero's head, as in *Slumdog Millionaire*. Sometimes a writer defers bringing on the hero until well into the first act and keeps his inner world mysterious to us for a good portion of the journey. That's what Mark Boal chose to do in *The Hurt Locker*. Both choices Beaufoy and Boal made, while worlds apart, proved to be the most dynamic, tension-inducing ways of thrusting us into their respective stories. The Hollywood movie thrives on such dynamism.

The Theme

In addition and very importantly, the Hollywood movie is dependent on an often near-invisible component: the thing that fuels all that speed, sound, and fury from the inside out. This is, in a word, the movie's *theme*: the larger meaning or universal truth that speaks to the audience on a personal, individual level. Tell me the story of an interesting person with intriguing problems and you can probably hold my attention for, say, one round of drinks. But go on about it for a couple of hours, and even the finest of lubricants won't keep me rapt upon my bar stool. I want to know what the overarching point is—how does this story make a difference? What does it show me about life—about *my* life?

Theme is often misunderstood as some fortune-cookie-like message that's arbitrarily imposed on material, but it's actually the lifeblood of a good script, permeating every aspect of a movie, from imagery to story resolution. In particular, it is expressed through what a given character learns over the course of a span of time. The "what I learned" of it all is generally what makes a given story worth telling. In movies, which need to reach a sizable audience in order to be profitable, the "lesson learned" element, speaking to audience-relatable truths and insights, is generally the province of *theme*.

For a supreme example of theme's potential depth, breadth, and power, take a look at *The Godfather*. In the movie's opening scene, the head of the East Coast's most powerful Mafia, Godfather Don Corleone, sits inside his somber inner sanctum while the revels of his daughter's sunshine-bathed wedding party go on outside. Another father, an immigrant who "believes in America" but has seen the two men who brutally beat his daughter freed on suspended sentences, has come to ask the don for "justice." After chiding him for not formerly behaving like a member of his extended family, the godfather agrees to help him out and then literally leads his new friend into the dark side of the room as he says, "Someday, and that day may never come, I will call upon you to do a service for me. . . ."

We're already in the realm of theme—the multiple meanings of family, of justice, of morality are now in play—and the movie continues to pull eloquently upon these threads. As it tells the story of the godfather's son Michael—who once claimed to his fiancée, "That's my family, Kay, it's not me," yet ends up inheriting his late father's bloody crown—Coppola's epic panoply of images keeps inexorably moving from the light into the dark. The movie ends with Michael Corleone, the newly anointed godfather, within that same inner sanctum of his father's. He is lying to Kay, now his wife, about the murder of her brother-in-law (which he condoned and conceived), then closes the door in her face as he continues to conduct his mob family's business.

In writer-director Francis Ford Coppola's hands, what could have been merely a sensational depiction of gang warfare became so rich in thematic resonance, exploring everything from the Mafia's code as a response to corrupt American society, to the hierarchical importance of weaponry and pastry ("Leave the gun—take the cannoli"), that its levels of meaning deepen upon repeated viewing. This is one reason that *The Godfather* is a classic and considered one of the greatest Hollywood movies ever made.

Using theme to organize and inform a movie isn't only the province of epic drama. When director Sydney Pollack took on the assignment of making *Tootsie,* a seemingly lightweight farce that's also become a beloved classic, he hung its masterfully constructed gags on what he called the "armature" of the script: the idea that its skirt-donning male protagonist, Michael Dorsey, became a better person when he was a woman than he'd ever been as a man. This simple but provocative thematic idea is what makes all the delirious high jinks that ensue in *Tootsie* (written by Larry Gelbart and Murray Schisgal) worth revisiting time and time again.

For screenwriters, a movie's controlling idea arises from discovering what a story is about, and once defined, helps articulate what the writer wants to say. Whether it seems spray-painted across the screen (e.g., *Avatar*'s simplistic "military-industrial greed, bad; indigenous-culture spirituality, good" notion) or feels organically inherent in a story's premise (e.g., *District 9*'s subtler but deeply resonant "we *are* the Other" throughline), having an idea to explore is what gives a good screenplay its depth and its universal appeal. For this reason I always encourage students to investigate what issue lies at the core of their projects, something that can often best be identified by figuring out what lesson is learned by their story's protagonist over the course of the film.

What do you want to know in the writing of your story? What question is your movie answering that will resonate with its audiences as the best Hollywood movies do?

The Dialogue

"Forget it, Jake. It's Chinatown."

When you look at these last spoken words from *Chinatown* divorced from their context, they appear relatively innocuous. Yet one could write a dissertation (and cinema studies students probably have) on the vast, dark subtext carried by fellow detective Walsh's casual dismissal as he leads a traumatized Jake Gittes away from the body of the love of his life, shot dead by the police as her evil, incestuous father looks on. The line signifies, among many other things, that the murderer will get away scot-free, that his kind always does, that nobody will even really take notice, and that Jake's entire reason for being has just been rendered null and void.

Another movie's ending: Phil, the antihero turned heroic protagonist of *Groundhog Day*, looks out on the snowy lawns of Punxsutawney, Pennsylvania; turns to his beloved Rita; and exclaims, "It's so beautiful! Let's live here." We, the audience, laugh deep and long, knowing that Phil has just spent a near eternity of infernally repeated February seconds doing everything in his power to get out of this godforsaken town. His closing lines, seemingly as mundane as they could possibly be, tell us all we need to know about his character's extraordinary transformation.

Therein lies the brilliance. The power of dialogue lies in its ability to do so much with so little, but this potent component of the screenwriting craft isn't simply about mastering brevity. What the form demands is compression. Duty-bound to rivet the viewer's attention for a scant two hours or less, the screenwriter constantly seeks a means to express as much information as possible in the shortest amount of time. And to this end, dialogue is an extremely versatile tool.

Witness the following iconic lines from *Rocky, The Lord of the Rings: The Two Towers, Pulp Fiction, The Wizard of Oz, Forrest Gump, The Silence of the Lambs, Gladiator, All About Eve,* and *A Streetcar Named Desire:*

When Rocky calls, "Yo, Adrian!" his words *reveal character,* as do Gollum's when he hisses, "My precious!"

When hit man Marsellus Wallace announces, "I'm gonna get medieval on your ass," he's *setting the tone and mood* of his character's world.

When Dorothy notes, "Toto, I've a feeling we're not in Kansas anymore," her expository line deftly *sets the scene.*

When Forrest Gump tells a stranger, "My mama always said life was like a box of chocolates. You never know what you're gonna get," he's *speaking to theme.*

When Hannibal Lecter tells Clarice Starling, "A census taker once tried to test me. I ate his liver with some fava beans and a nice Chianti," he's *revealing the past.*

When a gladiator removes his helmet in the middle of the Colosseum and proclaims, "My name is Maximus Decimus Meridius," his electrifying revelation *moves the plot forward.*

When Margo Channing announces, "Fasten your seat belts. It's going to be a bumpy night," her dialogue is *creating tension.*

In *A Streetcar Named Desire,* the classic line uttered by Blanche DuBois—"I have always depended upon the kindness of strangers"— reveals character, reveals the past, and speaks to theme in one fell swoop.

Given the seven different functions of dialogue demonstrated above, I always have my students put their scenes to one all-important test, as exemplified by the best Hollywood movies: Is their dialogue doing more than one thing at once?

The Imagery

Words are a great gift to screenwriters. Still, there's a reason why they used to call them *motion pictures.* We may not be able to quote a word of *The Dark Knight*'s dialogue, but its dizzying sequences of manic, explosive violence—or simply the look of the late, great Heath Ledger's crazed Joker face, smeared with running makeup—are hard to shake from our memory. Many people skipped the subtitles when the heroine of *Crouching Tiger, Hidden Dragon* went airborne with her magical martial arts moves, while both Pixar megahits *WALL-E* and *Up* contain first acts that boast virtuoso stretches of wholly nonverbal wizardry.

The expressiveness of images in motion is the core attraction of a Hollywood movie, and the job of creating such images starts with the screenwriter. The best of screenwriters *inspire* directors by investing the most seemingly mundane moments with powerful imagistic resonances.

It was John Patrick Shanley who came up with that indelible image in *Moonstruck* of Loretta reaching out to take Ronny's gloved wooden hand in the snowfall outside his tenement building, echoing how Mimi took Rodolfo's hand in the opera they've just seen at the Met. It was Alan Ball who created the complex image system of all things red (from wife Carolyn's garden roses to the final image of husband Lester's blood spattered on their kitchen wall) that made everyone talk about how brilliantly Sam Mendes had directed *American Beauty*.

Jaw-dropping visions of gravity-defying and time-and-space-shattering pyrotechnics made *Inception* the sensation of 2010. Yet it is the very last shot, a deceptively simple close-up of one small object in motion, that captures the true power of imagery. After nearly three hours of nearly nonstop action, we're left to contemplate a little brass top, spinning on a table. The significance of this totem will be well-known to anyone who's seen Christopher Nolan's mind-bender of a movie. Suffice it to say whether the top stops spinning and falls over or continues to spin is the most important question in a viewer's mind during the last seconds of the film. When I saw *Inception* in a theater during its opening weekend, and this final shot cut to black, the entire audience gave an audible gasp— along with some laughter and cries of incredulity.

Think about it: In fascinated suspense, millions of people have contemplated that spinning top (generating even more millions in revenue). A screenwriter thought it up.

Using evocative imagery can be the screenwriting equivalent of writing poetry, and the best scripts are so adept at cinematic storytelling— using the full arsenal of visual effects available to an alert writer to clearly and imaginatively articulate story ideas—that the reader really does "see the movie" on the page.

Exercise: Cut Dialogue, Use Imagery

One exercise I always have my students do is to take a scene that they've written as largely dialogue . . . and then put it aside and start again from the top. I tell them, "The director of your movie is running behind schedule and needs to cut those three pages, but he still needs to get the essence of that scene across—in a single shot. How would you express what's going on in your scene, without the aid of dialogue?"

It's worthwhile to ask this question of any dialogue scene you write: How can you *visually* speak to the audience in an even more direct and powerful way?

That's an art that flourishes in Hollywood moviemaking.

The World and Genre

While imagery has long been the substance of good storytelling in every genre, film has proven to be the most dramatic medium for putting you *in* the picture. Anyone who's seen *Fargo* has experienced the bone-chilling winter of northern Minnesota, just as an earlier American generation's first and most vivid experience of the Middle Eastern desert came from sitting, parched, through *Lawrence of Arabia*.

Environment, atmosphere, weather, tone, period, even time of day—all of these factors, as expertly manipulated by a skilled storyteller, collude to invoke a hyperreal time and space that an audience can inhabit and enjoy.

Mark Boal's script for *The Hurt Locker,* informed by his time spent embedded with troops in Iraq, was a stunningly executed movie on the page before later Oscar-winner Kathryn Bigelow lensed it. "The CRUNCHING of wheels traversing rough terrain, then SIRENS, HORNS, SHOUTS" is its first line of narrative information. Then we're thrust into the point of view of a close-to-the-ground robot cam—"A grainy, low-resolution view of a dusty dirt road"—that's zooming down a Baghdad street at dawn, "littered with the refuse of war: spent munitions, rubber bits, animal waste—all of which, from this odd, jarring perspective, looks gigantic, monstrous."

While directing on the page (i.e., including camera directions, cutting choices, etc.) is a tricky proposition and you will encounter several points of view on it throughout this book, in this instance, Boal is clearly "writing down a movie that pre-exists in his head," as screenwriter Robert Towne once put it, to great imagistic effect. Each page emblazons the world of war-torn Baghdad on the mind's eye of the reader with its "you are the camera" approach. "The desert sun glints off a nearby car and momentarily bleaches his mask bright white" as we walk with an armor-suited guy who defuses bombs, and provocative image systems are set in motion when our angle shifts: "Sanborn kneels down and guides Thompson's feet into the suit's black boots, then lashes up a series of Velcro straps to secure the armor, like a squire working on a knight."

Such screenwriting specificity gave director Kathryn Bigelow all the elements she needed to begin her work. Fully imagined, cinematically conceived envisioning of a specific place and time is one of screenwriting's smartest approaches to capturing the mind and heart of directors, directors of photography, and the entire range of interested talent, making the environment, however fantastical, actual.

With different but equal visual power, a fantasy landscape is made real on the pages of Charlie Kaufman's *Eternal Sunshine of the Spotless Mind* as its hapless hero is suddenly transformed into a baby version of himself, thrashing about in a sink and about to go down the drain. It's no surprise that such moments would be catnip to Michel Gondry, a point-of-view-on-acid video director.

World has proven to interact closely with genre when it comes to memorable screenwriting. In Hampton Fancher and David Webb Peoples's *Blade Runner,* a genre-reinventing combination of deliberately mismatched genres (futuristic sci-fi story played as a retro detective noir thriller), this is achieved largely through a wry series of trope reversals in the presentation of its world, such as the perennially sunny Los Angeles reenvisioned as a nighttime realm of constant rain.

Hand in hand with the dream-painting of *world* walks the reality of *genre*. Movies do fall into recognizable subcategories of storytelling: Action, horror, romantic comedy, biopic, thriller, and another two dozen disparate forms delineate even the most casual moviegoers' viewing choices. It behooves a screenwriter to be well aware of the characteristics and expectations every genre packs for the journey. Knowledge of a genre's history can help you build on its rich heritage and will inform how you choose to tell your story; unknowingly break or misuse a pivotal genre convention and you risk losing your reader, no matter how clever the tweak.

Do you know what genre you're writing in? I always ask students to identify their genre and to name at least three movies in that genre that have influenced and inspired them. Some classic Hollywood movies overturned the established rules of their genre (witness *The Godfather,* which overcame the fears of the studio that produced it, rebelling against the prevailing idea of what defined a "gangster movie" at the time). Studying genre is the best way to ensure that you truly understand the rules of the game you're playing. It prepares you for the task of tweaking those rules in your unique way.

The Sum of the Parts

Of course, the best scripts are those that combine all of these elements in such a seamless way that they're hard to separate in the mind of the enthralled reader. In a great screenplay, every component overlaps: Dialogue speaks to theme, while character moves the plot forward.

Scripts like these also utilize yet another element—call it *style,* or *voice.* A singular story expresses its writer's personality. At his writing-directing peak, Woody Allen established a personal style—verbally acerbic but rich in imagery, mixing flights of "What if?" romantic fantasies and aggressively absurd assaults on cultural norms—that influenced a generation of moviemakers.

You can see, for instance, *Annie Hall*'s inspired grab-bag of cinematic techniques in such recent romantic comedies as Scott Neustadter and Michael H. Weber's *(500) Days of Summer*. Similarly, Quentin Tarantino's postmodern fragmentation of narrative and audacious, blackly comedic dialogue have been nearly as influential on the modern-day crime, action, and thriller genres; the reflexive, self-consciously jokey oldsters wielding Uzis in 2010's action-comedy for adults *Red* are direct descendants of his *Reservoir Dogs*.

These are screenwriters who've left their indelible stamp on the ever-evolving Hollywood movie, a reflection of their expert grasp of the form's fundamentals and their willingness to push those forms past their conventional boundaries. In the realm of screenwriting, where the writer is essentially blueprinting a massive endeavor that often ultimately involves thousands of fellow craftspeople, how you meld together all of the storytelling components discussed here is, in a sense, your ultimate self-expression. Your personal voice is communicated through the sum of all the choices you've made concerning every screenwriting element we've discussed.

How will you translate your vision into words on a page, the kind that have inspired decades of great Hollywood moviemaking? You'll want to make sure that your use of all these screenwriting fundamentals is as creative and compelling as it can be. In the pages that follow, a virtual brain trust of screenwriter-instructors will hold you to that task. In the process, they will provide you with realistic advice, tips, exercises, insider knowledge, words of encouragement, and sometimes even laughs—all designed to guide you through the long and thrilling journey of writing your screenplay.

CHAPTER 2

Jump-starting the Screenplay

by Jon Bernstein

It can happen to anyone.

A woman on a crowded train has an idea, which comes to her "fully formed." She doesn't have a notebook with her so she thinks about it for hours and all the details bubble up in her brain. As soon as she returns home, she begins writing about a bespectacled boy who does not yet know he is a wizard.

It can happen anywhere.

In 1941, a businessman's imagination is sparked at a gambling table while he is on a layover in a posh Lisbon hotel. He constructs a scenario in which he is a spy and the other men at the table are German secret service agents, and he takes all their money.

It can happen anytime.

A suburban mother of two wakes up from a vivid dream in which two young people were having an intense conversation in a meadow by the woods. She gets up to make her kids lunch, sends them off to school, and then sits down at the computer to write about "an average girl and a fantastically beautiful, sparkly vampire."

It happened to them.

J. K. Rowling, with her infant daughter in a stroller, sat in coffee-houses as she pounded away at the story about a boy wizard named Harry Potter. Her slavish devotion to her inspired idea launched a literary and film phenomenon.

The scene set at the gambling table stayed with Ian Fleming for more than a decade. He finally sat down to write *Casino Royale* and placed his hero, James Bond, at a gambling table, immortalizing the exciting scene he had imagined all those years earlier.

Stephenie Meyer would be in bed and the voices in her head would force her to get up and go back to the computer. Six months later she sold the book, and the *Twilight* franchise was born.

These three people wrote massively successful stories that were ultimately turned into massively successful films. How did this happen? Why them?

They had an inspired idea, believed in it, and had the skill and discipline to bring it to life.

It can happen to you.

The Successful Screenplay: Creativity and Craft

Writing a screenplay is a fun yet complex process that requires two essential components: loads of creativity *and* a command of the craft. The screenwriter's creative mind dreams up a story, but it's the analytical part that must implement the screenplay form. When the universal elements of Hollywood storytelling are successfully in place, your story is transformed into an approximately 110-page screenplay with a passionate emotional core, a memorable hero, a dynamic structure and plot that thrust the hero into a compelling predicament, a fully realized world with dialogue that pops, and a theme that underlies the story and propels it forward.

Years ago, as a beginning screenwriting student in UCLA Extension Writers' Program, I was eager to take a swan dive into deep creative waters but resisted swimming within the lanes. I challenged my teacher: "What if I don't want conflict? What if I don't want an inciting incident before page ten? Maybe I don't want my hero to hit rock bottom." I wasn't interested in learning the rules. My mind-set was, *I'm a writer; don't rein me in, let me write!*

Three produced features (*Meet the Robinsons, Beautiful,* and *Ringmaster*) as well as numerous studio deals and assignments later, I have learned that these conventions don't rein in creativity and make screenplays rote and formulaic. In fact, just the opposite. Bold, original ideas flourish *within* what Eric Edson in *The Story Solution* calls the screenplay's "proscribed form." Once I embraced the power of creativity combined with craft, I not only became a better writer, I became a freer writer. And so will you.

This chapter helps you strike the proper balance of creative and analytical as you take your first steps to becoming a feature film writer. You first explore where inspired story ideas come from and how to generate them, and then learn to identify a movie's main story concept, commonly called the premise. You become acquainted with the major film genres and how they shape premise, examine how a great premise and strong theme work together to form the basis of a successful screenplay, and explore the importance of world and tone. Finally, you will begin to formulate your movie's "big picture" through the Ten Index Card Approach.

Sound like a lot? It is, but we are going to go step by step, and you'll get plenty of guidance along the way. Remember, writing a screenplay is a journey, not a race. It takes a while, and it's supposed to, so try to learn to embrace and enjoy the process. There will be breakthroughs, frustrations, low points, and exhilarating triumphs, just like in a good movie.

Story Ideas: Where Do They Come From?

The Mystery of Inspired Thought

Where does inspired thought originate? How exactly do we get our inspired ideas? Einstein closed his eyes and let his fingers wander over the piano keys. Ernest Hemingway swam; John Lennon napped. Steven Spielberg drives and Stephen King takes long walks.

If you are looking for ways to beckon your muse, here are a few suggestions:

Carry a notebook. Daydream actively. Eavesdrop aggressively. Think creatively and critically. Research a subject that fascinates you. Exercise. Drive. Read a book. Read a magazine. Read a newspaper. See a foreign film. Go people-watching. Pay attention to the world around you. Ask yourself, "What if . . . ?" Watch the news. Listen closely. Put a new spin on an old idea. Examine your life. Question everything. Think about someone you admire. Drive a new route. Think about someone you loathe. Take a different route. Bounce an idea off someone whose opinion you respect. Look deep inside yourself. Learn from your mistakes. Sit in the woods. Listen to a song you love. Think like a kid. Do volunteer work. Do some gardening. Ask yourself, "Wouldn't it be interesting if . . . ?" Display your excellent taste. Say to yourself, "If only . . ." Try something that's never been done before.

Exercise: Come Up with an Inspired Idea

You have twenty-four hours to come up with an inspired idea for a screenplay. When the time's up, write down your most viable idea and what you were doing at the moment inspiration struck.

The Open Mind: Be Ready for Inspiration to Strike

Sometimes when a great idea takes hold, we are under its thrall and powerless against its hold on our imagination. Be prepared to recognize that irrational yet instinctive moment when something clicks in your mind and you're not sure why, but it just *feels* right and you *know* you have to write it. As Stephen King puts it, "There is no Idea Dump, no Story Central, no Island of Buried Bestsellers. Good story ideas seem to come quite literally from nowhere, sailing at you right out of the empty sky: two previously unrelated ideas come together and make something new under the sun. Your job isn't to find these ideas but to recognize them when they show up."

When I was in high school, an idea gripped my imagination and wouldn't let go. It was an idea that stayed with me, and many years later during a meeting with Disney execs, I found a way to use it. The result was the animated feature, *Meet the Robinsons,* and that original idea is one of the movie's big scenes. Set at a school science fair, brilliant young inventor Lewis displays a revolutionary time-travel machine that is misunderstood by the judges and causes pandemonium. In the midst of the chaos, a mysterious boy from the future named Wilbur Robinson slips in and whisks Lewis away.

Once you have the big idea and can't stop thinking about it, what do you do next? Simple: Write it down. If you don't, it will drift away like smoke.

Exercise: Create an Idea File

Start and maintain an "idea file" to store away ideas and premises (which we explore below) as they arise. Just jot down the key words and main ideas, nothing more.

Story Ideas: Taken from Life

The Power of the Personal

We draw from our own lives in order to make our stories more personally meaningful and true. What compels us to tell certain stories and revisit certain themes tends to be rooted in who we are and what we have experienced.

For example, in the midst of writing the *Harry Potter* books, J. K. Rowling's mother died after a ten-year battle with multiple sclerosis. Her mother's death affected the author deeply, and consequently, the tone of the series darkened considerably as she delved into exploring Harry's loss of his parents.

Steven Spielberg drew the story of *E.T. the Extra-Terrestrial* from his own childhood. After his parents' divorce, young Spielberg filled the void with an imaginary alien companion. Spielberg said, "[E.T. was] a friend who could be the brother I never had and a father that I didn't feel I had anymore."

Everyone Has a Story. What's Yours?

What's your story? What do you have to say? You cannot write anything meaningful unless you are willing to delve inward to find the connection between yourself and your characters and the subject matter.

Be true to your own originality. What makes you laugh when you are alone? Did you move a lot when you were younger? Do you have a close relationship with your grandfather? Are you obsessed with the Elizabethan era? Do you love ballroom dancing? Are you a gifted ventriloquist? Do you run a dachshund rescue? These could be clues to the type of screenplay that you, and only you, are perfectly suited to write. Be true to your singular vision and tell a story that is uniquely your own. Write a screenplay that no one else could write besides you.

Exercise: Come Up with Ideas for Your Unique Story

In ten minutes or less, do the following: 1) Jot down five words that describe the kind of script you want to write. 2) List five subjects you are passionate about. 3) List ten things you do particularly well. 4) Describe in no more than two sentences the world you are interested in exploring. 5) Put into a sentence or two your main intention in telling this story. 6) List movies that are the most like the ones you'd like to write. Go!

Will Your Great Idea Make a Great Movie?

Premise

A good premise is vital. I would rather read a script with a great premise written by an inexperienced writer than a script with a dull premise written by an experienced writer. A great premise gives the script potential. If it's not a great premise, all the rewrites in the world are unlikely to save it.

When it comes to premise, there are no rules. The only limitations are those we place on ourselves. Now that you've generated ideas that have come from your own interests, passions, and unique life experience, it's time to figure out which will make the best premise for a movie.

The premise is the story concept that shapes your story and gives it purpose; it's the driving force behind your script's characters, plot, structure, theme, imagery, dialogue, and genre, and infuses all of these elements with action and emotion. A great premise will take you far. Sky's the limit. Try something the world has never seen.

Another Earth is a recent movie with, in my opinion, a fantastic premise: An Earthlike planet has been found and we all possess an identical twin living on it. The troubled protagonist enters an essay contest sponsored by a millionaire entrepreneur, who is offering a civilian space flight to this mirror Earth. She's chosen as one of the first explorers to travel to the planet, with the hope that her other self on the other Earth did not make the same mistakes she made.

When I first heard the movie's premise, my creative mind went wild imagining the story possibilities, and when I saw it, the clever, thoughtful story exceeded my expectations. Once you have a great premise, there are countless ways to explore it fully. Be sure you are maximizing your premise to its full potential.

Logline

So, what exactly is a logline? In her highly entertaining book *Hello, He Lied*, producer Lynda Obst refers to the logline as the "miniaturization of the idea." The logline's job is to give an immediate sense of the story and make us want more. A successful logline takes a story full of big ideas and complex plotlines and breaks them down into a simple sentence that can be quickly and easily understood.

The logline first came into use during the old studio days when screenplays were kept in vaults. A concise one-line summary was written on the script's spine, allowing studio executives, producers, directors, and actors to search quickly for a project that appealed to them without having to unstack the scripts.

Sometimes the creative process can become wayward and digressive, so the exercise of writing a logline can help rein you in and provide necessary focus. Nailing down the logline forces the writer to think clearly and succinctly about the idea. It is part of striking the "creativity and command of the craft" balance I spoke of at the outset of this chapter. Having the ability to articulate your movie concept in a sentence or two is a great way of beginning to identify and hone in on the core essence of your story.

These are the main things to consider while crafting your logline:

- **Characters**—Who is the protagonist? What does she want? What is her main goal?

- **Conflict**—Who is the antagonist? What is the protagonist's main obstacle in obtaining her goal?

- **Originality**—What is the unique element of your story that makes it stand out?

- **The World**—Does the specificity of the world give a clear sense of tone?

Let's take a look at two loglines:

An ambitious female FBI trainee matches wits with an imprisoned diabolical genius to learn the identity of a serial killer before he can strike again.

King George VI undergoes radical therapy for a stutter so he can deliver a speech to rally Britain during World War II.

Strong loglines contain action and a sense of excitement. Often stating the character's goal can be the way to convey the story concept. For example, the female FBI trainee is trying to "learn the identity a serial killer." King George has to "deliver a speech to rally Britain."

Are the characters, world, and main conflicts vivid in these loglines? Yes, and that may have something to do with what made *The Silence of the Lambs* and *The King's Speech* great movies.

Exercise: Create a Logline

Write a one-or-two-sentence summary of your movie that immediately conveys its premise, appeal, and unique twist.

Strong Premises in Every Genre: What's Yours?

As a beginning writer, it's a good idea to have a strong sense of the genre, or type, of the movie you are writing. Each genre comes with its own set of rules and every writer may have a slightly different take on what the major ones are, but here's my list of the Big Seven: drama, comedy, action, horror, romance, crime, and fantasy.

Drama

Broadly speaking, a drama is a serious story that involves a central conflict and intense struggles. The term *drama* comes from the Greek word *dran,* meaning "to act." Let's take a look at two loglines:

A working mother puts herself through law school in an effort to represent her brother, who has been wrongfully convicted of murder and has exhausted his chances to appeal his conviction through public defenders. (From the Internet Movie Database [IMDb].)

A faithful dog waits every day at a train station for his owner to return home from work, even for a decade after his owner has died.

Conviction and *Hachi: A Dog's Tale* demonstrate there is no need to be manipulative, contrived, or melodramatic when telling dramatic stories. Identify the true emotion in your story, tell it honestly, and capture its emotional punch in your logline, as in the examples above.

Drama subgenres include the social drama, whose central struggle is between a champion and a problem or injustice in society; the champion usually has a personal stake in the outcome of the struggle. Another subgenre is the coming-of-age drama, in which the central struggle entails the hero finding his place in the world. Finally, in the courtroom drama, the central struggle is to find out what really happened and expose the truth.

Comedy

Comedies are stories in which the central struggle causes hilarious results. Classic comedy is a twist on the expected: Create an expectation, and then flip it. What's the easiest way to flip the expected? Place your character in some sort of contradictory situation: a New Yorker in the country, a farmer in New York, a slob traveling with a clean freak . . . you get the idea. Here are loglines from the two comedies *The Hangover* and *Bridesmaids,* which explore this formula brilliantly:

> *Three hungover groomsmen awaken after a blowout Las Vegas bachelor party to find that the groom has gone missing and attempt to get him to the altar in time for his wedding.*

> *When broke and lovelorn Annie finds out her best friend is engaged, she tries to bluff her way through the wedding rituals.*

Comedy subgenres include screwball, romantic, fish out of water, horror parody, and gross-out.

Action

In the action genre, the central struggle of the story mainly plays out through a clash of physical forces, usually with an innocent hero pitted against a dangerous enemy. Screenplays in this genre are mostly plot driven, not character driven, with external action and a suspenseful story, and most of the scenes are written as action or with suspense that builds to action.

Here are loglines from *Speed* and *Mission: Impossible: Ghost Protocol,* classics of the genre:

> *A young cop must prevent a bomb exploding aboard a city bus by keeping its speed above 50 mph.* (From IMDb.)

> *The IMF is shut down when it's implicated in the bombing of the Kremlin, causing Ethan Hunt and his new team to go rogue to clear their organization's name.* (From IMDb.)

Horror

The central struggle in horror stories focuses on escaping from and eventually defeating a monster (either human or nonhuman). Let's take a look at two horror movie loglines:

A pregnant young wife and her struggling actor husband move into an ominous New York City apartment building with sinister neighbors who take a keen interest in her pregnancy.

A young journalist must investigate a mysterious videotape which seems to cause the death of anyone in a week of viewing it. (From IMDb.)

Creepy, right? And the movies made a fortune. It wasn't the production values that turned *Rosemary's Baby* and *The Ring* into monster hits. It was the right premise for the right genre.

Horror subgenres include ghost story, serial killer story, zombies, found footage, and horror-comedy.

Romance

The central struggle in the romance genre is between two people who must each overcome all obstacles in order to win or keep the love of the other. The most instantly identifiable subgenre is the romantic comedy, which is fun and lighthearted, with stories that always end happily ever after. Rom-coms require an inventive approach to the mix of characters and concept that addresses something relevant in culture, often pertaining to gender roles in relationships. Let's see if we can observe that formula in these loglines:

When a drunken hookup between a professional woman and a slacker has unexpected consequences, the reluctant odd couple attempts to transform their tentative connection into a lasting relationship, which they find much harder than making a baby.

While sharing a car trip from Chicago to New York, two recent college grads conclude it is possible for men and women to be "just friends"; however, their theory is seriously tested as they encounter one another over the years.

Knocked Up and *When Harry Met Sally* . . . demonstrate the basic rom-com formula involving two people who can't stand each other and can't stand to be away from each other. They meet, part ways, and then ultimately reunite as love transcends all obstacles.

Crime

The central struggle in crime stories is in catching a criminal. Usually the stories are a cautionary tale, rooted in a main character who commits a crime. Probably the most well-known subgenre is gangster crime, in which the central struggle is between a criminal and society. American filmmakers have been captivated by this genre for years and have used it to create some of America's most iconic movies. Can you recognize the loglines of these classics?

> *Henry Hill grew up idolizing the "wiseguys" in his neighborhood and is inducted into their world of petty crime, in which he eventually finds himself the target of both the feds and the mobsters, who feel that he has become a threat to their security with his reckless dealings.*

> *When a powerful gangster is gunned down, his reluctant son must seek revenge and take over the family business.*

If you guessed *Goodfellas* and *The Godfather,* you're right! Other subgenres include cops and robbers, blaxploitation, film noir, heist, and prison.

Fantasy

The central struggle in this genre plays out in two worlds—the "real" world and an imaginary world. There is usually a clash of great forces in the sweep of great historical change. The hero discovers hidden reservoirs of strength he never knew he had as his courage is tested against a formidable foe.

Many of Hollywood's biggest blockbusters have been in this genre, including *The Lord of the Rings, Star Wars,* and *Harry Potter.* All three of these fantasy adventures spawned sequels, resulting in multibillion-dollar franchises.

Fantasy's most popular subgenre is science fiction, whose central struggle is generated from the technology and tools of a futuristic world. Other subgenres include superheroes, alien invasion, mad scientist, monster, and mutant.

Animation and "Genre Switching"

Although most animated films fall into the category of comedy or fantasy, animation isn't considered a genre. Animated movies allow for the imaginative screenwriter to find stories in unlikely places. The premises of some of the top ten animated movies of all time involve ogres, jungle animals, toys, fish, a family of superheroes, and the secret world of monsters. Don't hold yourself back; the sky's the limit with animation. *Shrek, The Lion King, Toy Story 3, Finding Nemo, The Incredibles,* and *Monsters, Inc.* could only happen in animation.

Switching genres will allow you to see your premise in a whole new light. For example, if you turned *Alvin and the Chipmunks* into a drama, it would require a slight adjustment in the vision—but it could absolutely work! Imagine it: a searing drama about three rambunctious, hirsute musician brothers who lose their home and move to Los Angeles, where they meet a frustrated songwriter who sees their potential and turns them into superstars. Soon they are torn apart by the superficial glamour around them. In a town filled with sharks and sycophants, will the brothers discover what they truly value?

Wait a minute—I've seen that movie! I think you see my point. You can take an idea, flip it upside down, and turn it into something else entirely, which may or may not be a good thing. But at least it has you looking at your concept with an open mind.

Exercise: Create Ten Premises in Different Genres

Come up with ten premises and identify the genre for each. Which is your favorite? Now take each premise and mix it up and cast it in a different genre. Which one is your favorite now? Is your favorite the same or different?

World and Tone

Screenplays with a strong sense of place establish the tone of the movie and hook us in immediately. Let's take a look at a few examples.

Carthage, Texas, is the sort of place where Cadillacs veer off the road when the wealthy old widow drivers miss the brakes. If you drive down the main strip, you will see the Boot Scootin' Western Wear shop and a diner with a sign reading YOU KILL IT, I'LL COOK IT. Inspired by a true crime in the East Texas town of Carthage, *Bernie* tells the story of a popular funeral director who befriends an old widow before shooting her four times in the back with a gun she uses to kill armadillos in her garden.

There is an ominous tone beneath the cheery façade. We suspect something very bad may happen; we're just not sure *what*. The film opens in a mortuary science class with Bernie, a skillful and serene mortician, teaching the basics of beautifying the dead. He applies superglue to a corpse's lips in preparation for open-casket viewing. "Even the slightest hint of teeth can be disastrous," he cautions his students. "You cannot have grief tragically becoming comedy."

And we're off and running! Films with a strong sense of place have a way of hooking us in quickly. We understand—almost subliminally—what sort of story we are in for when the tone is established by the distinctive world. *Winter's Bone* is another example of a film with a strong sense of place. A constant threat of danger lurks beneath the surface as we see shots of a desolate corner of America. Banjos and acoustic guitars play as we meet a variety of grim, weathered characters who speak with strong regional accents. We feel a genuine sense of dread when our protagonist, a courageous teenage girl, goes looking for her father, a local methamphetamine dealer who has mysteriously vanished.

Exercise: Create a Vivid World

Take fifteen minutes to write about a world that is familiar to you. Capture the authenticity of your world by being specific. Feel free to jot down lines of dialogue if you have a strong sense of your character's distinctive voice.

Know What's Out There: Emerging Trends

The next step is to investigate what kind of premises are currently being sold and made. As Billy Mernit says in the preceding chapter, "Ask your average Hollywood player . . . what he or she wants in a story . . . and the most honest response will probably be 'The same, but different.'" What this means is that the film industry looks for properties that are similar to what's already proven to be popular, but with a new twist.

For example, the huge success of *The Blair Witch Project* paved the way for *Paranormal Activity, Cloverfield,* and most recently, *Chronicle,* and a new subgenre was born. Found footage, with shaky camera work, is a relatively new subgenre of filmmaking within horror, in which most of the film is presented as discovered film or video footage, often left behind by missing or dead people.

Keep an eye on the trades and blogs to see which movies are performing well and which ones are tanking. *Variety* and *The Hollywood Reporter* are the main industry trades, and most industry insiders rely on the *Deadline Hollywood* blog (Deadline.com) for their insider industry news fix.

Hollywood decides what screenplays to buy based on recent successes. After *John Carter*'s huge loss, you may want to set aside that script about a Civil War veteran who travels to Mars. However, after the big success of *Bridesmaids,* the time may be right for you to dust off that raunchy female ensemble comedy you wrote a while back. In Hollywood, timing is everything.

Another excellent resource for gauging Hollywood's fickle tastes is the influential Black List, an annual list of screenplay titles and their loglines identified as the favorite as-yet-unproduced screenplays by a group of more than three hundred film studio and production company executives. Both *Slumdog Millionaire* and *The King's Speech,* which won the 2009 and 2011 Academy Awards for Best Picture, respectively, were on the Black List. In fact, in one recent eight-year span, Black List scripts won for Best Original Screenplay and *The Social Network* for Best Adapted Screenplay. So it's worth a perusal of the loglines of some recent Black List scripts to pinpoint current trends and emerging genres.

By the way, UCLA Extension screenwriting student Terrence Michael made the 2010 Black List for *The Girl with Something Extra.* Check out the logline: "A dark comedy about a boy named Elda Winnows who is raised as a girl by his domineering mother, Mary. When Elda is forced to attend public school for the first time, 'her' search for love takes a surprising turn." This script got Michael an agent, a manager, and a deal with a production company.

Exercise: "The Same, but Different"

Go online and read the latest Black List (Blcklst.com/). Pick three loglines with stories that appeal to you, and write your own spin on them. Make them "the same, but different."

Theme

A successful screenplay always has a theme: a general underlying truth or main message that speaks to the audience on an individual level and is distinguished by the writer's personal, passionate point of view on the subject. Take two films that explore one of the most common topics—war—but whose themes differ significantly. *Apocalypse Now* (1979) shines a spotlight on the atrocities of the Vietnam War, fought by the United States in the name of democracy and freedom. Not specifically antiwar, the movie's theme is that there lies, in all human hearts, the potential for darkness and savagery. The theme of another war film, *The Hurt Locker,* explores what it means to be addicted to war. The film's main theme is clearly established by its opening line: "The rush of battle is a potent and almost lethal addiction, for war is a drug."

Screenplays with strong, well-realized themes have the power to raise awareness and create social change. For instance, *Erin Brockovich* is based on a true story of a working-class single mother who became a legal assistant and almost single-handedly exposed the deadly practices of a California power company. With its inspiring theme of "goodness and truth can prevail over greed and evil," this movie catapulted the topic of environmental safety into national awareness. More recently, *Milk* brought the topic of gay rights into mainstream movie theaters with its inclusive message that "all human beings deserve the right to live with dignity and without discrimination."

Even without major "opinion shaping" impact, it is through the exploration of theme that our writing becomes meaningful. In *The Best Exotic Marigold Hotel,* the topic of aging is explored with humor, bite, and compassion as a group of British senior citizens retire to India at what they expect will be a luxury resort, only to find that it has been exuberantly oversold by an earnest young man seeking to keep his father's dream alive. The way in which each character reacts to his or her new environment and life circumstances encapsulates the movie's underlying truth: "Life is continuously wondrous and meaningful to those who are open to it and who maintain their capacity for love and friendship."

Exercise: Delve into Theme

Write out the themes of three of your favorite movies. What appeals to you about these themes? How are these themes similar to the theme you will be exploring in your screenplay?

Theme and Premise

How Theme and Premise Work Together

Finding the proper balance between premise and theme is very important for a new screenwriter—in fact, for *all* screenwriters—to work toward. In my view, most great movies feature themes that *stem directly and organically from the premise.*

Let's take a moment to review the definitions we've learned so far: The premise is an original idea (or an original spin on a familiar idea) that is rooted in what a character learns over time. The theme is the story's larger message, whose meaning resonates with the audience and which you make your own with your own particular point of view.

For example, the premise of *Groundhog Day* is "A misanthrope is forced to relive the same mundane day over and over again," and the theme is "True satisfaction comes from living in the moment." The premise of *Toy Story 3* is "An old toy collection headed for the trash or attic lands in a day care center ruled by a tyrannical stuffed bear, and the toys must muster all their ingenuity and work together as a team to escape." The theme might be stated as "The power of togetherness and the ability to love and be loved transcend all of life's disappointments." In both cases, the movies' themes flow directly from their premises.

Building the Organic Relationship Between Theme and Premise

Finding a theme that ties in directly and organically with the premise is an important starting point for screenwriters. This doesn't mean that you need to insert your theme in every piece of dialogue and plot point. However, as you work your way through the long process of creating a screenplay, from developing your plot and characters to outlining and writing the first draft, through rewriting and layering in dialogue and deepening the visual storytelling elements, you will want to keep your theme in mind and to be alert to when and where you can convey your message and infuse it with your unique point of view.

One key to developing a strong theme is to make it understandable, which means giving it some sort of physical expression. Film is a visual medium and action drives story, so you will find that theme is best explored through the action in the protagonist's journey. To this end, the theme is often stated by one of the characters at some point during the movie. In *The Lord of the Rings: The Two Towers,* Sam's speech to Frodo at the end of the movie sums up its larger themes: "How could the world go back to the way it was when so much bad had happened? But in the end, it's only a passing thing, this shadow. Even darkness must pass. A new day will come."

In *Midnight in Paris,* Paul, the pompous professor, delivers the movie's main theme: "Nostalgia is denial—denial of the painful present. The name for this denial is Golden Age thinking—the erroneous notion that a different time period is better than the one we are living in."

The movie's main theme can often be found in the movie's opening lines. In *Little Miss Sunshine,* Richard's opening lines of dialogue establish the main theme: "There are two kinds of people in this world, winners and losers. Okay, you know what the difference is? Winners don't give up."

Exercise: Express Your Theme as Statement and Question

Theme is usually expressed as an affirmative statement on a subject or poses a significant question to explore. Try stating the theme of your movie's premise both ways.

You and Your Premise: The Beginning of a Beautiful Relationship

Here's the big moment: Pick your favorite premise. You and your premise will be spending a long time together—more than you realize—so choose wisely. Think of it as a relationship. You don't want to get too serious too early. See how well you and your big idea click. After hanging out for a while, you will know if you want to spend more time together or split up.

Be aware that you and your premise will experience plenty of ups and downs, and that most writers will hit patches where they want to quit. You need to love your theme and premise enough to commit to them and see them through the good and not-so-good times to the very end—or at least to the end of the first draft.

The Ten Index Card Approach to Imagining Your Screenplay

Guess what? You have taken the first important steps to jump-starting your screenplay! Are you ready for the next step? If so, good, because you'll need patience and perseverance here, and you'll need to resist the temptation to take your idea and type FADE IN. I promise your efforts will pay off, though, because this step is indispensable to writing the kind of feature film people want to read and see.

Now you'll take another, final step in the "jump-starting" process while maintaining maximum creativity. You are going to map out the big picture of your screenplay. This is not an outline—there's much more for you to learn about the conventions of Hollywood storytelling before you get to that stage. But by using the Ten Index Card Approach, you will begin to conceptualize the landscape of your screenplay, with all its contours, in its entirety. In a way, screenplay writing is like a long daydream, and the Ten Index Card Approach is a way of capturing it. These cards will also help you decide if you should stick with your idea or break up with it; in the process of working with these cards, you might discover a better idea floating around your head.

On the first index card, write the *title, genre,* and *logline.* (This will change over the course of writing your screenplay, but the goal here is to get something down now, before you start. Make your best guess.)

On the second card, describe the *world.* How well do you know the world you will be creating? Your screenplay may have a few different worlds. Write about your world in a vivid, evocative way. Capturing the look and feel of your world will help the reader "see" your movie.

On the third card, write the *story* in one neat paragraph. Six sentences maximum, ideally capturing the beginning, middle, and end. (This will also change—just give it your best shot!)

Spoiler alert: Some of the next six cards delve into topics discussed in the following chapters. Don't worry if you don't know all the terms yet; the point is just to take the very first pass at envisioning your story in its entirety.

On the fourth card, write about your *characters.* Who is the hero, the protagonist, at the beginning of the story, and who is he at the end? What does he want, and how does he change? The antagonist creates the drama and brings on the conflict. Who is the antagonist in your story? If the conflict is internal for the protagonist, then the antagonist is within your main character. A vivid, well-realized character dictates the screenplay's course of action.

On the fifth card, write your *theme.* What is the larger meaning of the entire screenplay? What "universal truth" speaks to the audience?

What's the personal point of view and passion that infuse your story, and why are you so uniquely well suited to tell it?

On the sixth card, write the *inciting incident*. What happens in the first ten to fifteen pages that sets your story into motion? Are we hooked in? Are the stakes clearly established?

On the seventh card, describe *act 1*. This is the setup, when we meet the hero and other characters and learn the main problem of the story. The antagonist is introduced, and the main conflict is established. This is also where the inciting incident takes place. Late in act 1, a plot point should occur that pivots the story in a new direction.

On the eighth card, describe *act 2*. Act 1's ending should deliver the story into the main conflict, complicating the initial problem. The hero gets pulled deeper into trouble, leading to the climax. By the end of act 2, the hero should be defeated, hitting rock bottom, and it should appear that all is lost.

On the ninth card, describe act 3. Act 2's final climax should lead to the resolution. The problem should be resolved in a surprising and unexpected way. The hero should learn a lesson and become her most authentic self as a result of successfully overcoming adversity.

On the tenth card, write short summaries of *three scenes* that you think will be very important to drive forward the story. Who are the characters in the scenes, what is the conflict, and where does it happen in the story? *Remember, conflict fuels story.* If you don't have enough conflict in your premise, your protagonist may not get a chance to be tested and grow.

When you have the ten completed index cards, know that you have taken a huge step: You have moved from *imagining* to *creating*. Now try talking through your story out loud and hear how it sounds.

As you move through *Cut to the Chase*'s first section, continue working on these index cards; they will give your story a structure and form. But do not cling too tightly to what you think the story is. Allow the story to expand. Surprise yourself. Once you reach the outlining stage, the cards will help clarify your objective and focus your story, and serve as a handy tool as you navigate the journey of drafting a screenplay.

Tips for Enjoying the Process

You are the hero on your journey of writing your first feature film. Goethe wrote, "In action, there is power, grace and magic," and every skill, every piece of knowledge you absorb, everything you do to put this knowledge into action, is moving you ahead toward achieving your goal.

There are a few parting words of advice I'd like to share that have helped and encouraged my students and have been instrumental for me in maintaining a positive state of mind throughout my own career.

Managing Your Inner Critic

The inner critic resides in each of us, an invisible gargoyle that knows exactly what to say to grip us with anxiety and paralyze us with self-doubt. What writer isn't familiar with the sinister whispers of the inner critic? *"You call yourself a writer? This is terrible. You can't show this to anyone or they will think you're a joke. You should seriously consider burning this. Maybe it's time to reconsider trade school."*

How many writers have stopped working on their screenplays because they believed their inner critics? It is the inner critic's dark victory when it convinces you to stop writing. Don't let it. Sure, everyone has an inner critic, but it's possible to disempower it by talking back. *"You know what? You're absolutely right. This draft really does suck. But guess what? All first drafts suck."*

This approach renders the inner critic speechless. *Victory!*

Recently, one of my students cheerfully told me that she wrote thirty pages in one week because she would say out loud before writing, "I am about to write some seriously sucky pages." It freed her up creatively, and she had more fun writing, too.

Resist perfectionism as you begin writing your screenplay. Be comfortable with the disorder. You can be a perfectionist later, while you are proofing your pages. At this stage, though, it hinders the creative process and prevents you from trying new things.

Take Risks—Be Willing to Fail!

There is nothing more boring than a safe writer. Be adventurous. Take risks. Write whatever you want. You can't please everyone, so you may as well please yourself. Try not to take your work or yourself too seriously. *You must be willing to fail.* There is no shame in failing. Failure is instructive. We need failure. There is no success without failure. This advice is something I have explored in my own creative work. I believe that we must keep moving forward and travel through our necessary failures into a bright future.

Trust the Process

In *Pollock,* a movie based on the life of Jackson Pollock, one of the giants of American abstract art, there is a scene in which the artist is working in his studio and accidentally spills some paint on the canvas. Instead of cleaning it up or painting over his "mistake," Pollock throws more paint on the canvas—again and again. Jackson Pollock's accident sparked his creativity and led to his signature style called "drip painting," for which he became an international sensation and one of the most revered artists of the twentieth century.

I feel the same way about screenwriting. It isn't tidy. In fact, you are going to get some paint on your shoes. Allow for chaos and disorder in the process and you will gradually learn to trust your ideas, and also your ability to write them. My greatest hope for you is that you'll discover your true voice and tell the story you were born to tell.

It can happen to you.

CHAPTER 3

"What Happens Next?": Structuring the Screenplay
by Andy Guerdat

"What happens next?" is the foundation of all storytelling. If you can get agents, producers, actors, and directors to ask themselves that question after the first page of your script, and then about a hundred more times as they flip through the rest, you'll have a screenwriting career. In fact, that's not a bad way to think about a screenplay: a whole bunch of ?s with an ! at the end.

Whether you get those potential readers to ask, "What happens next?" will be determined by how well you structure your screenplay. At UCLA Extension Writers' Program, I find that most of the flaws in my students' screenplays can be traced to poor structure. Professional screenwriters often spend more time plotting their story than they do writing the actual script. No one who writes for money can afford to waste time giving CPR to a screenplay that was dead from the start.

So in this chapter, I'm going to show you, step by step, how I (and most working screenwriters I know) get from a promising story idea to a viable screenplay structure. You'll learn the importance of withholding information and dispensing it to intriguing effect throughout the script, the successful execution of which is the basis of structuring a movie that works. You'll then learn how to take the seemingly random bits of story you've created, organize them into three compelling acts, and build your central conflict to a satisfying resolution, all in pursuit of one goal: to tease the readers who open your script and read that first page into wondering, *What happens next?*

The Power of Not Telling All

Let's start with this basic truism of storytelling: *Withholding information is more powerful than revealing it.* Don't think so? At the end of the chapter, I'll tell you the three simple words that are guaranteed to make you a successful screenwriter.

Okay, if you flipped ahead, you just proved my point. And if you didn't, you'll get it when you get there. Meanwhile, here are some examples of how professional screenwriters withhold information to get the audience wondering what happens next, the key to successful screenplay structure.

First: In *Fourth Story,* a movie thriller I wrote, the wife of a man who's mysteriously disappeared sets out to find him. But just as she leaves the house, the telephone rings. And rings. And rings. Who is it? The missing husband? The police with news of his whereabouts? Kidnappers? Starting to wonder? Well, I never revealed who it was; I chose to let the question hang over the story to give it a creepy sense of foreboding— which was a lot more effective than if I'd revealed who the mysterious caller actually was. Probably a telemarketer.

Second: I've seen the Coen brothers' *The Big Lebowski* many times, like millions of its admirers, but I still don't know exactly who did what to whom or why—nor do I care. *The Godfather: Part II* is an acknowledged masterpiece, but why did Hyman Roth try to kill Michael, and how exactly was Fredo involved? I'm not quite sure. But I sure couldn't wait to see if he survived. Same goes for the Dude and Walter.

Third, and perhaps the ultimate example: *Lost in Translation* earned more than a hundred million dollars, despite the fact that it practically *had no story*. No, really. Boy meets girl, boy doesn't do anything, boy leaves. Clearly, Sofia Coppola's screenplay was not a model of perfect story structure. Yet if you'd turned off the projector in the middle of any screening and asked the audience what they thought would happen next, I bet they'd have answered: A) The two leads will have an affair, but Bob (the Bill Murray character) will go back to his wife and leave Charlotte (Scarlett Johansson's character) wistfully alone; or B) They'll have an affair, but Charlotte will go back to her husband and leave Bob wistfully alone; or C) They'll have an affair and live happily ever after. I doubt that one person would've guessed that *nothing would happen*. But the catnip of "I wonder what's gonna happen next?" was strong enough to keep audiences engaged until the very end, when Bob whispers to Charlotte something that we never hear.

The power of "What happens next?" is so great that a screenwriter's cardinal sin is structuring a story in a way that lets the audience get ahead of the storyteller. You know the feeling: You're sitting in the theater and you instinctively sense that this is the part where the star's lovable buddy will be killed, thereby inspiring our noble hero to confront his archnemesis . . . and then that's exactly what happens. Groooan. Most movie executives would probably tell you that that story was "properly structured." But it wasn't, for the simple reason that it didn't create the desired emotional effect on the audience—that is, unless the screenwriter *wanted* them to roll their eyes in boredom.

Screenplay Structure: What It Is and Isn't

The purpose of story structure, whether it's a mainstream Hollywood movie or an edgy indie film, is to design into your story as much lively unpredictability as possible (all those ?s), even as it builds to a logical but emotional conclusion (the !). The purpose of structure, however, is *not* simply to hit some preordained benchmarks that give your script the artificial imprimatur of Proper Screenplay Form. That's not form; it's *formula,* which is a preconceived template intended to take the guesswork out of screenwriting. One can see why such formulas would appeal to screenwriters ("Wow! I just plug in my settings and characters and it's almost done!") as well as to screenplay readers ("Finally! A definitive way to tell a good screenplay from a bad one!"). But the problem is that formulas don't appeal to the most important element in the movie business: the audience.

There's a reason why movies like *John Carter* and *Battleship* and *Prometheus* were flops, and it wasn't the acting or ad campaigns or special effects. It's because the audience instinctively knew pretty much everything that was going to happen. You can practically see the producer's checklist for *Prometheus:* Gross slimy creatures, like all the prior *Alien* movies. Got 'em. Mysterious android crewmate, just like the others? Check. Time-tested false climax where the alien turns out to really be alive? Done. Standard-issue last-minute escape for the female protagonist? You know it. And the net result? Well, the audience I saw the movie with was bumping into those cardboard movie promotion things in the lobby as they sleepily trudged out of the theater.

You could watch every successful movie ever made, define everything they all have in common, and then apply each of those commonalities to your own script (and it's been done, believe me), and the only thing you're likely to achieve is failure. Why? Because the audience wants to be surprised, to see what they've *never* seen before. And, ironically, the very nature of any storytelling formula makes your story predictable and your audience bored.

Of course, withholding *too much* information can be confusing. For example, in *Winter's Bone,* Ree, an impoverished Ozarks teenager, is searching for her meth-dealer father among a clan of Dixie mobsters. In one scene we find her at a cattle auction, shouting something we can't hear above the mooing cows as she chases someone we've never met. End of scene. Later, we'll learn that she was trying to confront the local crime lord, but since that wasn't made clear before the scene, we weren't able to wonder, *Oh my God, will she catch up to him?* or *Oh no, what will he do if she catches up to him?* Instead, we were left to wonder, *Huh?* And yet *Winter's Bone* was still a fairly successful film by indie standards, despite its sloppy storytelling. It had some great performances, yes, but its story was such a gut-wrenching journey for the protagonist that we couldn't help but be hooked into wondering . . . *What happens next?*

The Ultimate Antiformulaic Screenplay Structure "Formula"

Good story structure, then, means dispensing dramatic information to intriguing effect. We want to reveal just enough information to keep the audience wondering what will happen next without giving them so little they start wondering if they're in the wrong theater.

So remember: Boredom is the screenwriter's archnemesis. Even confusion is preferable. But of course, to *intrigue* an audience is better than either. So, if **B** = Bored and **C** = Confused and **I** = Intrigued, then **I** > **C** > **B**. There. A formula.

How Do You Start Building a Movie Story?

So you've got this cool idea for a movie. Now what? You start by collecting all those "Hey, y'know what'd be cool?" scenes or characters or bits of dialogue you've been coming up with (and, I hope, writing down). And if you haven't, now's the time to do so, *before* you impose a prefab structure onto your story. You can't write a really cool story if you haven't first taken the time to think up the really cool stuff.

All those cool things are what screenwriters call *story beats* (not the same as a beat to an actor, which is a short pause, and to a drummer or a street thug, it's something else entirely). A beat is just something that happens to further the plot. If you told someone your story, every time you said, "So then . . . ," that would be introducing a beat. There are probably about fifty to eighty beats in a typical screenplay, but don't worry about that now. Later I'll tell you how to weed out the beats you don't need.

As you generate story beats, your brain may start naturally connecting some of them into a rough chronology. As it does, notice which beats connect with the conjunction *so* or *but,* as opposed to *and.* The words *so* and *but* are tip-offs to promising story roads. The reason? Because *so* implies that the beat you wrote *caused* the story beat that follows it, and *but* suggests the introduction of something that runs *counter* to the prior beat, or a plot twist. However, *and* often means that the beat is an unrelated event that may not be the result of what happened prior. (Aristotle called this storytelling concept the Theory of Causality, which sounds way smarter.) For example, in *The Social Network*, the protagonist is rejected by his girlfriend, *so* he trashes her online, *but* his new software program catches on in ways he never imagined.

So . . . *so* and *but* are good, but *and,* not so much.

Usually, after dreaming about your story for a while, you'll sense some of those beats fusing together to form the single most important concept in screenwriting structure . . . a *spine.* A lot of people call this a *logline,* which is fine, too (as long as you don't confuse it with those little blurbs on your TV's channel guide; those are often just really bad synopses or advertising taglines). I like the term *spine,* because just as a spine is the one bone in your body you can't do without (okay, a skull would be tough, too), you'll never make your story's skeleton work right without the backbone of *one central conflict.*

So whether you call it a logline, a spine, or a central conflict, this indispensable step in the process is the *one sentence that states what your story is about.*

That's right. One sentence. If it takes more than that, your story will almost surely be too disjointed for you to write well. *Lawrence of Arabia* is three and a half hours long; its spine is "A young English officer in World War I goes to Arabia and tries to become a god." That's it. Every story beat, every scene, every syllable of dialogue in Michael Wilson and Robert Bolt's great screenplay tells *that* story and no other. A TV movie I wrote called *Dance 'Til Dawn* (to go from the sublime to the not-quite-so-sublime) had twelve major characters and an extraordinarily complex structure of interweaving story lines. But its spine was simply "Three teenage couples and their parents have their romantic lives turned upside down on prom night."

Think of your spine this way: When little kids make poster art, they squiggle Elmer's Glue onto poster board, dump a bunch of glitter on it, and then slide the glitter off (and onto your rug). The glitter that sticks to the glue forms the pattern of the words or picture they wanted. So all those seemingly random story beats you wrote down are like the glitter. And the glue is the story spine buried under all of it, holding your picture together.

Assuming you've identified your spine, *write it on a Post-it and stick it by your computer*! We're going to use it to structure your screenplay.

Again, the spine or logline is the central conflict of your story, so seek out whichever character has the most conflict. That's probably your protagonist (or there may be more than one, as in the above-mentioned *Dance 'Til Dawn* or Richard Curtis's *Love Actually*, or in Stanley Kubrick and Arthur C. Clarke's *2001: A Space Odyssey*, in which the protagonist is humanity). Then, *so*-ing and *but*-ing away . . .

Follow Your Story's Conflict

Conflict Creates Emotion

Storytelling is the opposite of life, in which we try to avoid conflict, if we're smart. But when telling stories, whatever causes your protagonist the most misery is where you want your story to head. How so? Simple: Conflict creates *emotion,* and emotion is why audiences go to the movies. Am I sure about that?

Here's a little exercise: Make a list of every movie you can think of in the past twenty years with the word *wedding* in the title. Here's my partial list: *The Wedding Singer, The Wedding Planner, Wedding Crashers, Four Weddings and a Funeral, My Big Fat Greek Wedding, American*

Wedding, My Best Friend's Wedding. (And that's not counting *Brides-maids, Runaway Bride,* and *Father of the Bride* 1 and 2.)

Okay, now make a list of every movie you can think of in the past twenty years with the word *computer* in the title. Here's my complete list:

The point is, when you think of a wedding you think of kissing and crying and wedding-night sex and envious bridesmaids and horny ushers and divorced parents forced to sit together and embarrassing Uncle Murray getting drunk at table 7. All those wedding-themed movies got made (and were relatively successful) not because they were great, but because they were all about human *emotion.*

On the other hand, when you think of computers, you think of . . . a dude sitting in his apartment, typing away and, um . . . yeah. Even young males—the demographic group that most drives movie buzz by talking, tweeting, and texting about films (often while they're still in progress)—would rather see one about a wedding than a computer. They bought their tickets on the promise of passion, not technology. Movies that are about technology aren't even about technology; they're actually about people. How much time did James Cameron spend explaining the tech behind the avatars in *Avatar* (and who can remember any of it)? And Aaron Sorkin called his script *The Social Network,* not *The Story of Facebook.*

So we're going to need as much conflict as possible in order to create the full range of human emotions for our poor, put-upon characters: fear, anger, lust, heartbreak, grief, longing, pain, envy, greed, embarrassment, and unmitigated terror. The first words of Neil Jordan's 1999 version of Graham Greene's *The End of the Affair* are "This is a diary of hate." (If they'd been "This is a diary of love," the audience would've already been yawning.)

Even a love story as goopy as *The Bridges of Madison County* starts with conflict: the tragic death of a woman who'd made the agonizing decision to walk away from the one man she truly loved. Yes, your characters may feel positive emotions, too, of course—love, triumph, pride, etc.—but even joy feels more joyful with a healthy dose of conflict. Reuniting with a long-lost lover is more intense if your hero spent years crossing a war-torn continent than if he lost track of her for half an hour at the mall.

Picking Which Conflicts "Stick to Your Spine"

So you're following your protagonist's conflict, but chances are that trail may start to wander around a bit. Especially if you're trying to include all those cool beats you came up with. How do you know when you're going too far afield from your story? Okay, remember my glitter-and-glue analogy? Look at your spine and simply dump all those pretty-but-un-needed story beats off your poster board (but don't throw them away; you might decide to change your story and need them after all). The glitter that's left stuck to the gluey spine are the beats that tell only *that story*.

So your great scene where your hero trains a chimp to use a machine gun and fight Nazis? Well, if your spine is about a high school girl who must decide whether to go to Harvard or follow her dumber boyfriend to a less competitive college, that chimp-assassin beat probably belongs in the discard (but don't delete yet!) file.

Your story is probably starting to take a vague shape by now, but it still may feel like a succession of connected events, rather than a template for a screenplay. You may be starting to wonder . . .

How Do You Shape One Sentence and Some Beats into a Screenplay?

The ABCs of Three-Act Structure—with an X, V, and Z

Next step: Shape your story spine into *three acts.*

Almost all feature films are told in a three-act structure. There's a good reason for this, and it's not because it's just the way things are done. It's because of that diabolical villain of the darkened theater with whom we screenwriters do daily battle . . . General Boredom!

Try telling folks what happened to you today, and you'll find that no matter how amazing your day was or how entertainingly you tell it, your audience will be squirming after about twenty minutes (if you don't have refreshments, they won't last even that long). So screenwriters realized that the best way to tell a movie story was to give the hero a new conflict to deal with about a third of the way through the story, and then do it again roughly two-thirds of the way through. The three resulting story sections are called the acts.

Let me quickly add that you *don't introduce a new story spine* at the end of each act. Your central conflict must remain the same until the last frame of the film. Rather, you shift the protagonist's relationship to the central conflict, so that he or she has a fresh set of headaches.

A good movie to analyze in order to clearly see this effect is *Jaws,* which has a simple but almost perfect structure. First, what's the spine? Let's say "A sheriff who's afraid of the water must save his small coastal town from a predator shark."

In act 1, Chief Brody scans the water for the shark, offers a reward to anyone who kills it, hires shark watchers, etc. But when the shark slips past them and attacks his own son, Brody decides he must go to sea, hunt down the shark, and kill it himself. That's the start of act 2. Why? Because Brody now has a fresh goal within his larger central conflict. In act 2, Brody and his two fellow shark hunters find the shark, shoot it with flotation barrels, and chase it across the sea. But finally the shark turns on them and smashes a hole in their boat's hull, and, as dissension among the men grows, they wind up stranded in a helpless vessel. That's the beginning of act 3. Now the hero's fresh goal is just to survive the shark.

So the protagonist's shifting goals are: Act 1 = prevent the shark from attacking swimmers. Act 2 = find and kill the shark. Act 3 = survive (*HEEEELP!!!*). All three subconflicts are natural progressions within the larger central conflict. In fact, Brody doesn't resolve the spine of the story until he's just about to be eaten, a minute or two before the whole movie's over.

What makes an act, then, is not just Something Big That Happens. Something pretty darn big better happen every few scenes in any movie. What defines a new act is when the protagonist's relationship to the central conflict (the spine) shifts so that he has a new goal. Otherwise, the audience will surely get tired of their hero doing escalating variations on the same thing over and over.

But what if you decide it's easier to tell your story in just two acts? That tends to happen when a feature-length story is divided into a conflict (act 1) and a resolution (act 2), which often results in what many writers call the dreaded "up and back."

Consider some conflict you've faced in your own life. Let's create a story entitled *You Got the Flu*. How did this "story" progress? Rising conflict (you got the sniffles, you started sneezing, you stayed home from work, you went to the doctor, and he gave you a decongestant), followed by resolution (you took the meds, you felt a little better, you went back to work with a box of tissues, then you slowly got back to normal), and The End.

Great story. Not.

Yet that's the way most real-life conflicts—from sniffles to marital spats to wars—progress: a gradual buildup, a peak, and a gradual winddown. And since your hero needs to be actively trying to solve his conflict—just like you did yours in real life—he's also likely to solve it and start the descent toward conflict resolution about halfway through the story. Like this:

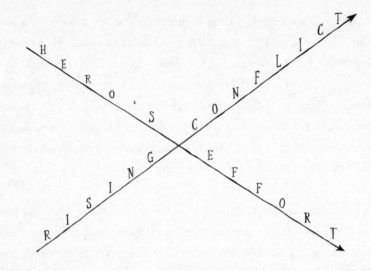

Which means your screenplay's central conflict is going to peak in the middle of the movie and leave you (and your angry audience) with a long, slow, boring, diminishing conflict to sit through, looking something like this upside-down V:

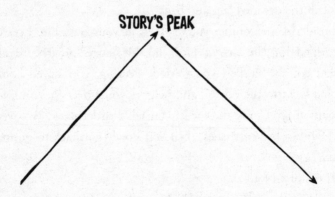

But don't worry! Help is on the way thanks to the three-act structure!

When you use three acts to keep shifting your protagonist's goal, you breathe fresh life into your story just before he can go and fix the nasty conflict you set up for him. So now your screenplay's structure looks something like this:

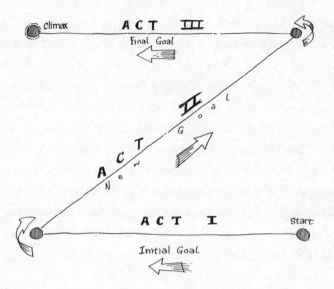

Just for fun, try restructuring our flu story in three acts. For example, it might read:

Act 1: You get the sniffles, start sneezing, go to the doctor, and call in sick. But then . . .

Act 2: Your boss decides to lay off someone in your department. Now you've got to go to work and pretend *not* to be sick. Hilarity ensues, but just when it looks like you've pulled it off, it turns out . . .

Act 3: You accidentally gave the flu to your boss—and you've been doing such a good job, you're named to replace him! So now you've got to prepare for a big presentation with the company's future and your career on the line, all while your flu meds are making you increasingly loopy.

Okay, I didn't say it was a *good* story, but at least the three distinct shifts in the protagonist's relationship to the central conflict may keep the audience who accidentally wandered into *You Got the Flu* engaged enough not to throw popcorn at the screen.

I find it helpful to envision the shape of a screenplay this way, as a Z instead of a straight line, with hash marks on it to denote where the acts should fall. Because a movie shouldn't feel like a straight line (that's even worse than an up-and-back, which at least has *one* twist); instead, it should be like a Z, or a broken-field runner on a football field, shifting directions to keep the audience off balance and wondering, *What happens next?*

But is it possible to tell a movie story in two acts? Well, Mel Brooks's original *The Producers* appears to have been structured in two acts, as were *Idiocracy, Sexy Beast,* and *The Artist,* to name a few. They enjoyed varying degrees of success (though it took thirty years and a Broadway musical for *The Producers* to catch on with general audiences). Most of the time, though, that lack of three major shifts in dramatic energy causes a movie to sputter out somewhere before the finish line. Despite all the filmmaking skill of Roman Polanski, for example, Yasmina Reza's wonderful play *God of Carnage* succumbed to no-third-act exhaustion when turned into the movie *Carnage.*

Pivot Points

Those points where the story turns from act 1 to act 2 or from act 2 to act 3 have different names—*plot points, act breaks,* or the *break into two (or three)*—but I prefer to think of them as *plot pivots.* That's what they should feel like to the audience—pivot points that spin the story off into an exciting, surprising, new direction. Think of when George Lucas had Luke Skywalker find his family dead and vow to become a Jedi knight like his father before him. Or recall exactly one-third of the way through Jeb Stuart and David Twohy's *The Fugitive* when Dr. Richard Kimble decides to head back to Chicago to find the one-armed man. In both cases, there's a subtle but palpable vrooooom in the theater, as the audience senses the engine of the story shifting into a higher gear.

The screenwriter I. A. L. Diamond (who with Billy Wilder wrote such great films as *The Apartment* and *Some Like It Hot*) was once asked about the three-act structure. He shrugged and said, "Act one, get your hero up a tree. Act two, set fire to the tree. Act three, get him out of the tree." That's a pretty good description. And take note of his instinctive use of "set fire to the tree." It's funny, it's scary, and it's *unexpected.* A plot pivot that doesn't surprise us isn't doing what it's supposed to do.

So as a general rule, the sharper, clearer, and more surprising those plot pivots are, the better: e.g., the hit man of Martin McDonagh's *In Bruges* discovering that his gangster boss has sent him to a Belgian tourist town so his partner can enjoy a day of pleasure before he's killed (new goal: how and when to whack his partner), or in Alexander Payne and Nat Faxon & Jim Rash's script for *The Descendants,* Matt King learning that his comatose wife was cheating on him (new goal: track down her lover so he can say good-bye to her).

By comparison, consider the fourth Indiana Jones movie (*Indiana Jones and the Kingdom of the Crystal Skull*): Act 1 ends with a motorcycle-riding punk asking Indy if he knows a Professor Oxley who has vanished in Peru after finding some artifact. Indy says the professor was his beloved mentor and sets off in search of him, fighting bad guys and delivering exposition along the way. But since the audience didn't yet care about the unseen professor or the doohickey he'd found, the impact of all the great action, comedy, and special effects in act 2 was tempered by a vague "Who cares?" feeling—and the story never recovered.

Indiana Jones and the Kingdom of the Crystal Skull made a lot of money, but with all its pedigree, megabudget, and massive marketing campaign, it was generally considered a disappointment. Despite its cadre of certifiably great screenwriters, my guess is that the cause of the film's tepid reception was primarily that sluggish pivot from act 1 to act 2.

I Can't Find My Acts!

Still having trouble finding your plot pivots among the many beats you've generated? Go back to your spine. That clean, simple logline should help you define those elusive three acts. A lot of audiences were stunned when act 3 of Paul Haggis's *Million Dollar Baby* took such a shocking turn. That's because they were used to seeing boxing movies (*Rocky, Raging Bull,* etc.) in which the fighter was the protagonist.

But the spine of *Million Dollar Baby* wasn't "A young woman struggles to become the female boxing champion" (if it had been, the film would've likely opened with Hilary Swank in a trailer park, not Clint Eastwood in a gym). The spine was something like "An old boxing trainer, guilty about once allowing one of his fighters to be blinded, tries to help a young woman become champion *without getting her hurt*." Given that spine, it made perfect sense that the end of act 1 was the trainer reluctantly taking on the young woman as she's getting pummeled in the ring, and that the end of act 2 was her being paralyzed, thus forcing the trainer to decide whether to accede to her wish to be euthanized, the ultimate form of "hurting her."

So by knowing what your story is about—your central conflict—you can more easily locate your three acts in the maze of twists, laughs, scares, and surprises you've dreamed up for us. And those moviegoers who were confused by *Million Dollar Baby*'s abrupt twist? Well, remember, **C**onfusion beats **B**oredom. And they must have ultimately liked the story, because the movie was a big hit.

Once you've got your three-act Z laid out, you should be starting to see the shape of your story. But hang on a bit longer. You're not quite ready to start writing.

Original or Adapted Material: Structuring Them Isn't All That Different

Before diving further into the specifics of structuring a screenplay, I've thus far used a number of films—some original and others adapted—to illustrate points. *Winter's Bone* and *John Carter*, for example, were based on novels; *Prometheus* was based on the earlier *Alien* films and *Battleship* was based on a board game(!). Throughout *Cut to the Chase*, you will encounter the same mix with only a rare distinction made between the two. In the context of discussing structure specifically and screenwriting in general, it's important for you to know that there isn't all that much difference between writing an original screenplay and adapting one based on what the Writers Guild calls "source material."

Even when a screenwriter adapts an existing property, he or she must make crucial decisions about what existing material to include, what to chuck, what to keep but alter, and what will just have to be made up. These decisions are often as difficult as simply writing a script from scratch, since the screenwriter usually must jettison or rethink structure, characters, or scenes from the source material that simply don't work in this incarnation. The great playwright/screenwriter Tom Stoppard said it took him as much time to adapt the BBC/HBO movie of Ford Madox Ford's *Parade's End* as it would have to write a new play; he had to borrow bits from other Ford novels as well as from history in order to find "dramatic events" that would show cinematically many of the subtle, internalized moments from the novel.

As a credit consultant for the Writers Guild, when I judge a script to determine which of its several screenwriters gets credit for what, I am mandated to consider more than simply who wrote what original material. The decisions made concerning what parts of the source novel, play, TV show, prior screenplay, or whatever should be left in or cut out also are inherently creative. And for further insight into the often-maddening process of turning existing work into movies, watch Charlie Kaufman's *Adaptation*.

Fleshing Out Your Three-Act Structure

How Do You Get This Thing Started?

The answer: Quickly. Anyone who tries to tell a little kid the story of Hansel and Gretel and doesn't get them lost in the woods pretty dang fast is going to look up to find his audience chasing the dog around the backyard. So your first order of business is to:

1. Briefly establish the world you're asking us to enter with you.

   By *world* I don't necessarily mean the geographical landscape (although it may include that, especially if your tale is set on another planet or in another period of history); I mean the *emotional* landscape. For example, the world of *Brokeback Mountain* as defined for us by Larry McMurtry and Diana Ossana is the rural West of the early 1960s, where men were heterosexual or else. That is the fundamental fact the audience needs to know, and the storyteller needs to dramatize, in order to tell the spine of that story. In the original *Star Wars,* that opening shot of a teeny spaceship being pursued by the GIGANTIC Star Destroyer established not only that we were "in a galaxy far, far away," but that there was some kind of really, really scary power dominating it. Then . . .

2.   Help us locate your protagonist.

This character is going to be our emotional guide through the movie—we're going to feel whatever he or she feels—so the sooner we find and connect with that person the better. Sitting in a dark theater at the beginning of a movie is like waking up in a strange bedroom. We ask ourselves: Where am I? Who am I with? Do I care about them? That imaginary bedmate is your audience's protagonist. And if your audience finds themselves in bed with multiple protagonists, well, what happens in the movies stays in the movies. But make sure to . . .

3.   Force us to identify with your protagonist.

Major point: The audience doesn't need to *like* that character so much as *identify* with him or her. Many of the movies' great protagonists are pretty rotten people, like Michael Corleone in *The Godfather.* But how did Mario Puzzo and Francis Ford Coppola introduce us to Michael? Escorting his cute, white-bread girlfriend to his sister's wedding, where he's embarrassed by his family. Who hasn't experienced that feeling? And how can anyone feel empathy for a pompous, short-tempered royal? We did in *The King's Speech* when David Seidler introduced us to George VI being humiliated as he speaks in public. Murderous gangster or English king, the screenwriters made the audience feel for them as human beings. They're our boys, whether we like it or not.

Once you've briefly established who your protagonist is and made us feel empathy for him or her, get on with it! The initial event that forces your protagonist into action is often called the *inciting incident.* Put more simply: Start the story already! By the last of the opening credits in *The Fugitive,* Richard Kimble's already been interrogated, arrested, tried, and convicted of his wife's murder, and he's just about to escape from his prison bus (the inciting incident).

Brit Marling and Mike Cahill started their independent feature *Another Earth* with a young woman partying after being accepted into MIT. Then as she's driving home, a radio DJ mentions a new planet has been discovered in our solar system, and as she looks up to see it . . . *bam*! She plows into a family's car, kills the wife and child, and puts the husband in a coma. She stares in horror at what she's done, the sirens approach, and we're all of maybe five minutes into the movie. That's a heckuva start.

Now start laying out your beats (using index cards, a legal pad, or typed bullet points) as you head toward your first plot pivot at the end of act 1. So far so good, but . . .

Solving the Mystery of the Middle

The trick to successful second acts, I think, is not to look at them as some kind of bridge between your beginning and end, or worse still, as a clothesline upon which you hang a string of preconceived beats, but rather as a road trip. The audience is in the backseat and has no idea where they're going; you're in the driver's seat and know where your destination is, even if you're not entirely sure what route you'll be taking to get there. In other words, once you've defined your spine and shaped your story into three acts, your goal is simply to *tell that story.* Take us on a trip that's as cool as you can make it, so long as each scene and joke and shock and reversal is *moving the story forward*—that is, keeping the protagonist on his or her quest to solve the central conflict of the story.

And as you do, keep in mind what we're always trying to make the audience ask: "What happens next?" That's why I find it helpful to *think of all stories as mysteries.* A detective follows clues to solve a riddle. This is pretty obvious if you're writing, say, *Shutter Island,* but what if you're writing a romantic comedy or a personal drama?

Well, at the start of Woody Allen's *Annie Hall,* the protagonist tells us he broke up with his longtime lover and states the "mystery" of the comedy-drama: "I keep examining the pieces of my life and trying to figure out 'Where did the screw-up come?'" The rest of the film provides him (and us) with clues to that mystery, and if you pay attention, you can solve it (though the protagonist never quite does). When he buys Annie philosophy books, makes her see depressing European films, and encourages her to go back to school (all clues), he inadvertently expands her intellectual horizons to the point where she realizes she doesn't need him anymore. Mystery solved: He made her into someone so like himself that she reflected his own self-loathing (or, at least, that's my theory).

Or in *Doubt,* John Patrick Shanley plants a critical clue in his "mystery" when a boy yanks his arm away from a priest's grasp. But then there's another clue: The priest keeps his fingernails long. Did the boy shrink from the priest's touch because he's a molester or because he accidentally scratched the boy's arm? It's a mystery . . . inside a dark, dramatic character study.

Mysteries are sort of like fun minefields: Mini-explosions of information keep going off, each of which should surprise the audience, give them some fresh insight into the truth, and then immediately raise some new question. So try answering this simple question as you move ahead, plotting out your story: Does each new beat contain a *surprise,* an *insight,* and a *question*?

After the opening D-day scene in Robert Rodat's *Saving Private Ryan,* we see the bodies of hundreds of dead men, fish, and equipment on

Omaha Beach, until . . . *surprise:* We finally focus on one dead man with RYAN stenciled on his backpack. *Insight:* There must be something special about him. *Question:* I wonder what it is? Now we cut to a typing pool as a woman writing letters to the families of dead soldiers recognizes Ryan's name and takes three such letters to her supervisor. *Surprise:* Two other Ryan brothers died that same day. *Insight:* Their poor mother will be devastated. *Question:* What is the big brass going to do about the fourth Ryan brother who's alive behind enemy lines?

And on and on the screenplay goes—surprise-insight-and-questioning away—until it finally reaches the final surprise and insight of its mystery: the discovery of who the old soldier was at the Normandy cemetery.

If, as you advance your way through your story, you stop amazing, illuminating, and alluring your audience, they'll start checking the time and wondering what to order at the Cheesecake Factory. Remember, your job is to keep your audience intrigued. So put on your sexiest metaphorical clubbing outfit and start seducing them through your story. In storytelling, playing manipulative mind games is not only acceptable behavior; it's required.

The Midpoint: Your Protagonist Shows the Way

About halfway through your second act, you'll probably find your protagonist's efforts to accomplish his or her goal coming to a head and transitioning into some new phase of the quest. In act 2 of Peter Hedges and Paul and Chris Weitz's *About a Boy,* for example, Hugh Grant's character Will is trying to balance his emotionally isolated playboy lifestyle with the unwanted intrusions of a needy twelve-year-old boy, Marcus. Will avoids him, ignores him, and then grudgingly accepts him into his life. But when he sees Marcus bullied mercilessly, Will decides to try to make the nerdy boy look a little cooler. Will's second-act goal is still basically the same, but his balancing act has shifted as he gets drawn deeper into Marcus's life while still trying to maintain his emotional distance. This is the midpoint of the story.

Personally, I don't ever think about midpoints when I'm writing a script. The reason I don't think about them is because by roughly midway through your story, the natural flow of the narrative will likely build to this transitional peak anyway. If you're keeping your artistic antennae tuned to your audience's potential boredom, you'll sense that your hero's quest will need to have peaks and valleys, and Mount Midpoint is just one major peak.

The problem comes when writers attempt to *write to the midpoint,* and often wind up creating an off-putting lump of plot that doesn't feel natural to the reader. The worst thing a writer can do is to force a story toward artificial benchmarks; it's like putting a dam in a naturally flowing river. The people you should be listening to when you're midway into the storytelling process are your *characters*.

Characters have a way of morphing on us as we write them. A successful screenwriter friend told me that when he gets partway through a script and a character feels like he wants to go in a different direction from the plot, he changes the plot, not the character. There's a very practical reason for this: The audience doesn't watch movies with story outlines in hand. They are engaging with the protagonist on his or her emotional journey. So if the characters aren't doing what feels right to you, the audience will probably feel that way too—and disengage from the story.

Subplots and How to Use and Not Use Them

Sometimes referred to as *B stories,* subplots involve secondary stories and characters and can be used to excellent effect. For example, Woody Allen used a B story in his masterpiece *Crimes and Misdemeanors* to provide comic relief from its dark A story and brilliantly wove them together at the climax when the unpunished murderer of the A story coolly "confesses" his crime to the clueless loser from the B story. John Sayles (*Lone Star, Sunshine State*) regularly uses multiple protagonists and story lines to keep his films fast-paced and to help his complex themes resonate. And intercutting between Richard Kimble's escape and Sam Gerard's pursuit creates a tremendous sense of mounting tension in *The Fugitive*.

But it's hard enough to tell one good movie story, so add *only those characters and secondary plots that help you tell the spine of that story*. If it helps your story to add a sleazy rival who lights a competitive fire under your straitlaced hero, do it. Need a gal pal to listen to your heroine's nutty plan to win her heartthrob? Fine. If it makes the story funnier to contrast your hero's offbeat scheme to get a promotion against a "normal" character's more rational plan, so be it.

Too often, however, beginning writers muddy up their stories with superfluous subplots and characters to disguise the fact that their spine is too weak to hold up a feature-length story.

If you find that's the case for your own story, go back and heighten the protagonist's inner dilemma ("raise the stakes" is studio executives' mantra), as screenwriters Alexander Payne and Jim Taylor did in *Sideways*. Paul Giamatti's character Miles is a frustrated author with a dead-end job and an ex-wife he pines for. That's too bad, but it wouldn't have been enough to hang a movie story on—except that Payne and Taylor made sure we knew that if Miles didn't learn to accept his life the way it was, warts and all, he'd lose his soul—and maybe even kill himself.

Almost Famous was equally well made, but its story (based on the writer-director Cameron Crowe's life) is about a high school kid who covers a rock band's tour for *Rolling Stone* over his mother's objections. And if he doesn't? He'll have to go back to high school, I guess. Like the rest of us. Boo flippin' hoo. The story had to shift to the problems of the band's leader and a groupie since the protagonist's emotional journey would never be compelling enough to affect most audiences.

So shore up your spine if it's necessary, but *never add a subplot unless you really need it*. And if you want some examples of B stories that *didn't* work in movies, they're hard to find—because almost all of them wound up cut in editing.

Hey, how about that? You've almost finished structuring your story.

But What About the Ending?

That's the "almost."

Endings don't have to be as daunting as they may seem, for one simple reason: You don't have to tie up all the plotlines; *you only have to resolve the spine of the story.* There, don't you feel better now? In fact, attempting to create tidy resolutions for every character and subplot often makes your ending feel, well, too tidy. And too long.

What's the resolution of Tony Gilroy's *Michael Clayton*? It's Michael's decision to trash his high-paying career as a sleazy legal "fixer" by wearing a wire and bringing a murderous corporation to justice. He still owes money to the mob, probably lost his job, and has a messed-up personal life, but he resolved the spine of the story: He found out who he was.

The end of *Million Dollar Baby*? The old trainer mercifully injects his boxing protégée with a fatal serum, then quits boxing. Did he ever reunite with his estranged daughter? We'll never know. That wasn't the spine of the story.

Or how about *Sideways*? The story ends with Miles summoning his courage to knock on the door of the woman he loves in order to tell her just that. Movie over. Fade to black. On his knocking fist. We never hear him say he loves her, much less her response (pretty good chance it started with, "I'm really flattered, Miles, but . . ."). It didn't matter what her response might have been; the *spine* of the story was resolved when Miles decided to accept the truth of his life, whatever that might turn out to be.

In fact, it's better if the audience *doesn't* get answers to everything; they'll have something to talk about over dinner. They may even pay to see it again.

But do you need to know what your ending is before you start writing? Yes and no.

I can't imagine starting a screenplay with no idea how it's going to end—although there are screenwriters who swear they do this. My guess is they may not *consciously* have an ending in mind, but their writing experience is making them subliminally move their tale toward a likely resolution. Starting a screenplay half-blind is certainly not a strategy I would advise a beginning writer to adopt. One screenwriter I know likens knowing his ending to hanging a lantern on the end of a pier so he can always find his way if he gets lost on the dark, misty lake (in the fog of storytelling, in case the metaphor's a bit tortured). I think that's a pretty good way to look at endings.

So that's the "yes" in the "yes and no." But . . .

You have to be ready and willing to adjust your lantern when you reach it, or even move it to a different pier sometimes. Or, to return to my road trip analogy, you as the driver may know we're all going to wind up in San Francisco, but you don't necessarily know if we're going to take Interstate 5 or the 101. And you might just decide it'll be more interesting to hang a left and go to Carmel instead.

In other words, when you get there, *change your ending if it's not working the way you imagined it would.* Just make sure you then go back and adjust your beginning and middle if need be so they still make sense with your new finish.

Most importantly, in order for the ending of your story to resolve your spine—and hence send the audience out of the theater feeling satisfied—the protagonist must have an emotional catharsis. And you can probably guess why: because *emotion* is the product our clients (the audience) have paid for.

And for the audience to leave the theater with that emotional rush, your protagonist almost always needs to *face his greatest fear.* In *Jaws,* it's the water and the unseen horrors lurking beneath. In *Million Dollar Baby,* it's killing a surrogate daughter. In *Sideways,* it's the painful reality of a life of failure. In *Brokeback Mountain,* it's the truth about one's sexuality.

Which raises one last point: The protagonist doesn't necessarily *conquer* his greatest fear. Ennis Del Mar in *Brokeback Mountain* doesn't, and he pays a heavy price for it. But the screenwriters did force him to *face* it, and in doing so created a poignant and tragic resolution. And would the ending of *The Godfather* have been better if Michael Corleone had told his wife the truth about his murderous rampage, saved his soul, and devoted his life to doing good deeds?

Probably not.

So What Are Those Three Words Guaranteed to Make You a Successful Screenwriter?

Write great screenplays.

See? I told you withholding information was more powerful than revealing it. And by the way, it's also the absolute truth. After thirty years as a professional writer, I've never known one writer with talent *and* perseverance who didn't have some measure of success in Hollywood.

So, what happens next? That's up to you.

CHAPTER 4

Building Characters
by Cindy Davis

A few years ago, I asked my agent what studio execs were looking for in a screenplay. He said, "Simple plot, complex characters." The answer seemed too rational, so I polled a few others in the film industry. *The exact same words* came out of their mouths: "Simple plot, complex characters." They said it reflexively, almost robotically, the way you'd answer "What's two plus two?"

I knew I had to take notice.

Since then, I've become obsessed with figuring out how to create complex characters—and how to do it efficiently. As a working screenwriter (I've written features for Pixar, Working Title, Miramax, New Line, Disney, and Fox), I'm often asked to generate full-fledged pitches in a matter of days, so I don't have time to screw around.

Many screenwriting books urge screenwriters to concoct detailed backstories for each character and to fill out long questionnaires. As a film student, I spent hours doing this stuff. And it never helped. I was certain I was doing it wrong (being female and a screenwriter, self-flagellation comes naturally). But now that I teach classes at UCLA

Extension and I'm all cocky and full of myself, I know better. These exercises are what I call "decaf, nonfat lattes." Feel free to try them, but really, what's the point?

Instead, I've attempted to craft a more efficient method of building stylish, complex characters. The eight major steps include: defining the character's broad stroke, finding the paradox of the character, selecting signature traits for the character, getting the audience behind the character, adding the internal layer, showing new sides to the character, making the character "actor bait," and, lastly, keeping it real. What follows is a more detailed description of how to execute these steps.

If you execute all eight steps, you should end up having a big, juicy, complex character on your hands.

Step 1: Define the Main Character's Broad Stroke

First, decide on your main character's broad stroke (i.e., how the character will act most of the time). When I begin a script, I fill in the blank in this sentence: "Most of the time my character will act like _____." Seriously. I fill in that blank. Locking this choice down is a critical step in creating a strong, consistent character.

Trick: If you're waffling on what your main character's broad stroke should be, try inserting different character descriptions into your logline to see which description makes the logline most compelling. For example, the logline for *Finding Nemo* is "A clownfish must travel across the ocean to find his son." The writer could have chosen any broad stroke for the main character: bossy, bored, lazy, insane. But he chose to make the clownfish ocean-fearing. This choice of broad stroke works brilliantly: It's relevant to the logline, it's ironic, and it ensures that the main character is going to have a big, life-altering journey.

Once you've decided on your main character's broad stroke, you need to make sure you deliver on it when writing the script. To do so, take the following three steps.

Craft a Pithy One-or-Two-Line Character Introduction

I highly recommend taking the time to write a precise, stylish sentence when introducing your main character. Introductory descriptions tend to be strongest when they not only describe the character's appearance but also the core of the character's personality. One of my favorite examples is from the pilot of the TV show *Gossip Girl*, which describes Blair Waldorf this way: "Pretty. But will never feel beautiful enough." Simple, yet it says volumes.

Many of my students look distressed when I give the above example, because they've had it drummed into them that describing feelings is verboten. Dozens of screenwriting books preach that screenwriters are only allowed to describe what a viewer can see and hear, verbatim, on-screen. But in my experience, screenplays are becoming more and more like novels, and less and less like blueprints of a film. Readers are busy. They don't have time to infer what's going on in the script. They need the writer to spell it out for them. Now, more than ever, it's up to the writer to get the reader to experience the film. I honestly believe that learning this *one piece* of information could mean the difference between having a career as a screenwriter and being a struggling, bitter, whiny writer.

So just in case it didn't sink in, I'm going to repeat it another way: *It's your job, screenwriter, to get the reader to see and feel your movie through what you've written on the page.*

Reiterate the Main Character's Broad Stroke Multiple Times Within the First Few Pages of Your Script

A friend of mine recently got engaged, but she was concerned. Her fiancé had told her *once* that he loved her, but he'd never said it again. She finally mentioned this issue to him, and he explained that he didn't see any reason to repeat it. If the way he felt about her changed, he'd let her know.

When I tell this story, most people (especially women) grimace. Why did my friend need her fiancé to reiterate his love for her? Because people change. And people lie. And you never know when they might decide to do so.

This is especially true for characters in a script. When readers first open your script, they've never met your characters before. They have no idea if your character is about to change or if he's a pathological liar. Therefore, right off the bat, you need to solidify who your main character is in the eye of the reader. After you've described your main character's broad stroke with your pithy introductory sentence, you need to reiterate it. Multiple times. In both the character's dialogue and his actions. *Without being redundant.* Here are three ways to sell your character's broad stroke.

The Mini-Montage Method

In *The 40-Year-Old Virgin,* the writers described the main character, Andy Stitzer, as a boyish forty-year-old man. Then they delivered on it:

On page 1, we get a mini-montage of Andy's morning routine: Andy wakes up in a room dominated by sci-fi posters and action figures; Andy does a lame workout with equipment he bought from late-night TV; Andy takes a bubble bath; Andy tucks his pant leg into his sock, preparing to ride his bike to work. On page 2, we learn that Andy regularly spends his evenings watching *Survivor* with his eighty-year-old neighbors. Once Andy leaves, the neighbors discuss how obvious it is that Andy needs to get laid. On page 3, a gorgeous woman with massive cleavage enters the electronics store where Andy works; Andy doesn't notice. And on page 4, Andy tells a coworker about his weekend: He spent it making egg salad.

Four pages in, and readers know exactly who this character is—which they find overwhelmingly satisfying. (To fully appreciate why this is so satisfying, try reading ten unproduced scripts a day, like readers do. You'll see that a script with a consistent main character is a *godsend.*)

Do be aware, however, that producers often cringe at montages—one producer explained to me that *montage* is French for "a big waste of money." So here are two other strong methods of introducing a main character.

The Defining Scene Method

To use the defining scene method, introduce your main character doing an action that defines him. *About a Boy,* for example, opens with such a scene. We meet Will, an extremely hip bachelor, visiting an ex-girlfriend who has a new baby girl. Will is thoroughly awkward around his ex-girlfriend's kids and horrified by the mess they make. Then Will's ex-girlfriend asks if Will would like to be the baby's godfather. Will replies, "I am truly, truly . . . touched. But you must be kidding. I couldn't possibly think of a worse godfather for Imogen. I'd drop her on her head at the christening, then I'd forget about her birthdays until her eighteenth, when I'd take her out, get her drunk, and try to shag her. Seriously. Very bad choice."

This scene defines who Will is—a confirmed bachelor who dislikes kids—and it sets up how difficult the rest of the story is going to be for Will, who'll be forced to befriend a young boy.

The Mini-Story Method

This is also a strong way to introduce your main character, especially for an action film, because it starts the story off with a bang. With the mini-story method, the writer opens the story on the main character tackling a mini-goal that is different from (but usually related to) the main goal he'll tackle later on. For example, *Saving Private Ryan* opens with a mini-goal. The main character, Captain John Miller, has landed with his troops on Omaha Beach during World War II, and his mini-goal is to get them to a safe overhang.

Within this nine-page mini-story, we see Miller make jokes and put his troops at ease, despite all the death and chaos around him. We see him forge ahead with his military objective, even though he's fully aware that it's insane. We see him draw fire so two of his men can dive for cover. Once the mini-story has concluded, we are in awe of Captain Miller and know without a doubt who his character is.

Continue to Remind the Reader of the Broad Stroke Throughout Act 2

You've written your pithy introductory sentence; you've reiterated the character's broad stroke multiple times throughout the first few pages. And you're still not done. For your character to be memorable and consistent, you need to sprinkle in beats that remind the reader of the character's broad stroke *throughout the entire second act.*

Andy Stitzer engages in more man-boy behaviors throughout act 2 of *The 40-Year-Old Virgin,* Will acts like a shallow bachelor throughout *About a Boy,* and Captain Miller awes us with selfless acts of heroism throughout *Saving Private Ryan.* If these main characters didn't repeat their defining actions throughout their stories, their characterizations would feel muddy, inconsistent, and disappointing.

Step 2: Find the Paradox of the Character

Once you've crafted your main character's broad stroke, you may want to add a paradox to the description. This may seem contradictory, especially since I just blathered on in previous paragraphs about how writers need to keep their characters consistent. However, if you pick an intriguing, believable paradox for your character, it can take your character from being run-of-the-mill to being truly fascinating.

For example, the main characters in both *Shrek* and *Erin Brockovich* have strong paradoxes. Shrek's broad stroke is that he's a disgusting ogre, *but* the paradox of his character is that he has a soft side. Erin Brockovich's broad stroke is that she's a broke single mom who dresses like a bimbo, *but* the paradox of her character is that she's razor sharp. For both of these characters, the paradox gives them great dimension.

WARNING: Do not "over-*but*" your character. I had a student who was so eager to make her main character dimensional that she gave the character multiple paradoxes, all within the first few pages of her script. Instead of being dimensional, the character was unbelievably confusing.

Remember: Whenever you apply any screenwriting tip to your writing, *keep it real*. If the change doesn't feel believable or organic, don't do it.

If you've decided to give your character a paradox, you then need to decide when to reveal it. The timing of this reveal can significantly impact how readers relate to your character. In *Erin Brockovich,* for example, the fact that the busty, blond main character is actually very intelligent is revealed right off the bat. We're introduced to Erin at a job interview, where she reveals that she's a fast learner, she fell madly in love with geology at her last job, and she helped design part of the Alaskan pipeline. This makes it much easier to believe a major plot point that is soon to come: Erin will take on a lawsuit against a major corporation, despite having no formal legal training. If the writer waited until that plot point to reveal Erin's smarts, we might find the entire story an eye-roller.

In *Election,* the main character's paradox is revealed later. We're first introduced to Tracy Flick as her high school's most eager, ethical, ambitious Goody Two-shoes. Then on page 9, the writers reveal Tracy's paradox: Tracy is sleeping with one of her teachers. It's a jaw-dropper of a reveal, which makes the reader even more intrigued with Tracy. If the writers had chosen to begin the story with Tracy in bed with her teacher and *then* shown her to be ambitious, readers would perceive Tracy as primarily duplicitous, rather than primarily ambitious. When writing your script, try experimenting with revealing your character's paradox at different times to determine which placement gives you the effect you wish to achieve.

Step 3: Select Signature Traits for the Character

Truly memorable characters usually have signature traits. Here are four categories of traits to consider when crafting your character.

Repeat a Word or Phrase

Try giving your main character a catchphrase. Cuba Gooding Jr. repeats the phrase *Show me the money* in *Jerry Maguire*—a memorable facet of his

Oscar-winning performance. Or, if a catchphrase feels wrong for your character, try giving him a word he repeats. Tracy Flick, for example, uses the word *travesty* three times in the movie *Election*—a perfect word for a young overachiever who's desperate to be taken seriously. It's a subtle detail, but readers feel smart when they pick up on these things. And who doesn't love a writer who makes them feel smart?

Repeat an Action

Try giving your main character a specific action to repeat. Jimmy Stewart's character in *Harvey* always hands out his business cards, while Sarah Jessica Parker's character spends a lot of time twirling in *L.A. Story.* Both are memorable traits that make the characters endearing.

Repeat a Behavior

Try giving your main character a distinctive way of behaving around others. In *The Silence of the Lambs,* Hannibal Lecter has a habit of verbally dissecting anyone in his presence. When Clarice Starling first visits him, he hisses, "That accent you're trying so desperately to shed—pure West Virginia. What was your father, dear? Was he a coal miner? Did he stink of the lamp? And oh, how quickly the boys found you! All those tedious sticky fumblings, in the backseats of cars, while you could only dream of getting out. Getting anywhere, yes? Getting all the way to the F . . . B . . . I."

Later, a senator visits Lecter, and he dissects her, too, asking, "Did you breast-feed [your daughter]? . . . Toughened your nipples, didn't it?" And as the senator leaves, he adds, "Oh, and, Senator . . . ? *Love* your suit." This repeated behavior helps make Lecter one of the most memorable characters in film.

Clothing

Try giving your main character a unique way of dressing. In *Legally Blonde*, Elle is defined by the fact that she always wears fashionable clothes and that her signature color is pink. Similarly, in *Fast Times at Ridgemont High*, Spicoli's unique, laid-back attitude is clearly underscored by his choice of obnoxious black-and-white checkerboard slip-ons.

Once you've chosen signature traits for your character, liberally repeat the traits throughout your script. When I first read the script for *Erin Brockovich*, I was shocked by how many times the writer reiterated Erin's manner of dressing. On page 2, she's described as wearing a miniskirt and a tight top, looking beautiful but "clearly from a social class and geographic orientation whose standards for displaying beauty are not based on subtlety." On page 4, Erin is in "a teensy, leopard-print mini-dress. As she jiggles a spike-heeled foot, everything about her shimmies gloriously." On page 5, Erin is dressed for court wearing "the most conservative thing she owns: a red, form-fitting mini dress."

Three examples in five pages. Wouldn't the reader find that redundant? Nope. The reader *loves* it. Five pages in, and Erin Brockovich's signature trait is firmly etched in the reader's brain.

Step 4: Get the Audience Behind the Character

One of the more annoying things a producer can say after reading your script is "Why should we care?" But it's a good question. When a screenwriter presents a feature film script to a producer, the writer is essentially asking that producer to raise somewhere between ten and three hundred million dollars to turn the script into a film. In order for the film to make money, the story needs to connect with millions of people. Not thousands. *Millions.* Therefore, the story's main character must display traits that are likely to inspire a big chunk of the human population to care. Here are eight ways to boost the likelihood that your main character will be universally embraced.

The Main Character Has a Clear Goal

At the end of act 1, have your main character decide on a concrete goal, and then, *for the entire second act,* keep your character pursuing that goal. When crafting my first act break, I fill in the following blank: "My main character *decides* to _____." This protects me from crafting a passive main character. Because readers *hate* passive main characters. Why? Try reading a script where the main character takes little action and has no clear goal, and see how many pages it takes before you start eyeing your paper shredder.

The Main Character Is Picked On, Screwed Over, Humiliated, or Harmed in Some Way, *but* He Stands Up for Himself

If your character is victimized in some way, but he keeps forging ahead, virtually every reader will want to root for him. Liam Neeson's character in *Taken* is a prime example of this. Not only is he dissed by his ex-wife and her new rich husband; he's forced to listen on the phone as his daughter gets kidnapped by members of a sex-slave crime ring. When Liam Neeson takes matters into his own hands to get his daughter back, the audience gets behind him.

The Main Character Is Trying Hard to Improve, but No One Will Let Him

Hard workers are universally loved, and they're even more inspiring when others thwart their efforts. In *American Beauty,* for example, Kevin Spacey goes to great lengths to get some feeling back into his life—he quits his degrading job; he starts working out. He's making real progress, and yet his wife tells him, "You will not get away with this." Similarly, in *Working Girl,* Melanie Griffith does everything she can to improve her low-class life, but her best friend keeps pooh-poohing her efforts, saying things like,

"Sometimes I sing and dance around the house in my underwear. It doesn't make me Madonna. Never will." Both of these slights instantly inspire an audience to cheer on the main character.

The Main Character Is Passionate About His Goal

Passion is infectious. When a character pursues a goal with unbridled passion, the audience invariably gets sucked into hoping the character achieves that goal, no matter what the goal is. In *Bottle Rocket,* Owen Wilson has so much enthusiasm for becoming a thief, the audience gets behind him, even though his goal is stupid and illegal. In *Four Weddings and a Funeral,* the audience is dying to see Hugh Grant win over Andie MacDowell—even though she's a bit on the slutty side—because *he* wants her so badly. Add passion to your main character, if possible. Characters who waffle about what they want are much harder to get behind.

The Main Character Is Funny

Audiences will forgive almost any mistake a character makes if he's funny. Look at *Iron Man*. The writers purposely opened the movie on Tony Stark rattling off witty lines of dialogue, cracking up all the soldiers in his Humvee. The movie then flashes back to the true beginning of the story, where Tony screws over his best friend by not showing up for an awards banquet. Pretty rude behavior, but the audience instantly forgives him, because they've already been charmed.

The Main Character Is Uniquely Clever or Skilled

Try beefing up your main character's skill level, if in doubt about his appeal. In *The Bourne Identity,* for example, Jason Bourne is a trained killer. Not the most likable occupation. But he's so phenomenally good at it, he's fascinating to watch.

The Main Character Has Humility

You may have noticed how many actors make appearances on *Saturday Night Live* after they've made jerks of themselves in public. When characters make fun of themselves, audiences will forgive most any indiscretion. This is true both in real life and in film. In the film *Arthur,* for example, Dudley Moore may be a spoiled drunk, but he is kind to everyone he meets, including hookers and bums. He's also self-deprecating, saying heartbreaking lines like "Everyone who drinks is not a poet. Some of us drink because we're not poets." This humility makes him one of the most lovable alcoholics on film.

The Main Character Helps Others

Jack Nicholson in *As Good as It Gets* may be a jerk, but when he pays for a high-end doctor to help Helen Hunt's son, it's hard not to soften toward the guy. Bill Murray's character in *Groundhog Day* is similarly unlikable. But at the end of the movie, he selflessly helps out dozens of townsfolk, ensuring that the audience feels good about Bill's character once they leave the theater. Try having your character help others to ensure his likability.

Once you've decided on what universally loved traits from the above eight categories you're going to give your main character, try to reveal one of these traits *within the first few pages of the script.* If readers immediately fall in love with your character, they will be much more likely to forgive any flaws you reveal later on.

Learning how to get the audience behind your main character is so important that you should take pains to build this mental muscle. Generally I hate exercises that I find in screenwriting books because they're usually filler that the author himself would never waste time doing. But here's an exercise I recommend and actually do myself.

Make a list of films that have characters you adore, rewatch those films, and note the *exact moment* the "I *love* that character!" feeling hits you. What evoked that response? Tease it apart—was it *one* specific line of dialogue? Two lines? Three? Was it an action? Learn what techniques work on you, and then use these techniques for your own characters. You'll be able to execute these techniques most believably, because they resonate with you.

Step 5: Add the Internal Layer

All of the above steps addressed who your main character is from an external point of view. This step will address what's going on inside your character's head. I wholeheartedly believe that by constructing a strong internal layer for your main character, you can turn an average movie into an Oscar-caliber one. So, in other words, don't skip this step.

Give the Character One Big Problem to Solve

Start by coming up with one big personal problem that your main character will struggle with *for the duration of the story*. In *Saving Private Ryan,* for example, Captain Miller struggles with the fact that he is risking six men's lives to save one—a microcosm of the insanity of war. Almost every scene raises this issue, and amazingly, it never feels redundant. Just the opposite. The story feels cohesive and meaningful because of it.

Have a Character Spell Out What Your Main Character's Big Problem Is Early On, Somewhere in Act 1

Once you've decided what your main character's big problem is, make sure to spell it out early on in your script. Seriously. Don't be subtle. Try having a friend of the main character point out the problem to him. For example, on page 4 of *About a Boy,* one of Will's many ex-girlfriends points Will's problem out to him, saying, "You're 38, you've never had a job, or a relationship that lasted more than two months, except for me, and I chucked you because you were hopeless. . . . You're a disaster. I

CUT TO THE CHASE

mean, what's the point of your life?" Will struggles with this problem for the duration of the movie.

You could also have the main character reveal his problem to the audience himself. In the opening of *American Beauty,* for example, Lester Burnham sums up his problem for us in a voice-over: "Both my wife and daughter think I'm this gigantic loser. And they're right. I have lost something. I'm not exactly sure what it is, but I know I didn't always feel this . . . *sedated.* But you know what? It's never too late to get it back." Within the first few minutes of meeting Lester, readers know exactly what his problem is—as opposed to the movie *The Weather Man,* starring Nicolas Cage. *The Weather Man* is similar in tone to *American Beauty,* but the writer never spells out what Nicolas Cage's problem is. We see Cage gets hit by food repeatedly, but we never find out why. Cage seems to be distraught about his life, but we never learn what's he's distraught about. Many questions are raised, but never answered.

Guess which movie won the Oscar for Best Picture?

Know What Led the Main Character to Having His Big Problem

If you have time to create a detailed backstory for your main character, that's great. But if you don't, there's one bit of backstory I recommend you know: how the main character came to have the big problem he's struggling with. Why? Because this information is so intriguing, you'll most likely want to put it in your script. Here are three strong ways to utilize this backstory: as a prologue, as a flashback, or in small bits throughout the script.

In *Finding Nemo,* for example, the main character's problem is that he's overprotective and fears the ocean. In the prologue, we learn why: His wife and kids were eaten by a barracuda. In *The 40-Year-Old Virgin,* we learn through a hilarious flashback why the main character is forty years old and still a virgin: He had three mortifying sexual experiences when he was younger, which turned him off sex altogether. Lastly, in *In the Line of Fire,* the backstory of the main character (played by Clint Eastwood) is revealed in bits throughout the story. Through a series of phone calls with his nemesis (John Malkovich), we learn that Eastwood's character is a secret service agent who failed to protect JFK from being assassinated. The story culminates with Clint Eastwood retelling his backstory in detail—a cathartic moment that enables him to forgive himself and move on.

All three of these methods are equally effective. Choose whichever works best for your story; just be sure to keep the information entertaining and to the point.

Regularly Let Readers into the Main Character's Head

For readers to easily understand what's going on inside your character's head, don't be afraid to spell it out for them. Here are three methods I recommend.

Use "Wilson's Method"

Try having one character analyze another character. I call this "Wilson's Method," because Wilson on the TV show *House M.D.* is always analyzing Dr. House. The audience would have no idea how clever House is without Wilson theorizing about House's manipulations. Another master of this method is Hannibal Lecter. He regularly pries information out of Clarice's head and extrapolates from there, saying things like, "You still wake up sometimes, don't you? Wake up in the dark, with the lambs screaming?" The best part of this method: It adds depth to both characters involved.

Describe What the Character Is Feeling

I know many screenwriting books ban this technique, but look at what the Oscar-winning writer of *The Departed* put in his script. In the scene where Billy (played by Leonardo DiCaprio) first meets Captain Queenan and Sergeant Dignam, we get the following descriptions of Billy's mental state: "Billy has no idea why he is in this room with the brass"; "Billy doesn't want to answer unless he can answer correctly"; and "Billy wouldn't normally take crap from this guy, but he does." We are in Billy's head, and it makes for a great read. This is not verboten. This is necessary.

However, it is important to be judicious when using this powerful tool, because it's easy to use it badly. If you find yourself explaining specific events that happened in the past (e.g., "Billy took a yoga class prior to meeting with the brass, so he's able to handle the meeting more calmly than usual"), you're writing a novel, not a screenplay.

End a Scene off a Character's Look

To remind yourself to address the emotional layer of each scene, you may want to borrow a trick from TV writers. They often end scenes with "OFF [insert character's name here]" and then describe what's going on in the character's head, followed by an ellipsis. For example, "OFF ROBERT, feeling like a movie star . . ." Or "OFF SUSAN, wheels turning in her mind . . ."

Step 6: Show New Sides to the Character

To create a truly dimensional character, guess what? You need to show that the character has more than one dimension. We've already discussed adding a paradox within the first few pages of the script. To keep the reader intrigued, continue to reveal new facets of your character as your story progresses. Here are four ways to do so.

Show a Moment Where the Main Character Behaves Differently from His Broad Stroke

Once you've *firmly* established the main character's broad stroke, it's surprisingly effective to have the character behave in the opposite manner, but only for a brief moment. Try having a tough character show a hint of vulnerability, or have a meek character lash out for a second. See how much more intriguing this character becomes. For example, Erin Brockovich is one of the toughest, most resilient characters on film, even threatening that she won't leave her lawyer's office unless he gives her a job. But then, on page 15 of the script, we get a glimpse of her vulnerable side. In a low, desperate voice, she tells her lawyer, "Don't make me beg. If it doesn't work out, fire me . . . But don't make me beg"—a memorable, Oscar-winning moment.

(To clarify, this differs from the character's paradox, which is a trait that defines the character for the entire film. Erin Brockovich's paradox is that she's an uneducated bimbo who's razor sharp, not an uneducated bimbo who's vulnerable. The vulnerability is a small, rare moment.)

Show the Character Having a Private Moment

I always try writing a scene where my main character is by himself, just to see what my character will do. This "private moment" scene often reveals a unique side to the character, and, since the moment is supposed to be private, it's usually titillating for an audience to watch. For example, one of the most riveting scenes in *American Beauty* is of Annette Bening, by herself, slapping her face and calling herself a big baby. Try writing a scene where your main character is alone. Chances are, that scene will end up in the final draft of your script.

Show the Main Character Interacting Differently with Different Characters

If your main character seems to act the same with everyone in your script, try throwing a curveball character into the story. For example, if your main character always acts cool and hip, try writing a scene of him with his mother. Or if your character is always nice to everyone, try a scene where he runs into someone who makes him furious. For a memorable example of this, watch what happens when the super-nice hotel receptionist in *Forgetting Sarah Marshall* runs into her ex-boyfriend. Contrasts like these are fascinating to watch and make a character feel much more real and alive.

Stick the Character in an Intense Situation

A new facet of a character often reveals itself when a character is placed in an unfamiliar or intense situation. For instance . . .

A Big Ethical Decision to Make

Try sticking your main character into a situation where he has a big ethical decision to make. In *Election,* for example, Tracy Flick, in a fit of rage, shreds her competitor's campaign posters; afterward she has to decide— should she tell the truth or cover it up? Her choice reveals a whole new layer to her character.

A Life-or-Death Situation

Placing your character into a life-or-death situation can be particularly revealing, especially when the character has never encountered a situation of this intensity before. For example, it's thrilling when pampered, feminine Elizabeth Swann gets attacked by pirates in *Pirates of the Caribbean.* She doesn't cry and wait for a strong man to save her. Instead, she fearlessly kicks some butt.

A Fish-out-of-Water Situation

Fish-out-of-water stories are favorites among Hollywood producers. Try plopping your main character into an environment that's the opposite of that to which he's accustomed, and see how he reacts. *Legally Blonde* contains a great example of this. When blond sorority girl Elle arrives at Harvard, she could easily be disdainful or threatened by all the snobby, unattractive law nerds. Instead, Elle maintains her bubbly, social nature and treats all the nerds like her best friends. This makes Elle's character even more endearing.

Step 7: Make the Character "Actor Bait"

A script is much easier to sell if the main character has a big, juicy role that famous actors will kill to play. Here are a few ways to make "actor bait" out of your main character.

The Big Introduction

To create a big, showy introduction for a character, try having other characters talk about the character before the audience meets him. Miranda (Meryl Streep) in *The Devil Wears Prada* gets an introduction like this. Not only does Miranda's assistant gloat about what a legend Miranda is, but the entire office goes into full panic mode when Miranda is about to arrive. Rick in *Casablanca* is also introduced this way. Everyone in Casablanca talks about Rick and has an opinion about him. Even before the audience meets Rick, they're already fascinated by him.

The Character Experiences a Wide Range of Emotions

Nothing makes a role actor bait like Oscar potential. For a role to be showy enough to catch the Academy's attention, the character generally has to display a wide range of emotions. Try to place your main character in a variety of scenes that allow the actor to express a vast emotional range. And go for broke. Don't just make your character mad, make him enraged; don't just make your character happy, make him ecstatic. Actors will love you for it—and jump at the role.

Killer Dialogue

Most importantly, give the main character multiple lines of dialogue that an actor will be dying to deliver.

The Main Character's First Line

Take care with the first line of dialogue that your main character says. See if you can craft a line that encapsulates who this character is. In *The Dark Knight,* for example, the first line the Joker says is, "I believe that what doesn't kill you . . . simply makes you stranger." Not only is the line intriguing; it gives great insight into who the Joker is. That's serious actor bait.

A Few Great Lines Within the First Few Pages

Give the main character a critical mass of great lines within the first fifteen or twenty pages, and the actor will be on the phone with his agent before he finishes reading the script. Check out what Kyra Sedgwick's character says within the first twenty pages of the pilot for the TV show *The Closer:* 1) "I'm sorry, Detective, but if I liked being called a bitch to my face, I'd still be married." 2) "Mother. Listen. You always ask that. . . . And it ends up being an argument about what I do for a living and it's just too late to go back and try the ballet." 3) "You know, right now they may dislike me just because I'm new. Or because I hold a position above their old boss. But I want you to relax, Henry. Because once I roll up my sleeves and go to work, and they see me in action, why, they'll have a whole list of other reasons to hate my guts. Feel better?"

No wonder the show ran for seven seasons and earned Sedgwick an Emmy Award.

Creating great dialogue is so important, we devote an entire chapter to it in this book. At this point, suffice it to say that people in Hollywood tend to think that anyone can craft a great story (ha!), whereas writing great dialogue is a gift. So if you want a career as a writer, take the time to make your dialogue sparkle.

Step 8: Keep It Real

Finally, here are three simple words that have taken me years to learn: *Keep it real.* I write comedies, and early on in my career, producers would prod me to make my story "bigger" or to "amp it up." I had no idea what they meant, so I tried adding physical humor or more obvious jokes. Wrong. I tried adding set pieces. Wrong. What ultimately worked was *keeping the story real*. When the characters were dimensional and felt like actual human beings, that's when producers got excited. So here are a few ways to prod yourself into keeping your story real:

Stick a Big Sign on Your Computer That Reads "KEEP IT REAL"

I'm serious. And then deliver on it. In each scene, make sure your characters behave realistically and make believable choices. Also, make sure each character's behavior tracks from one scene to the next. For example, I just read one of my students' scripts—it started with a girl panicking because she discovered her psychotic ex-boyfriend was on an airplane with her. In the very next beat, the girl was rocking out to her iPod and flipping through a fashion magazine. Huh? She's on a plane with a psycho stalker! How can she be this cavalier? It's your job as a writer to comb your script for these inconsistent behaviors, and having a constantly present reminder will help you do that.

Base the Character on a Real Human Being

When you first create a character, basing him on a real human being is a great place to start. Often, it helps to combine characteristics of a few people you know. Borrowing from real life is a great way to find fresh details that crackle with authenticity. There are a few flaws to this technique, however: Sometimes, what people do in real life is just too weird and unbelievable for a script. You have a built-in sense of what seems real and what seems fake—you must utilize this sense, even on *real* details. You're not allowed to use the defense "But that really happened!" if everyone who reads your script says it just doesn't ring true.

Also, only base a character on yourself if you're certain that you're self-aware. (Here's a test to see if you're self-aware: Did you immediately think,

"Oh yeah, I'm totally self-aware," after reading the previous sentence? If so, you're probably not self-aware. I'm just saying.) I've had multiple *un*self-aware students write autobiographical stories, and it's not pretty when everyone in the class gives the comment "Why is the main character such an asshole?" Therefore, use this technique at your own risk.

Hang a Lantern on It

Sometimes you need a character to do something that is just not true to his or her nature. How can you do this and still keep the story real? As a last-ditch effort, try "hanging a lantern on it." In other words, try shining a light on the flaw in your story. When you point out to the reader that you know there's an inconsistency, sometimes you can get away with it. Here's an example from *Casablanca:* Ferrari is a businessman who only looks out for himself. Ilsa and Laszlo come to him for letters of transit. After they decline his offer, Ferrari generously offers them another option—which is *totally wrong for his character.* So the writers "hung a lantern on it" by having Ferrari say, "I am moved to make one more suggestion, why, I do not know, because it cannot possibly profit me."

Here's a more modern example, from *Reservoir Dogs:* Steve Buscemi's character arrives at a prearranged meeting place after his team's bank robbery goes bad. He's certain that someone set them up, and whoever did so must know about this meeting place as well. So *why in the world* does Steve Buscemi show up at the meeting place? It's a completely illogical move on his part. So Quentin Tarantino "hung a lantern on it." He had Buscemi's character say, "What the f**k am I doing here?" Because Buscemi's character points out that he made an illogical move, the audience still feels like they're in good hands.

Only Use Tips That Feel Organic

Now that I've given you all these tips on how to build complex characters, I'm going to give you one final tip: Don't use any of these tips *unless* they make your character stronger. Screenwriting tips aren't rules for you to obey; they're tools for you to try. If any tip directs you toward something that feels inorganic, throw it out. Many beginning writers force screen-writing "rules" onto their scripts and then they complain that using these rules made their script formulaic. It's not the rules' fault. It's up to the writer to understand, on a gut level, why these "rules" exist, and to use them responsibly, always keeping the characters real and the story beats organic.

So that's how you *build* a complex character in the beginning of your script. What do you do with your character for the rest of your script? For the answer, read the next chapter: "Deepening Characters and Defining Their Arcs."

For easy access, here's a checklist of the above tips, listed in order of how I personally use them when I'm crafting a script.

Building Complex Characters Checklist
In the Outline Phase

- Define the main character's broad stroke.

- Find the paradox of the character.

- Select signature traits for the character.

- Get the audience behind the character.

- Give the main character one big problem to solve; figure out what led the main character to having this problem.

In the Script-Writing Phase
ACT 1
- Craft a pithy one-or-two-line character introduction.

- Reiterate the main character's broad stroke multiple times within the first few pages.

- Craft multiple lines of dialogue that an actor would kill to say.

- Have a character spell out what the main character's big problem is somewhere in the first act.

ACT 2, FIRST HALF

- Continue to remind the reader of the main character's broad stroke throughout the second act.

- Regularly let readers inside the character's head.

- Show new sides to the character.

CHAPTER 5

Deepening Characters and Defining Their Arcs

by Billy Mernit

> The secret subject of any story worth telling is what we learn
> or fail to learn over time.
>
> —Robert Penn Warren

The 3-D comic book superhero action blockbuster that zoomed past Batman, Harry Potter, and the *Star Wars* clan in 2012 to become the third-highest grosser of all time ($623 million domestic and counting) featured some spectacularly explosive pyrotechnics. But I don't remember its fans waxing ecstatic about how well *The Avengers* blew things up. No, people were most excited about how this movie finally got the Hulk (Mark Ruffalo) right, how awesome the wit and cool of Iron Man (Robert Downey Jr.) was, how they liked seeing the sexy and sophisticated Black Widow (Scarlett Johansson) kick ass, and what a compelling creep Loki (Tom Hiddleston) was. What most wowed its audience were the movie's people.

The Avengers is a character-driven movie. True, it's full of eyeball-filling sci-fi set pieces, but writer-director Joss Whedon's most significant achievement lies in bringing a slew of two-dimensional comic book creations to life as believable human beings distinctly set apart from each other. There's no confusing Captain America's World War II–era naïveté with Thor's Viking-prince loftiness, or Hawkeye's solo sniper mentality with Nick Fury's paternal team-leader sensibility. Each superhero has a unique point of view and most of them start from a competitive, every-man-for-himself position—which is what makes their ultimate teaming up so emotionally involving.

The preceding chapter expertly delineates a host of effective approaches to your creation of compelling characters, and you can see many of them put to use in Whedon's epic hit. In this chapter, we'll look at ways to deepen your characters and to create active, involving journeys for them. How are your protagonists affected by the turns in your story? What discoveries do they make at each juncture, and what decisions does it lead them to? These beats make up a character arc. Such arcs drive, shape, and add substance to your story, and they create the kind of riveting read that can get a project sold.

Four Essential Ways to Deepen Your Characters

Over the course of many years of work as a screenwriter, studio story analyst, script consultant, and instructor, I've come to the conclusion that there are four essential components to the creation of a compelling character: *purpose* (the character wants something—the more specific, the better), *credibility* (the character gives on-screen evidence that he's capable of achieving this goal), *empathy* (the character encounters relatable difficulties in achieving this goal that make us root for him), and *complexity* (the character has an intriguing inner life, with inner conflicts that increase our emotional involvement in his story). Obviously, other factors can help enliven the construct, but if these four are in place, your character will inspire a stronger rooting interest.

What ultimately binds an audience with purposeful, credible, empathetic, and complex protagonists is a sense that they're active, as opposed to static. What really makes us care are protagonists who may be capable of learning something from their experience—ones who may grow and even change their ways over the course of their story. We all like to think we could be that conscious and open to life's lessons, instead of being rigidly fixed in our positions.

We're going to explore how such growth, or a "lesson learned" for the protagonist, can be activated in a screenplay. But first let's take a closer look at each of the character-component fundamentals I've cited, to see how you can build on them to create a truly compelling heroine or hero for your movie.

Purpose: Wants and Needs

The cliché question that any actor asks when presented with a piece of material to play is "What's my motivation?" And it's wise to be as specific as you can in answering this question. Tell an actress who's about to meet a guy in a café, "In this scene, you want to be happy," and you leave her at a loss, for how does one play "I want happiness"? On the other hand, tell the actress, "All you want in life is a pair of Christian Louboutin Maralena Flame Sandals ($2,445 at Neiman Marcus), and the guy sitting at that table—he's your Louboutins," and she enters the café scene with a motivating idea (however sexist in conception) to work with.

Confusion often reigns in the realm of purpose and goals, because *want* can be a deceptive term. Human beings are inherently complicated creatures, propelled by impulses both conscious and unconscious. We can say, speaking to novelist Kurt Vonnegut's great quote ("Every character must want something in a scene, even if it's only a glass of water"), that our protagonist Matthew wants Joe's bottle of Evian, but such a desire can signify something other than thirst. Maybe he wants to show Joe that he's like Joe ("I admire your taste in water"). Maybe Matthew wants the Evian because he wants to prove that he can convince Joe to give him anything.

The character's want is usually conscious. The character's *need* is often hidden to him or her. The writer has to know both.

Much of our characterization work involves manipulating a character's wants and needs. Sometimes these motivations are in harmony, but often they're at odds. When you set a protagonist in motion with this inner dichotomy at work, you're actively involving the audience in a kind of psychological hide-and-seek. We enjoy the privileged position of understanding characters' needs while they chase after their wants. So your job as a screenwriter is to define your character's wants and needs—both in the overall arc of the story and within specific scenes.

In my role as a story analyst at Universal, I gave a multitude of notes on the many drafts of *Bridesmaids* when it was in development. In working with Kristen Wiig's character, Annie, I identified her version of the want vs. need conflict as a self-esteem issue. Annie *wants* to be a great maid of honor for her best friend, Lillian. In outshining her rival, Lillian's new friend Helen, Annie *needs* to prove that she's worthy of her task.

In the infamous bridal shop set piece, Annie has taken the bridesmaids to a questionable restaurant, and everyone's violently ill from food poisoning. The havoc they wreak in this pristine, all-white environment creates great laughs, but the scene peaks in a showdown between Annie and her rival. In their confrontation, Annie refuses to acknowledge that she's ill. She *wants* to keep from being sick in front of Helen, and so she *wants* to successfully chew and swallow the Jordan almond that Helen proffers to her. That's the specific task at hand. But what does Annie need? Annie needs to deny responsibility for the debacle that's unfolding around her, and so all of her energy in the scene is dedicated to somehow being absolved of her role in it. To be the winner and not the loser, she needs to be in denial. *Annie needs to be right.*

Asking what the character wants and needs in a given scene is an effective way to keep your protagonists true to their primary purposes and personalities, and to track these essential attributes throughout your script.

Credibility: Making It Real

If a reader is going to understand your character's wants and needs, and going to believe that your character may be capable of achieving the goal that you've set out for him, you've got to back him up. The time-honored methodology that most screenwriters utilize in making their characters credible is twofold. One, you research. Two, you use what you've garnered from this research to paint in details, as exhibited by the character in word and deed, to convince us that he is who he's advertised to be—and that he may even be able to get what he wants.

Susannah Grant, speaking of her research for *Erin Brockovich,* told a *Salon* interviewer in 2004 that she spoke with the real Erin's lover, kids, and boss-turned-partner, Ed Masry. She interviewed the plaintiffs in Masry and Brockovich's case accusing Pacific Gas & Electric of chromium poisoning; she watched hours of videotape and pored over dozens of legal documents. Grant was obviously fortunate in having a real-life character and event from which to draw such information.

The same principle applies to a fictional character. In a 2000 issue of *Scenario,* Danny Rubin described how research informed his writing of *Groundhog Day.* He and star Bill Murray flew to the town of Punxsutawney so that they could witness the actual celebration of the holiday. He'd originally spoken to the town's Chamber of Commerce and looked at their literature, but said, "After we actually saw it [Groundhog Day], there was a whole different feel to it than we had imagined. It was delightful, really delightful—a wonderful civic event. We incorporated a lot of that into the movie. Everyone there knew it was a goofy ritual—it was almost sophisticated in its hickyness. What was so much fun about the festival is, it's the middle of the night, zero degrees, they've got bonfires going—and they're playing Beach Boys music."

Meanwhile, what if you don't happen to have mountains of court case files or a round-trip ticket to Punxsutawney on hand? Writers are researchers by nature, tending to be naturally inquisitive. To ground the believability for a character, often all you need to do is observe people—intimates and strangers both—and ask the necessary questions. If I were researching a mountaineer taking on an Alpine range, I'd send an e-mail to a friend of mine who lives in Joshua Tree and is fond of climbing the boulders there. Her experience is vastly different from that of my climber in the Alps, but her answer to the query "What's your favorite part of rock climbing? What gets you off on it the most?" could supply the personal POV that a diploma from the University of Google can't provide. Think deeply on what it feels like to freeze your butt off while you're doing a physical chore, and you can reasonably fill in the rest of the scene.

Once you've researched your characters and the world they inhabit, it's time to apply the information you've gathered and put it to work creatively. In my UCLA Extension Writers' Program classes, my students have found one exercise particularly helpful in this task.

Credibility Exercise: A Day in the Life

Laurence Olivier once insisted that he couldn't capture the essence of a role until he actually wore the shoes of the man he was going to portray. But as such props aren't often available, this imagination workout provides a useful way to "put yourself in the character's shoes."

Write this exercise in whatever form you wish, either as shorthand notes or as a linear story, but write it in the first person and in the present tense. Select a span of time within the framework of your movie, either at the start of the story or from well within the action. You're not necessarily looking for a dramatic plot point—any day in the life of your character will do.

Begin with the sentence "I wake up."

Take it from there, but do it as incrementally as possible. You're not going for "I wake up before noon and grab lunch before I go to the library." No, force yourself to break down the character's actions into units of detail as small, slow, and incidental as you possibly can make them. "I wake up. I shut off the alarm, pull off the covers, and get out of bed. I plod down the hall to the bathroom. . . ."

And yes, go to the bathroom. It's not ordinarily what we see in a movie, but remember the opening of *The 40-Year-Old Virgin*? Judd Apatow got the first laugh of his movie by showing Steve Carell's character having to lean over the toilet at an angle because being a forty-year-old virgin, he evidently had what we call "morning wood."

The idea here is to think through every detail. You may already be inaccurate—doesn't your character wear glasses? If so, would she have put them on before she walked down the hall? And what about those bedcovers—isn't it the dog days of August in your story? If so, the covers—no, scratch that, the sheet—may already be scrunched at the foot of the bed, and maybe the very first thing your character does, even before her feet touch the floor, is open the window above her head.

You get the idea. Do this in stream-of-consciousness style if you wish, adding in thoughts and feelings, but do your best to concentrate on the specific physical details of your character's actions. All of this is in the service of inhabiting your character's world. The "day" you write about will probably never appear within your actual screenplay draft, but it's likely that some telling detail—some insightful bit of a life really lived—will come out of this exercise, a detail you can put to good cinematic use.

The audience can sense it when a character behaves as if he comes from a genuinely lived-in past, when he resonates with a specific milieu. A man who comes from the world of espionage walks into a room with a certain heightened awareness. You can recognize a guy who's been in prison from the way he eats a meal, protecting his plate and wolfing it down fast enough to fend off rapacious fellow inmates. In *The Last of the Mohicans*, we see hero Hawkeye (Daniel Day-Lewis) deftly load the powder into his Revolutionary War–era musket, and in record time. His almost unconscious, casual mastery of the task came out of writer Michael Mann walking in his character's moccasins . . . in his mind. And what's been created is a vital sense of authenticity.

Empathy: Making Us Care

We root for characters who encounter relatable difficulties in achieving a goal. This has led to some confusion in screenwriting circles over the idea of "likable characters." Many writers think that to empathize with a character, he has to be someone who's easy to like. But in truth, we don't have to like your character. We have to *relate to* your character. Raoul Silva, the Bond villain played by Javier Bardem in *Skyfall,* is nobody's idea of a fun guy to have a beer with, but his perverse sense of humor, the wit with which he masks a lifetime's inner pain and rage, make him fascinating company whenever he's on-screen. Somewhere within us, we relate to both the wound Silva carries and the defenses he's constructed to counteract it.

Nonetheless, giving protagonists *positive attributes* remains an effective way for getting us on board with them. You can increase the audience's empathy for your characters by giving them positive attributes that encourage identification. We relate to kind characters, and to smart ones; courageous characters are always a good bet, and characters that retain an air of mystery work well, too.

What's addressed less in the pursuit of creating character empathy is the empathy that needs to exist between a protagonist and its creator. Often what gets an audience to bond with a character stems from a sense that the character's energy and life are personal to the writer of the story. You can sense it when a movie "knows" its protagonist, the way you or I might know ourselves or someone close to us. And I've come to think that the key to such knowledge comes from seeing the world not only through the protagonist's eyes but through the protagonist's imagination as well. How does the character see herself? Who does *she* think she is?

Empathy Exercise: Working from Within

One of the best-known standard movie clichés is the third-act scene where the villain, shortly before dispatching the hero or heroine (or so the villain thinks), explains in bald expository dialogue all the whys and wherefores behind his or her nefarious behavior. More often than not, what these evil-incarnate characters reveal is that they see themselves as the *hero* of the story: All their reprehensible actions support a plausible agenda in which they are the ones who've had the bravery and ingenuity to do the right thing all along. Such speeches reflect an observable truth about the human condition: Our lives are to some degree defined by who we believe ourselves to be.

In this exercise, have your protagonists describe themselves as *they see themselves*. You can do it as a monologue, a journal entry, or an e-mail to a close friend. Any form will do, and stream of consciousness works well. It's description from the inside out. Your character removes his public-persona mask and owns up to who he really believes he is, for better or for worse. Thus the character who's perceived by all who know him as a mean-spirited, spiteful, and offensive jerk reveals that from his own POV, he's the only *honest* person he knows: His unique ability to tell the truth is a brave, heroic trait. Why is everyone always giving him a hard time?

Or maybe a character who seems admirably altruistic to the world at large, a "people person" who's constantly at the service of others, might describe herself from the inside as a weak and pathetic coward: She's never learned how to ask anyone for what she wants.

The takeaway from this exercise is an essential trait or quality that becomes a part of your character-depiction arsenal. In any given scene, who the character believes she is can be the go-to default for her. So long as your character is true to this belief, we can feel the truth and consistency in her behavior. And since this bedrock belief is so often at odds with how everyone else views this character, it deepens the scene with a subtext that can surprise and intrigue your audience.

Complexity: The Sum of the Parts

Maybe you know someone who's always striving for a certain kind of success and always failing to achieve it. You know what he wants, you believe he's capable of getting it, you empathize with his struggle in overcoming the obstacles in his way . . . only to be brought up short when you see him self-destruct and destroy his chance at happiness. You may eventually find yourself wondering, *Does he really want that thing he says he wants?* Maybe he's more invested in never being able to have it.

Such a psychology is evidence of a character with an inner conflict. Take Pat, the bipolar protagonist played by Bradley Cooper in David O. Russell's *Silver Linings Playbook*. After a stint in an institution, Pat claims he wants to reconcile with his estranged wife. All he needs to do, in order to have a shot at this, is to take his meds and stay out of trouble. But throughout the movie's first half, Pat is his own worst enemy. In one key scene, he's nearly arrested when he starts to get into a street fight, and his bad behavior is triggered by something that's literally "inside him"—

he's hearing a song in his head, the song he heard playing when he discovered his wife with another man.

In some way, shape, or form, all of us move to our own inner music. And the movies that get us to understand a character's inner conflict tend to be the ones that really get under our skin. Our sense of a character's *complexity* arises when his inner life is brought into play and warrants an entire section of its own, as it brings us to the all-important topic of character arc.

Defining and Activating Your Character's Arc

At its most basic, a story that sustains an audience's interest features a protagonist with a goal who encounters obstacles but ultimately achieves that goal. Another way of looking at this is to say that in any story, a status quo is established, threatened, and more often than not, ultimately replaced by a new status quo. In a "high-concept" movie—one with a story premise so simple that it can be summed up in a few words—that status quo is primarily external, with the main action largely enacted on an external playing field. Character will be a factor in how the situation is resolved, but in a high-concept movie like *Air Force One* ("a terrorist hijacks the president's plane"), what's immediately compelling is the external conflict. Drama is inherent in the power dynamics of the situation, no matter what the individual personalities of the president or the terrorist might be.

In a "character-driven" movie, where the external situation may not be so remarkably dramatic, generally the status quo that's established, threatened, and altered is internal—meaning, the protagonist's inner conflict creates the core interest of the story. The obstacles that come between the protagonist and a goal have the most impact *within* the protagonist. In *American Beauty,* what seems to be the story concept (a middle-aged married man wants to sleep with his teenage daughter's friend) is an external manifestation of a larger drama within: An "already dead" man in midlife crisis wants to feel alive again, to regain his passion and freedom, and to be reborn as a more honest and conscious human being.

The best movies are motored by strong story concepts where the conflict is external (e.g., in *The Avengers,* aliens from another dimension seek to take over the world) but there are internal, character-driven conflicts as well (e.g., to save the world, a group of fiercely independent superheroes must become a united "family"). The key to making your movie as emotionally involving as possible is to make sure that your protagonist's inner conflict is as strong and intriguing as your story's external conflict. And the element that needs to be identified and tracked, in this process, is the nature of what *changes* within your characters . . . and ultimately, what they *learn.*

Generally, the lead character in a story begins in one position, with a defined viewpoint. How the character's position and viewpoint shifts or changes over the course of the story is thought of as the *character arc.* If a protagonist is a fully developed character who possesses an inner life, then how a protagonist's inner conflict interacts with the story's exterior conflict is the basis of the character's arc, and this arc is the true "driver" of an involving story.

Character Change and Growth

Change in the status quo and the results of this change are an eternal fascination to the audience. The movie *127 Hours,* based on the true story of Aron Ralston, makes its change a literal matter of life and death: Aron, played by James Franco, begins his journey intact and ends it minus one limb but alive. What sustains our interest is the "how" of this. We want to see not merely the external mechanics but the internal process. How does a man marshal the bravery to cut off his own arm? *How the character changes* is the true subject of the movie.

The nature of this change is the substance of the character arc. A character starts in one position—call it "Point A"—and ultimately ends up in another, "Point B." The arc is the shape of her shift.

Change comes in all manner of shapes and sizes. For example, while a character might occasionally "change her essential nature," a far more common kind of change is when we see dynamic characters radically alter their behavior in the course of a story. Jake, the soldier hero in *Avatar*, changes his side in the movie's battle, joining his supposed enemy. Another kind of change occurs when a character is forced, or given the opportunity, to reveal and build on his true nature, which previously hadn't come to the surface. The true change in Jake is that he allows his innate compassion and humanity to overcome his warrior persona.

Alternatively, many a popular movie character is beloved precisely because he or she *doesn't* grow over the course of a story. James Bond and Milla Jovovich's Alice character in the *Resident Evil* series are protagonists of this kind. The target audience for these genre stories isn't primarily interested in inner conflicts. Instead, fans of action movies and thrillers want to see a character with a specific skill set go up against ever-more-formidable adversaries in exciting set pieces. But the popularity of the trio of Matt Damon *Bourne* movies demonstrates the effectiveness of internally driven character arcs in action movies. Jason Bourne, an updated James Bond–like hero, is made memorable because he does in fact have inner conflicts and actually "changes" in some ways over the course of each of his franchise's three installments.

A Theory of Character Growth in Time

The average theatrical feature has a running time of about two hours, more or less (comedies and action genre movies tend to run somewhat shorter). Despite recent debates in screenwriting circles over whether all movies must conform to a three-act structure or not, this structure is perceived as the generally accepted way one deals with the average feature's length, from both sides of the buyer and seller equation. Studio executives want to know what the first and second act breaks are in a given script, and most writers outline their stories in these terms; even the most experimental indie script can be roughly divided into a beginning, middle, and end. In broad strokes, the "protagonist-with-goal meets obstacles and overcomes them" structure generally lends itself to this form.

Most screenwriters would agree that there are certain basic plot points that are the most structurally vital, with an organic function within the screenplay's skeletal structure. A three-act structure includes: 1) a *setup;* 2) a catalyst, or *inciting incident;* 3) a *first-act turning point,* or break; 4) a *midpoint;* 5) a *second-act turning point,* or break; 6) a *climax;* and 7) a *resolution.* The exact placement of these plot points within the three-act structure can vary. For example, some movies play climax and resolution beats practically on top of one another, while other movies have extremely short first acts.

With this context in mind, how does a character's arc play out within such a ready-made armature? More often than not, the character arc has a structure that tends to run parallel to the structure of the plot.

The screenwriter who has created a heroine or hero not only has created a backstory and larger context for the character but has deliberately chosen the most dramatic (or comedic) event in the life of this protagonist for us to experience vicariously. In most stories, the protagonist will move from Position A to Position B over the course of this designated event, whether B is a radically different position or merely a more consciously reaffirmed version of Position A—an original position now owned and understood more fully.

What does it take to make a person change or grow? Often it's a crisis, a trauma, a life-altering dilemma. We're generally so resistant to change that only an extreme situation can prompt such movement, and a good movie capitalizes on this basic human truism. To create a believable, compelling character arc for your protagonist, your job is to *track the character's inner (i.e., emotional, psychological, spiritual) reaction and response to the beats that make up the story's events.*

If you accept, as I do, the wisdom in the Robert Penn Warren quotation at the head of this chapter—that what the character *learns* (i.e., the realization that has prompted him or her to change) is the real subject of your story—then what needs to be determined is the causal relationship between the exterior developments of the story and the interior developments that occur within the character.

After looking at character-driven movies of all kinds (biopics,

coming-of-agers, buddy movies, romances, family ensemble movies, et al.),
a certain similarity in the trajectory of such stories became apparent to me.
This structure, based on these viewings and on my years of working within
the studio system, has its basis in a fact of human nature. We don't progress, as people, in one fell swoop. Think, for example, about your attempt
to break a bad habit. Did you declare smoking, alcohol, or sugar consump-
tion off-limits and then instantly achieve success? More often than not, it
took more than one attempt. The same holds true for learning. We study,
we try—we *fail*, and then, with renewed effort, we get it right.

With this in mind, let's examine the functions of a three-act structure's
basic plot points. What will these beats represent for your hero or heroine,
and how will they lead to his or her ultimately learning a lesson in life?

1. Setup: Character Defined

Your movie's setup is a scene or sequence that establishes the story's status
quo. You introduce us to your protagonist and her world. You want to
give the audience a strong, vivid sense of who she is and what she wants.
And often what you define (or indicate) is the character's inner conflict.
The protagonist need not have self-awareness at this point—but you want
the audience to get "what's wrong with her picture."

2. Inciting Incident: Character Questioned

The inciting incident acts as a catalyst for your story, throwing its external
world into flux. This disturbance in the status quo also upsets your protagonist's inner world and requires some kind of response, raising a character issue. How will she react to this situation? The inner conflict that
you've indicated for your character in the setup is likely to be challenged
by this external development.

3. First Turning Point: Growth Opportunity

The first act break represents a literal and figurative turn for the protagonist; it's the plot beat that forces your heroine to make some sort of choice.
A new goal is defined, one that will begin your story in earnest. In

character terms, this newly defined goal implies a change or possible growth for the protagonist: She'll have to leave her comfort zone and step up to the plate. Will her inner conflict defeat her, or . . . ?

4. Midpoint: Change Activated

Often a reversal of fortune or a revelation that enlarges your story's central problem, this plot point enlivens the middle of the movie by raising the stakes. It's an event that hooks your protagonist more deeply into the central conflict and most often signifies a new approach for her. In making this commitment, she directly confronts her inner-conflict issue. Is your heroine capable of doing things differently?

5. Second Turning Point: Change Tested

Just as your protagonist made a decision to act at the first act break, the second act break requires her to make another decision. Whatever choice is made here will determine the nature of the story's climax. For the protagonist, this choice most often puts her growth or change to the test, and it often results in a seeming defeat for the "new me," because her inner-conflict issue hasn't been entirely resolved.

6. Climax: Epiphany and Its Result

In the climax, your story's external conflict reaches its peak. For your protagonist, the approach of the climax, the climax itself, or its immediate aftermath triggers a realization: an epiphany. This is where your character's self-awareness catches up with the audience's understanding of her inner conflict, and a change in the character becomes manifest; her achievement (or in some cases, seeming defeat) signifies growth.

7. Resolution: New Awareness

In the world of your story, a new status quo, whether subtly adjusted or vastly different, is established. For your protagonist, some inner transformation, however incremental or monumental, is implied and acknowledged. Something has been learned over the course of these external events that has resolved the protagonist's internal conflict. Things will be a little different for her from now on.

This structure represents the integration of a character's learning experience within the trajectory of a story. While it's not the only conceivable form such a story can take, I encounter it (or variations on it) both in the screenplay specs that I read for the studio on a daily basis and in most of the theatrically released features I see: *A major event in a person's life forces this person to deal with an inner issue. Resolving that issue requires responding in a new way to the situation, and a real change often only occurs after some initial failure . . . but perseverance and a commitment to changing the situation facilitate change, with a lesson learned, in the end.*

The beats of the character arc in such a story roughly correspond to the beats in the exterior story as used in a three-act structure. Sometimes a plot beat and character beat are simultaneous. More often than not, there's a one-two relationship, meaning that the character's emotional reaction either creates the action in a given beat or is the direct result of an external action. Significantly, the one beat that seems to "float" is the character's epiphany. In some stories, the epiphany follows the second-act turning point and precedes the climax; in other stories, the epiphany occurs within the climax or even directly follows it. But the larger structure holds; generally, the big beats in a character's arc are linked to the major beats in the overall structure of the story.

Case Study: *The King's Speech*

An Oscar winner for its screenwriter (David Seidler), director (Tom Hooper), and lead actor (Colin Firth), as well as the Best Picture winner for 2010, *The King's Speech* begins with trauma. In 1925, the Duke of York, second son of King George V, attempts to deliver a speech to thousands of British subjects for a ceremony in Wembley Stadium and is defeated by his own stammer. His listeners are visibly disturbed, while his loving duchess can only watch helplessly, mortified. It's a devastating public humiliation.

The movie ends more than a decade later in a triumphant reversal of this debacle, with the duke (now King George VI) having successfully delivered a vital speech to the nation, being cheered by a crowd as he waves from the royal balcony, his happy queen by his side. Also present at the scene of his triumph is a commoner named Lionel Logue, and therein lies the tale. In *The King's Speech,* a duke who never expected to become a king becomes one and overcomes a lifetime disability with the help of a speech therapist. It's the story of how an unlikely friendship develops between two men from disparate worlds. And at its core, *The King's Speech* is about how a man faces his deepest fears. The character arc for the duke who becomes king is simple and powerful: He begins the story as the cowering prisoner of these fears and ends it as their master.

Let's look at the major plot points in the story of Bertie (as he was known to his family) in terms of how his growth—from fear-based to fear-conquering—is enacted.

Character Defined: The "What's wrong with this picture?" of Bertie's world is vividly established in that nightmarish opening sequence, and the story's setup is filled out in subsequent scenes: Bertie is an introvert stuck in an extrovert's role, a public figure who'd prefer to live in private.

Character Questioned: The duchess convinces the duke to see Logue, a speech therapist. In the film's inciting incident, Logue breaches royal etiquette by insisting on calling the duke "Bertie," and his familiar, down-to-earth approach infuriates

Bertie, especially as Logue intuits the fears at the root of his problem. This shock to his status quo shuts Bertie down. Afraid of admitting to his fears, he's defeated by his prideful anger and stomps out, ending his relationship with Logue before it's properly begun.

Growth Opportunity: Years later, Bertie's father, fearing that Bertie's older brother David won't prove to be a suitable successor, forces Bertie to try to read one of his speeches. Unable to do it, and shamed by having failed his angry father, Bertie decides to return to Logue (the first turning point). His agreeing to work with the therapist implies a change to come, signifying possible growth. Bertie will face his fears.

Change Activated: In their work together, Logue breaks down Bertie's resistance and uncovers the painful story of how he was demeaned by his father and brother. As England moves toward war with Germany, Bertie's father dies, and David is too in love with the American divorcée Wallis Simpson to claim the throne. Bertie is terrified by the prospect of having to accept the crown instead. At the movie's midpoint, Logue tries to rally him and goes too far, accusing him of being "governed by fear." Bertie turns apoplectic. "You're nobody," he rails at Logue. "These sessions are over!" But in the wake of his brother's abdication, Bertie realizes that to become the king he must be, he has to do things differently. So he needs the help of the man he has rejected.

Change Tested: Student and teacher reconcile and set to work in earnest. But in the second turning point, Logue shows up at the next rehearsal to find that the archbishop, resentful of Bertie's insistence that this Australian commoner be allowed to run the show, has exposed his lack of proper credentials and wants him fired. An upset Bertie accuses Logue of being a fraud who only sought to enhance his reputation. Bertie's growth has been put to the test and his "new me" has failed. But Logue stands up for himself, and for Bertie, provoking him into a fit of rage—in which his stammer disappears. And Bertie has his epiphany: At last comprehending what an ally he has in Logue, he decides to reinstate him, defying the archbishop and taking command of his fate.

Epiphany's Result: When war is declared, Logue is summoned to the palace. Bertie must address the nation on the radio. Logue does his prep work, goading Bertie past his anxieties to exclaim, "I have a right to be bloody well heard!" Now Bertie stands in the shadow of the looming microphone. In this climax, he must definitively conquer his fear, and with Logue silently coaching him through every phrase of the speech as an anxious nation (along with Bertie's wife and family) listens on . . .

New Awareness: Bertie comes through. The film's resolution is particularly satisfying in its recapitulation and reversal of his earlier failure. In his new status quo as King George VI, Bertie waves to his cheering subjects, a man who's come into his power. In the film's last moments, he turns back to acknowledge Logue, his therapist and his friend.

Logue has a character arc that echoes and resonates with Bertie's. He's been unable to translate his limited stage experience into a career, so their first meeting is that of an unsuccessful speaker with an unsuccessful actor. Though he has been an effective speech therapist, now Logue fears that he's not worthy of this task, and at two crucial points he fails. Yet he ultimately succeeds

> in asserting both his ability and his humanity. In "fixing" Bertie, Logue forges a friendship that transcends class.
>
> The intertwining of Bertie's and Logue's character arcs, which dovetail with the story's every significant plot point, creates the movie's thematic spine. The story begins with royalty and common man set apart, in a world out of balance. It's in facing a common enemy that the two spheres unite, and the new status quo is directly stated in the movie's final moments. "Well done, my friend," Bertie says, his hand on Logue's shoulder. "Thank you, Your Majesty," Logue replies.

Variations on the Theme of Growth

Do all character arcs conform to this one design? Of course not. But most memorable movie characters enact some version of this basic trajectory. A protagonist confronting an exterior conflict is forced to grapple with an interior conflict: This reflects life as we know it. And overcoming such dual conflicts is usually not achieved in one quick, direct route. We try, we fail; we try again, and perhaps again, before we succeed. There are infinite variations to how this archetypal story plays out. Your job as a screenwriter is to define the specific nature of your unique character's struggle.

The Hunger Games, an action-thriller with a sci-fi/fantasy twist, introduced us to Katniss Everdeen, one of the most popular female characters in decades. Living a life of poverty in one of twelve districts ruled by a small plutocracy, Katniss is established as a young woman of some complexity. As a hunter, she demonstrates an impressive set of traditionally masculine skills while being classically feminine in her compassion for her vulnerable little sister. Katniss is fiercely independent, but we see that she feels a deep allegiance to her community.

All of these qualities make Katniss a more fully realized heroine than the norm. But when she bravely volunteers to take her sister's place in the annually televised games, a ritual fight to the death between "tributes" from each district that will yield a single victor, the one conflict that's most essential to Katniss's nature comes to the fore: Katniss is a rebel. She detests authority.

So how does someone so rebellious stay alive, when survival in the Hunger Games hinges on working *with* the powers that be and not against them? If you track Katniss's inner conflict throughout the movie, you'll see that this question of "change"—will the rebel conform?—is the thematic glue that holds the story together. The major story beats we've presented are all in place, and at every significant juncture, Katniss resists and then gives in to the idea of playing by the rules. Though, tellingly, the instances where she tests the limits—for example, when she gets the attention of her potential sponsors by firing an arrow right into their midst—set up her epiphany and the resolution of the story. Katniss wins by ultimately defying the Panem authorities; she's prepared to die to prove her autonomy, and thus outsmarts the rulers, who want a victor of the games to emerge alive.

Unlike Bertie in *The King's Speech,* Katniss doesn't grow or change in the sense of conquering an inner conflict. Her growth is signified by the ultimate assertion of her true nature. So her struggle isn't about the emergence of a "new me"; it's about the emergence of a "real me." She has tried to be like the others, and in fact has stayed alive in large part due to her willingness to conform, but in the end, she must be who she is. This "I am what I am" declaration—owning her true nature—is the resolution to her arc.

Is there such a thing as a complex, compelling character who ultimately *denies* any growth or change? Many tragedies feature this sort of protagonist, who could change but sadly won't or can't. *There Will Be Blood*'s Daniel Plainview (Daniel Day-Lewis) is an utterly ruthless oilman, so fixated on acquiring power that there's little room in his life for anything, or anyone, else. The one time he's forced to compromise, to acquire some land he covets, he's humiliated by the pastor who owns it

(Eli, played by Paul Dano). Plainview carries this defeat within him, a hidden wound. In the story's violent climax, having exacted revenge on Eli by sucking his land's oil out from under his feet ("I drink your milk shake!"), Plainview beats his onetime rival to death.

This isn't a story of "change" unless one considers the progression of a driven, homicidal nature to even grislier crimes a kind of growth. It's an arc of someone becoming more of who he is, with his essential nature played out to its logical dark conclusion.

A similar, less harrowing version of this kind of arc can be found in *The Social Network,* where the fictionalized Mark Zuckerberg (Jesse Eisenberg) resists any real growth; what we witness is a character struggling against his more humane and loving impulses. In the end, the hunger for control in this isolationist is what wins out.

In the realm of protagonists who do learn a lesson and do evince some significant change in the story's resolution, there are further variations. In *Bridesmaids,* for example, the epiphany that Annie's character experiences doesn't come from her own actions—she's literally slapped into self-awareness by a supporting character, the hilarious and endearing Melissa McCarthy's Megan.

More recently, in the comedy *Ted,* we see an example of a character arc that's actually bogus—it's a bait and switch in which the protagonist *seems* to grow, and thus achieves his goal, yet the ending reveals this growth to be largely symbolic. John (Mark Wahlberg) has "grown up" to satisfy the more mature needs of his girlfriend Lori (Mila Kunis). But because his buddy the talking teddy bear Ted is resurrected in the end (largely, I suspect, to enable the studio to make a sequel), the new status quo isn't really all that different from the one at the story's start.

All of these variations nonetheless share one common thread: They set their protagonists on a path in which their inner conflicts are tacitly the true subject of their story. As we've seen, by wrapping such inner conflicts around the major beats in your exterior story's progression, you can enact an effective character arc that excites and sustains an audience's interest.

The Sum of the Parts and the Arc

What do we really want to see when we go the movies? Beyond the adventures and the spectacles, we want to see ourselves. We want stories that we relate to, that have things to tell us about what it's like to be a human being in this world. As screenwriters, we seek to translate our personal experiences into something universal, and the key to this translation is an acknowledgment that all of us are shaped by our experiences—that we grow and learn from what we live through.

This is why it's so important to do the extra work that signifies digging deeper into the characters we create. When you make a protagonist's purpose more specific and enliven it by setting both wants and needs in motion, you're bringing us closer to life as we live it. When you learn enough about your characters to be able to make us believe that we're walking in their shoes, when you get us to empathize with them by showing us how they see themselves, you're involving us more deeply in our own struggles. And when your characters enact the arc of that essential human drama—how we strive to move from darkness into light, from lack of awareness to compassionate insight—you're inspiring us to become the better people we hope we can be.

All this and a tub of hot popcorn to be earned in the bargain—doesn't that sound like a worthy pursuit?

CHAPTER 6

Outlining the Screenplay

by Juliet Aires Giglio

Introduction (AKA, "It's Never Good If You Haven't Outlined It First")

When I first started writing this chapter, I was about ten pages into it when I realized it was coming out terribly! Even worse, I was almost out of gas and I had no idea what I was going to write for the remaining ten pages. And then I hit the wall. Seriously, I hit the wall in my office. And irony set in as I realized that I was writing a chapter on outlining, but I had neglected to do just that: *outline*.

I have outlined countless screenplays and pitches. I've made a career of selling scripts that always begin with an outline. I do so because if I don't, I lose steam somewhere in act 2.

So now, I'm going to go off and outline this chapter.

I'll be right back. . . .

Whew. The first thing in my outline is the introduction. Check! In all seriousness, when you start to write, it's never good if you haven't outlined it first. The first script I wrote with my writing partner/husband, we outlined. I can still see the outlines taped to the wall in our East Village rent-controlled apartment.

After getting my MFA at NYU's film school, I was very lucky to find work rather quickly—my classmates and I often joked that *NYU* stood for *now you're unemployed.,* My first job was at Tribeca Films, where I got to read scripts and analyze them. More importantly, I got to ride up and down the elevator and pass lots of offices, each of which had a giant cork-board or dry-erase board. And on them were script *story beats,* which are the major events in the screenplay, divided into three acts. What I learned from seeing those story beat sheets is this: Rare are the writers who don't outline their stories. Some might say they don't, but that's probably because they're so seasoned, they can do it in their heads.

When it came time to move to Hollywood, my husband and I were polishing our first script as we maneuvered our U-Haul truck across Route 40. We had an old laptop (even then it was ancient) with a screen that was incredibly hard to read. But that didn't stop us because we were determined to finish our script! By the time we hit the Los Angeles free-ways, our script was done.

We gave that script to everyone we knew—all four people. Luckily for us, my former NYU classmate Claire was a D-girl. ("D" stands for *development,* which refers to the developing of script projects for film and TV. D-girls and D-boys are always on the lookout for script properties for their bosses, usually a producer or studio executive.) Claire actually liked our script, and while it didn't sell right away, it did get us our first agent. It also got us lots of meetings. One of those meetings was at Walt Disney, and that's how we set up the animated *Tarzan* movie. CUT TO fifteen years later, we've had: eleven studio assignments, six options, five spec sales, four produced movies, and two Writers Guild cards. The lesson is this: Always outline first.

In past chapters, you discovered how to create a strong premise for your script and turn it into a viable screenplay structure, build compelling characters, then deepen them and define their arcs. Now it's time to pull all of this knowledge together into outline form, so that you are prepared to *write your first draft*! As my fellow *Cut to the Chase* author Steve Mazur tells you in the next chapter, "Writing Through the First Draft," "your outline is meant to establish the *general* parameters of your plot, characters, emotional through-line, theme, and overall structure. Within those parameters, however, there's *lots* of room for discovery, exploration, and experimentation."

This chapter guides you to create this all-important tool: a four-to-five-page outline that clearly delineates your script's beginning, middle, and end—*step by step*—and gives you guidelines for mapping out the main elements of your script. I believe the methods I'm going to share, including my favorite—"carding it out"—will work for you, as they have for the Writers' Program screenwriting students I have taught.

Step One: Refine Your Movie's Logline

The first step in outlining is to make sure that your logline, that one-or-two-sentence summary of your movie you first created in chapter 2 ("Jump-starting the Screenplay"), is the best that it can be in capturing what your movie is about *now*. As you have heard repeatedly by now—because it's true!—screenwriting is a process; the logline is a perfect example because at the very beginning of dreaming up a feature-length script, you create a logline that best encapsulates your whole movie and its genre, and then refine it as you work through developing your plot, characters, theme, and world.

I first became acquainted with loglines when I was a "reader"; readers, as you have learned, are people hired by producers and studios to read scripts for them because they just don't have time to plow through the mountains of material their offices receive. If a script is deemed great by a reader, a development exec will read it. If he or she likes it, the producer *might* read it.

The process went like this: The studio or producer would assign me a script to read, and I would then write a one-page summary called a script coverage page and comment on whether the script should be assigned a

"Pass," "Consider," or "Recommend." Sometimes the script wasn't worth buying, but the writing was so good that the writer would be considered for another project. Finally, at the top of the script coverage page, I'd create the logline. I'd usually start out the logline with: "When _____ happens, then [something else] happens." *When* is a good word to begin with, because it implies that some sort of change will happen in the story—that the main character will have a problem to solve that will change his or her life.

I learned from this experience how important it is for me, at the point where I am ready to outline my script, to nail down my logline. That way, I'm positive that I have a good story, complete with problems and conflicts, and that I *stay focused on the story I am telling*. There are many formats you can use to write a good logline. (The one I currently use is: "When _____ happens to [your hero], he must do _____ in order to solve his problem.") The trick is to create a logline that works best to remind you what your movie is about and prevent you from straying from it. Once you have finalized your logline, write it down and keep it in clear view of your computer, as you will refer to it often as you outline—and then write—your script.

To make sure you have a firm grasp on what makes an effective logline at this stage of the process, let's create a possible logline for *Black Swan* (screenplay by Mark Heyman, Andres Heinz, and John McLaughlin), one of the most acclaimed movies of 2010: "When a timid prima ballerina gets the dual role of black/white swan, she must learn to get in touch with her feelings in order to keep the part." Okay, did I make you want to see the movie? Maybe. But maybe not. What about this logline: "When a repressed ballerina gets the role of a lifetime, she must discover her evil, out-of-control side in order to keep the part." Now the movie is more enticing, right? "Repressed ballerina" pulls us into the story more than "timid," and "evil, out-of-control" is more exciting than "get in touch with her feelings." Your logline should make us want to see the movie but not tell us the ending. (If you do, your reader won't want to read the script.)

Step Two: Create Your Movie's Poster

Once I've got the logline in good shape, I often create a mock movie poster, because when pitching a movie idea, a producer or executive will often ask, "What's the poster?" I can't draw and I'm hopeless with computer graphics, so I create my poster the old-fashioned way: I cut and paste pictures from *Us* and *People* magazines. I think about my dream casting and then come up with a picture of an actor for each important part in my movie.

Why do I make this poster? For one thing, it gets me thinking about the tone of the movie and how to sell it as a story. Also, making a poster is fun, can be a good way to procrastinate, and usually forces me to come up with a really good title. Sometimes I think I have a great title, and then I put it on my poster and I can see that it's not so great. Most importantly, I create the poster because it can be inspirational when writing the script, and it keeps me focused on who I think the characters should be like.

Most of the time, you don't get the actor for whom you wrote the movie. But sometimes you get lucky. The first two spec scripts that I sold with my husband were written for very specific actors. We wrote a script titled *Welcome to the Family,* with Bette Midler in mind for the lead. Her company bought the script. Even though the movie was never made, it helped us pay our rent and buy lots of stuff. Next was a movie called *The Broadway Brawler.* It was about a washed-up hockey star, and we wrote it with only one actor in mind: Bruce Willis. We were ecstatic when he became attached to the project, and it sold. Then the movie went into production for twenty days before it was shut down. But that's another story for another chapter. My point is that you should always aim high and write a script with particular actors in mind. You never know . . . you just might get them attached.

Exercise: Make a Poster

Create a poster for your movie. Include your title and give the movie some kind of "tagline," which is something that the marketing department uses to sum up the tone of the movie. For example, the tagline for *Aliens* was, "In space, no one can hear you scream . . ."; for *Jaws 2* it was "Just when you thought it was safe to go back in the water . . ." Tape your poster to the wall next to your computer, right next to your logline.

Step Three: Outline Your Movie

You've got your logline. You've got your poster. Now it's time to learn how to create the best possible four-to-five-page outline, because this is going to be key to ensuring that your story can be turned into a *feature-length* movie with characters whose problems, conflicts, and ultimate transformation will grab your readers and viewers from beginning to end. Plus, sitting down in front of a blank computer screen can be intimidating.

The "Forty-Card" Method: Carding Out Your Movie

Writers can employ a variety of methods to create an outline. Some summarize their movie into act 1, act 2, and act 3. Others make up a *beat sheet,* which is a list of events that will happen in the movie. Still others create a grid, listing the key points such as the inciting incident that kicks the movie into gear and laying out the act breaks. These methods are valid, but my favorite method for outlining a screenplay is to use forty three-by-five white index cards to "card out" the important story beats of the movie. The number forty is important—and not just because Moses wandered for forty days and forty nights in the desert, and Jesus fasted for forty days in the wilderness, and Noah got seasick on the ark for forty days and nights.

I use forty cards because it gives me ten cards for act 1, which typically runs twenty-five to thirty pages; twenty cards for act 2, which typically runs fifty to sixty pages; and ten cards for act 3, which typically runs—like act 1—twenty-five to thirty pages. Each card covers approximately two and a half to three script pages. My goal is to write a *first draft* that's less than a hundred and twenty pages; if you find your draft ranging from one hundred to a hundred and ten pages, that's fine too—particularly if you are writing a comedy.

This "forty-card" method allows you to map out the whole script in a simple, visual way: Literally, you see the character development, plot, and structure of your script lined up in four columns on your dining room table or on a bulletin board. (The first column is for act 1. The second and third columns are for act 2. The fourth column is for act 3.) It's a quick way of seeing where your script works and where it doesn't. Forty cards work particularly well because most beats of a story run about two and a half to three minutes. Remember that one page of a screenplay = one minute of screen time. (Of course, there are exceptions. Aaron Sorkin's script for *The Social Network* ran longer because the characters spoke super fast.)

If you only used twenty cards, you wouldn't have enough beats for your story, and if you used sixty cards, you'd have too many story beats, which would culminate in a hundred-and-fifty-page script. Plus the number forty is a nice, balanced number, and when things are in balance, life is good.

A screenplay is often looked at as the blueprint for the movie by the production folks—the lighting, design, and camera people. In much the same way, your forty index cards will be your blueprint for your script. Hence, the blueprint for the blueprint.

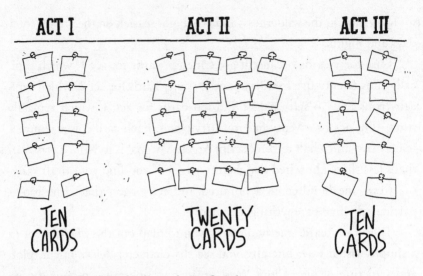

ACT I · ACT II · ACT III

TEN CARDS · TWENTY CARDS · TEN CARDS

"Carding It Out" in Action: *Juno,* Act 1

To see how this method works, let's break down act 1 of *Juno,* winner of the 2009 Academy Award for Best Original Screenplay, into ten cards. I chose this film not only because it's a terrific script, but also because it serves as an inspiration for unknown writers who don't live in Los Angeles. Diablo Cody was living in Minnesota, blogging about her exploits in a strip club, when a film manager happened to read her blog and encouraged her to write a screenplay. The rest is history—and if she can do it, so can you.

That said, here's act 1 of *Juno* in ten cards:

Cards 1–5: The Main Characters

Card 1: Opening Hook

Meet your hero doing something interesting or involved in a big event. Movies often open this way in order to hook us into the story. Flashbacks, voice-overs, and prologues are great too.

Meet Juno in a flashback having sex with a guy.

Card 2: What Is Your Hero Doing When We First Meet Him or Her?

This action is important, as it usually reveals something particular to each character. This is often called the setup and gives us a strong sense of who they are and what they want at the outset of the movie. Be as specific as you can here.

Juno takes several pregnancy tests and learns she's pregnant.

Card 3: Meet the Mentor

When a character has a problem, he needs to have someone to talk to—and this is where the mentor comes in. The mentor doesn't have to be an elderly bearded gentleman; in fact, the mentor is often a best friend and could be a peer. The mentor gives your hero someone to talk to about his problem. Sometimes there is more than one mentor.

Juno tells her best friend, Leah, that she's pregnant. (Juno's father will also emerge as a mentor.)

Card 4: The Hero's Life If Nothing Changed

We need to establish what the hero's life is like before the movie really gets going. Why? So that we can better understand the character arc and watch our hero go through a satisfying change.

Bleeker (the father of Juno's baby) and Juno are lab partners in science. They act as if they're not pregnant. At home, we meet Juno's dad (acting as mentor here), her stepmom, and her younger half sister. Juno makes an appointment for an abortion.

Card 5: Something Happens, Interrupting the Hero's Normal Life

This is often known as "the inciting incident" and is the catalyst for the changes to come.

At the abortion clinic, a pro-life teen tries to convince Juno to keep her baby.

Cards 6–10: The Plot

Now that we've gotten to know our characters, it's time to get that plot moving using the remaining five act 1 cards. This will become your main plot, also known as the *A plot*. (Later we'll get to the B plot.)

Card 6: The Hero Reacts to What Just Happened

Often this means, to borrow from Joseph Campbell's theory of the Hero's Journey, the hero "refuses the call." The hero, or someone close to the hero, expresses reluctance—a fear that what is happening is not a good idea. At this point, the hero chooses to reject the "call to adventure" because she wants to maintain the status quo. The hero is afraid of change.

Juno ignores the pro-life teen and goes into the clinic. She wants to get rid of the baby in order to keep her status quo of being a carefree teen.

Card 7: The Hero Meets with a Mentor or Best Friend

Usually at this point, the hero is in denial or disbelief and needs to talk with that mentor or a best friend again about what he should do.

Juno tells Leah, her best friend, about her change of heart and decision to have the baby. Her friend gives her advice: Read the PennySaver *newspaper to find adoptive parents.*

Card 8: State the Question of the Movie

Every movie has a problem that needs to be solved. That problem needs to be clear at this point in the movie before we go into the second act.

Will Juno find good parents for her baby?

Card 9: The Hero Reacts
to the Decision He or She Just Made

Movies are all about characters reacting to what has just happened.

Juno tells her parents she's pregnant and that she's going have the baby and put it up for adoption.

Card 10: The Act 1 Break:
List What Happens at the End of Act 1

This is a major turning point in your script. The hero's new goal propels us into the next act. It is the point at which she recognizes the goal or task and makes a conscious choice to pursue it. Now we know what's going to happen in the movie.

Juno decides to meet with Vanessa and Mark, the attractive couple from the PennySaver. *If she likes them, they will be the adoptive parents.*

A Couple of Tips About the First Ten Cards

The first five cards were all about Juno and her character, and the second five cards were more about plot (Juno is pregnant and what is she going to do?). While all ten cards must be about the character and the plot, and in almost every genre, establishing the hero is first and foremost, they don't necessarily have to be in the *exact* order that I've laid out. The important thing is to make sure you have the story beats that are included in cards 1 through 10. For example, you want to be sure to have a mentor, to have a problem for your hero, and to have a status quo scene.

The only exception is card 10, because it signifies the act break and therefore always needs to be in the tenth-card position. If you're looking at your cards in their four columns, card 10 should appear at the bottom of the first column (i.e., act 1), so that, at a quick glance, you can see what happens at the end of act 1.

Second, notice that the index cards don't necessarily tell us where the scene takes place or everyone who is in it. It's very bare bones. Just remember what Sergeant Joe Friday said in the classic *Dragnet* TV series: "All we want are the facts." At this point, these cards will most likely only make sense to *you* and nobody else. Once you've finalized the placement of your index cards, you'll type them into the computer; it's then and *only* then that you will begin to flesh out your story.

Third, as you write up your cards, you don't have to think of them in order. If you come up with an idea for act 2, write it on a card and throw it on the board in column two. Later, you can figure out where it goes. In fact, that's the beauty of figuring out your story with index cards first. You can easily maneuver story points and visualize the entire script.

Exercise: Write Up the First Ten Cards

Write down the first ten beats of your story on index cards. Be sure to have a strong card 10—your first act-break beat. You don't need to list a lot of information—just enough to remind you of what is happening.

Carding Out Your Movie: Act 2

We'll have approximately twenty cards in this act. Remember, it's all about balance. The trouble with writing act 2 is that it often can come up short. You start out enthusiastically writing act 1, and it's all going great. Then the second act begins, and by page 60, you've got nothing left to say. Why is that? Because you have no road map. You don't know where you are going. That's why outlining is so important and why the carding method is so useful: You can see in advance where you may come up short. These index cards will keep you honest and keep your pacing on track.

Act 2 is *why you write the movie*. It's when your hero starts trying to solve his problem. And lots of obstacles are thrown in his way. I like to tell my students to "start small and go big": Make the initial obstacles in act 2 small. And as the act continues, make the obstacles bigger and bigger so that by its end, your hero has much more to lose than she did at the beginning of the second act.

Cards 11–20: Act 2 Begins

Card 11: The First Step into the New World for Your Hero

This is the first card in the bright shiny new act, and because of what just happened at the end of act 1, this card represents a potentially major shift or change in your hero's life.

Juno visits Vanessa and Mark, the prospective adoptive parents, for the first time. It's a totally new world—not only because of the implications of giving up her baby, but also because she's out in what her stepmom calls some "godforsaken" suburb.

Card 12: Describe How the Hero Might Initially Try to Solve His or Her Problem.

When we try to solve problems, it's only human nature that we try to solve them in the easiest way possible.

Juno is going to solve her problem of being pregnant by finding a suitable couple to take her baby. She checks out the house and likes what she sees. Juno thinks it will be easy to have the baby and hand it over.

Card 13: New Rules and Appearances

At this point, the hero typically has to learn new rules or pretend to be someone else to deal with his new problem.

Juno plays guitar with Mark, the man she thinks will be the father of her baby.

Card 14: The B Plot

The B plot, also known as the subplot or the secondary story to the A plot, is introduced and functions to illuminate or in some way clearly support the A plot. Often the B story is the love story.

Bleeker invites Juno to the movies but she can't go because of the ultrasound appointment. It's obvious they still like each other in spite of the pregnancy. This is the beginning of their courtship post–pregnancy news.

Card 15: The Hero Is Tested and Often Gains Allies and Enemies

Whenever you've got a problem you're going to have some trials and tribulations. This is exactly what should be happening at this point in the movie.

Juno is getting her ultrasound and the technician is nasty to her. Stepmom Bren sticks up for her. It's a fun scene because we see Juno gaining an unusual ally in her stepmom.

Card 16: The Hero Hits a Snag in His or Her Effort to Solve the Problem

It's too early for the hero to solve her problem at this point in the script, so you need to throw her a curveball.

Juno drives an hour to see Vanessa to show her the ultrasound but she's not home.

Card 17: The Hero Is Confused and Makes a Mistake

Your hero needs to mess up at this point in the story, adding some conflict.

Juno hangs out with Mark, watching movies and treating him like a boyfriend instead of like the father of her baby.

Card 18: Cut Away to the B Plot

Just like your A plot, your B plot also needs to have a beginning, middle, and end. Be sure to include cards that have the B plot.

While hanging out with Mark, Juno talks about Bleeker (the B plot).

Card 19: A Scene That Builds to
the Halfway Mark of the Script

This point in the script is all about ramping up to its mid-point.

Vanessa returns home and finds Juno and Mark alone. It's awkward.

Card 20: The Midpoint—Something
Important Happens!

I know what you're thinking here: Every scene in my movie is important! And you're right—but the midpoint is even bigger. It's often a point of no return for your hero. It also marks the moment at which the hero starts to change in a significant way.

Juno begins to have feelings for Mark, the potential adoptive dad, and wants to spend more time with him. It is clear that Juno has switched her affections from Bleeker to Mark. Her stepmom tells her it's inappropriate to hang out alone with a married man.

A Few More Thoughts on the Midpoint

The midpoint marks the halfway point in your script. It comes around pages 55–60 in the middle of act 2. It's true that we think of scripts in terms of three acts: act 1, act 2, and act 3. However, I believe the second act should be broken in half, giving scripts a four-act structure. The middle of the script, or the midpoint, is often just as important as the other act breaks. For that reason, I break up act 2 into two parts, act 2A and act 2B, and view them as two separate columns.

Exercise: Write Up Cards 11–20

Now take out your Sharpie and index cards. Using the guidelines I've given you, write up cards 11–20. Introduce the new world for your hero. You should have lots of obstacles in these cards. Don't forget to introduce the B plot. And most importantly, don't forget to indicate the midpoint.

Cards 21–30: Act 2 Continues

Card 21: Show How the Hero Is Really Starting to Change

After the midpoint, there's always a major character shift for your hero. At least there should be, in order to keep your story interesting.

Juno is physically changing. She's very pregnant at this point. Her belly is huge, or as Bleeker says, "I sort of noticed that you kept getting pregnant-er, yeah."

Card 22: The B Plot Continues

This is the middle of the story line for the B plot. It's often when the romance really develops.

Juno visits Bleeker at home. He wants their relationship to continue. Juno rejects him, encouraging him to date another girl.

Card 23: The Hero Learns It's Not Just About Him or Her

The hero has been focused solely on his problem up to this point in the story. This card reminds the hero that he isn't the only one with needs.

Mark and Vanessa disagree over what color to paint the baby's room. There's tension, and also a hint planted that trouble lies ahead for this couple.

Card 24: The Hero Struggles, but
We Feel Closer to Him or Her in the Process

We need to empathize with our hero.

Juno tells Leah she's tired of being pregnant and feeling hungry all the time.

Card 25: Then the Unexpected Occurs,
and It's Usually a Big Surprise

At this point in the story, we need a big turning point that takes us into the end of the second act.

Juno is at the mall with Leah when, totally out of the blue, she sees Vanessa playing with a child. Juno realizes what a great mom Vanessa will be. Then Vanessa talks to the baby in Juno's womb and feels the baby kicking. It's an important moment for both Vanessa and Juno.

Card 26: The Hero Is Pushing Forward Again,
Toward Solving His or Her Problem

At this point in our story, we're suddenly thrown back into the main plot.

A title card tells us it's SPRING. Juno is now very pregnant. Her stepmom adds an elastic band to Juno's jeans. At school, Juno is the subject of much curiosity as we see everyone staring at her.

Card 27: Something Bad Happens to the Hero

As we get closer to the end of the second act, everything will start to go downhill for your hero.

Juno learns Bleeker is going to the prom with another girl. She's upset and angry.

Card 28: The Hero Becomes Truthful

Often this is when she owns up to what the real problem is.

Juno confronts Bleeker about the prom. She finally admits how she feels: tired of being pregnant; tired of kids staring at her belly. She tells Bleeker, "You don't have to have the evidence under your sweater."

Card 29: The Calm Before the Storm

Typically, this is a heartfelt scene, heavy on character and not much plot. It's also a reaction to what has just happened.

After her fight with Bleeker, Juno puts on some lipstick and goes to see Mark. They slow-dance. He misinterprets her schoolgirl crush. She reveals she thinks of him as old.

Card 30: End-of-Act-2 Beat and Another Major Turning Point

This is where it all goes wrong for your hero. He is further than ever from achieving his goal; it's often called the "all hope is lost" moment. (In romantic comedies, for example, it's usually when the couple breaks up and it seems like they'll never get back together.)

Mark tells Juno he's asking Vanessa for a divorce. Juno realizes that she no longer has the perfect adoptive parents for her unborn child.

Exercise: Write Out Cards 21–30

Write up the second ten cards for act 2. Be sure to weave in/introduce your B plot.

Carding Out Your Movie: Act 3

As you get to act 3, the proverbial "ticking clock" should be getting very loud. In comedies, the ticking clock is usually an impending life event, such as a wedding or the birth of a baby. In dramas, it's often the trial or the battle scene. No matter what the genre, act 3 always includes the Big Culminating Event that will solve the hero's problem or alter his or her life in some way. If your plot and characters are all working, it gets very exciting to card out act 3.

Card 31: The Hero Is Faced with One Last Great Decision

Sometimes she makes the wrong decision here, or the decision comes too late.

Juno tries to convince Mark not to divorce Vanessa.

Card 32: The Hero Experiences
a Real Downer Moment

It seems like all is lost.

In front of Juno, Mark tells Vanessa he wants a divorce. There is no longer any doubt. Juno has lost a family unit for her baby.

Card 33: The Hero Struggles with an Identity Crisis

The protagonist has doubts. He wonders if he's ever going to solve his problem.

Juno isn't sure what to do about the baby. After crying, she has an epiphany and writes a note to Vanessa on a Jiffy Lube receipt. We won't know what she wrote until the end of the movie.

Card 34: The Mentor or Best Friend Steps in to Help

The mentor comes to the hero's aid one last time. Notice how the mentor has been there for the hero throughout the script.

In Juno, *the mentors have been the best friend and Juno's father. At this moment, we have a heartfelt father-daughter scene: Juno talks with her dad about couples, and in the process realizes she's in love with Bleeker.*

Card 35: The Last Big Problem to Solve

Before the final battle or climactic moment, the hero has to resolve one last issue in his life in order to move forward.

Juno finds Bleeker and confesses her love for him. They make out in front of everyone at the high school track practice.

Card 36: The Big Moment for
Which We've Been Waiting

Commonly called the climax or showdown, this is where the external conflict reaches its peak. In a war movie, this is the major battle scene; in a romantic comedy, it's a proposal or a wedding. The hero's inner conflict is resolved here as well.

Juno's water breaks. She is going to have her baby! Finally!

Card 37: All the Plotlines Come Together

This is always a very satisfying moment for the audience!

Juno is rushed to the hospital with her parents and best friend. Juno has the baby. Even Bleeker shows up after his track meet.

Card 38: The Hero Makes a Sacrifice

This is the moment when the hero gives herself up—either a thing or a part of herself.

Vanessa arrives at the hospital. Juno gives up her baby and decides not to see him. Vanessa is blissfully happy with the baby. Reveal what's written on the Jiffy Lube note: "If you're still in, I'm still in."

Card 39: The Hero Realizes Something
Important—AKA, the Epiphany

After the sacrifice, the hero comes to a positive conclusion.

Juno's dad tells her, "Someday you'll be back here again—on your own terms." Juno realizes he's right.

Card 40: Closure

The ending of your movie, in which we see the hero has achieved success.

We see Juno playing guitar with Bleeker. Singing. More in love with him than ever. It's a sweet ending.

Exercise: Card Out Act 3

Write down cards 31–40. At this point, you will have forty index cards. Make sure they are arranged in four columns. You can now easily look at an overview of your script. You'll see the pitfalls and where it's working well.

Color-Code the Cards

You can take this carding-out process one step further with some color-coded cards. If you have multiple subplots, give them different-colored cards. Or you can use different-colored Sharpies. The latter method works really well with an ensemble movie when you have multiple characters with multiple story lines. If each character is written in a different-colored Sharpie, it's easy to spot when one character has been out of the story for too long. It also helps you to weave plots more easily.

Rearrange the Cards

Using the cards and talking out loud, tell yourself or someone else the story. If something in the story seems out of place, move the card around. These cards are now the new road map for your script.

The Next Step

Once you're satisfied with your story, it's time to take the cards and type them into your computer. At this point, you can keep them numbered from 1 to 40.

Then the fun begins as you start to flesh out each card into your four-to-five-page step outline. (Generally speaking, the first page is for act 1, pages 2 and 3 are for act 2, and page 4 is for act 3—with a fifth page "just in case." Interestingly enough, when you watch a movie and break it down into forty beats or forty index cards, it will always take about four, sometimes five, pages to write them out.)

In addition to connecting the dots as to how one event "steps" to the next, this is when you can finally write all those extra things about your character—where she's from, what she likes, what her hopes and dreams are. It's also where you begin weaving your movie's emotional through-line and theme, and in the process, take the time to discover, explore, and experiment as you create your "working blueprint" from which you will write your first draft.

Creating Your Own "Bottled Water Tour"

The professional screenwriter's agent will often want his client to pitch her story before she actually writes it. The agent will set up meetings with development executives who liked Ms. Screenwriter's previous script, which became her "writing sample." The execs call this "testing the waters," but I call it the "bottled water tour," because once a screenwriter's career gets rolling, she'll tour the town, pitch at various producers' offices, and accept bottled waters as she goes from place to place: flat or bubbly, Evian or Voss. But besides drinking a lot of expensive water, the screenwriter pitches her story to hear how it sounds: what works and what doesn't. When she gets back to her office, she adjusts her outline.

As a new screenwriter, you can create your own "bottled water tour" by pitching your story to as many friends as possible. Do this *before you write the script.* Don't be intimidated—remember that, at this early stage, you are with trusted friends, and looking ahead, know that agents are very wise to have their clients get out and tell their story ahead of time because it forces them to realize what isn't working. So start practicing now! Just think, down the road . . . envision how exciting it will be when you are pitching for real and you're confident that your story is working, because the development execs are excited. And once in a while, when you're really lucky, you actually sell the story ahead of time.

Wrapping It Up

Now you're ready to sit down and write!

I'll show you the outline for this chapter on outlines:

Introduction

The Logline

The Poster

Card It Out

> Act 1—Ten cards
>
> Act 2—Twenty cards—don't forget the all-important midpoint
>
> Act 3—Ten cards

Use cards to write a four-to-five-page step outline

Pitch story to friends

Adjust your outline

Flesh out your outline

Start to write

You are now officially prepared to write your script and you're surrounded by the tools to help you get started: the movie poster to give you inspiration, your logline taped above your computer to keep you focused. And best of all, you have a four-to-five-page outline that has all the important beats of your story already laid out for you in script order. I promise that page 1—and many more in your first draft—will breeze by.

SECTION II

Writing Your First
Draft Feature Screenplay

CHAPTER 7

Writing Through the First Draft

by Steve Mazur

The Goal

You've come up with a premise that you're excited about. You've run it by a few friends and they agree—it's a terrific idea. You've constructed an outline, laying the groundwork for the most effective and compelling way to say what you want to say. And now you're ready to start your first draft.

First, congratulations!

Second, let's be clear on terminology: The first draft is the step in which you convert your outline into screenplay format, complete with scene headings, stage descriptions, dialogue, and transitions, ideally totaling somewhere between 95 and 115 pages. It's just step one in a longer process, with subsequent passes through the script required to make all the changes, additions, and cuts needed to arrive at a finished screenplay ready to show the world.

Third, there's something important you need to know about your first draft before you get started:

It's gonna be rough. It's gonna be messy. It's gonna be, well . . .
Bad.

Yeah, you heard me right. Your first draft will be bad.

Now, how can I possibly know that, given that I know nothing about you, your idea, or your writing? It's simple: *All* first drafts are bad.

Repeat after me: *All. First drafts. Are bad.*

Am I saying this to depress you? To make you run screaming from your keyboard, never to return? No, quite the contrary—my goal is to *liberate* you. Liberate you from false expectations. From unattainable goals. From the belief that every word you put on paper must be perfect.

To steal a line from a movie I cowrote, *Liar Liar,* you can trust me. Of the more than forty screenplays I've written or cowritten over the last twenty years, every single one of them started out bad. Beyond bad, actually. *Terrible.* Sadly, a few of them ended up that way. But most didn't; they got better and better and better over multiple drafts until they were actually kinda good (with a few of those becoming really good, I'm relieved to say).

Look, very early on, I realized I wasn't my generation's Faulkner or Hemingway (thanks a lot, Paul Thomas Anderson and Charlie Kaufman). Instead, I knew I was part of "the great unwashed," the 99 percent of screenwriters who need to write multiple drafts, who need to get the craft down before finding the art, who need to "write bad before rewriting good."

The truth is, every great screenplay started out as a first draft in need of a *ton* of work. It doesn't matter if you're Billy Wilder. Or Preston Sturges. Or Tony Gilroy, Steve Zaillian, or Susannah Grant. Even P. T. Anderson and C. Kaufman need to rewrite. Your first draft is going to be messy, disorganized, too long (or too short), uninspired, and/or uninteresting. In a word: bad.

But that's no problem. Because—*tada!*—you get to rewrite your script. You get to take another pass at the material, then another, and another—as many as are necessary to gradually and steadily improve every element until your script becomes *good.* (And maybe, just maybe, *great.*)

Why am I bringing up rewriting now, when you haven't even launched into your first draft? *Because knowing you're going to rewrite changes the way you approach your first draft.*

First drafts are a time to focus on the biggest elements of your screenplay: premise, theme, plot, main characters, and story structure. Then, in subsequent drafts, while refining and sharpening these elements, you also add nuance and detail to your scenes, dialogue, visual imagery, and stage descriptions.

So, please, don't waste your time and energy on the lie that your first draft needs to be perfect. Structure off? Main character muddled? Scene not working? Don't get discouraged—remember, you get another bite at the apple. In fact, you get as many bites as you need to get it right.

And that's the whole point of a first draft—to move from the general notions of your outline to a rough first pass (with emphasis on *rough*). It's only *after* you complete this rough pass that you're in a position to add in the details and finishing touches that lead to a final draft you can be proud of.

I can hear you now: "Okay, smart guy, then what *is* an appropriate goal for your first draft?"

Well, according to an old cliché, "Close only counts in horseshoes and hand grenades." You can add first drafts to that list. That's right: Your goal is simply to *get close*. In percentage terms, if I can get my first draft within 50 percent of my final draft, I'm pleased. And if it's 60 percent there, I'm *ecstatic*.

Much more important is to use the writing of your first draft to *explore* and *discover*. *Explore* your premise freely and fully; *discover* a workable structure that creates a build up throughout your script; *explore* your theme and what you want to say; *discover* a compelling, fun, and fascinating way to tell your tale. If, by the end of your first draft, you've found the real heart and soul of your story, that's a big win, *even if every specific detail in the script needs reworking.*

See, your first draft is a time to cut loose, try things out, dive into your plot and see where it takes you. Do you have an edgy and outrageous idea? Give it a shot! If you go too far, no problem; you can always pull things back in your rewrite. As noted wild man David Crosby advised, "Let your freak flag fly!"

Getting Started

So what do you need to do before you begin your first draft? Here are seven essentials.

Have Something to Say

There's only one reason to write, and that's to say something—an idea, a feeling, an emotion (better still, all three!). Great movies don't just entertain; they *speak* to us. So say something worthwhile!

Appreciate Great Screenplays

If you haven't already done so, read the screenplays of movies that you admire. Pick something in the genre you plan to write in. Working on a comedy? Find a copy of *Groundhog Day* or *Little Miss Sunshine*. Writing an action movie? Get your hands on *Raiders of the Lost Ark* or *The Bourne Identity*. And be sure to read the screenplays in their original formatting to get the full flavor. It won't take long (usually two hours or less per script), and you'll get a real sense of the look and feel of a top-notch screenplay.

Where do you find these screenplays? Just search the Internet—you'll find almost any script you're looking for there. (The Daily Script is a good place to start.) In addition, popular screenplays may be available in a bookstore near you (with the added benefit that you'll be putting some well-earned money in the pockets of the writers).

A word of caution: Established screenwriters can get away with things you can't, like sloppy formatting and poor grammar. Emulate their art but not their lapses in craft (at least not until you get a few of your own hundred-million-dollar blockbusters under your belt).

Command the Tools of a Writer

Just as a carpenter wouldn't arrive at a work site without his or her toolbox, a screenwriter needs to be equipped with the tools of the trade before beginning work. Our job is to communicate clearly, concisely, and effectively, and that's only possible if we have a strong command of grammar, punctuation, and spelling.

The fact is, even if you managed to write something wonderful without those basic skills, it wouldn't matter. No agent, producer, or studio executive will take the time and energy to wade through an unknown writer's script if it's filled with mistakes. You'll be summarily dismissed as an amateur, one who doesn't take pride in his work.

And, no, I'm not suggesting you relive eight years of elementary and middle school, à la *Billy Madison*. Instead, get hold of *The Elements of Style* by William Strunk Jr. and E. B. White, and also read books on grammar like *Woe Is I: The Grammarphobe's Guide to Better English in Plain English* or *Eats, Shoots and Leaves*. These are required reading for my screenwriting students and they'll be invaluable reference tools for your writing.

Learn the Rules of Formatting

A screenplay needs to work on two levels at once: as literature (providing an entertaining and compelling read) and as the blueprint for the making of a movie (guiding the director, actors, crew, etc.). To best accomplish this second purpose, screenplays require strict adherence to proper formatting.

Formatting refers to the many rules and customs used in the presentation of scripts. Things like the correct number of lines per page; the proper margins for stage descriptions, dialogue, and parentheticals; the right way to specify whether a scene is shot indoors or out—there are rules for *everything*. Making matters more complicated, there are different conventions for different types of scripts. (For example, teleplays use different formatting than screenplays.)

Why do these rules and customs matter? Proper formatting helps professional readers see your screenplay as the movie you intend it to be. Specifying "DAY" or "NIGHT" in each scene heading may seem cumbersome, but it's important information to filmmakers trying to understand the "feel" of your scene. Likewise, strict rules regarding lines per page and margins enable producers to accurately estimate the length of the finished film. When a minute of film costs half a million dollars or more, time is literally money and producers need to be able to rely on proper formatting to plan schedules and estimate expenses.

On the other hand, failure to format correctly will likely distract your readers from your content, causing them to lose focus as they struggle to navigate your poor presentation. And, as with the use of incorrect grammar, punctuation, and spelling, failure to follow the rules of formatting will make it less likely that your script will be taken seriously in the marketplace.

So, how *do* you properly format?

Don't panic—the rules and customs are readily available and easy to grasp. Get hold of a screenwriting software program. Many are available, the most prevalent (though not necessarily the best) being Final Draft, which includes a template for "Warner Bros. Style," the style most often used within the industry and the one I require my students to use. With the proper software and a little diligence, you should have no problem mastering the arcane art of formatting.

Set a Writing Schedule (and Stick to It!)

In screenwriting, "steady wins the race." A script can't be dashed off; it takes time—and multiple drafts—to get it right. Of course, you may already have a lot on your plate—a nine-to-five job, a full load of classes, a family to raise (and/or any combination thereof). So where does screenwriting fit in?

My advice is to treat your writing as if it were a second job (though one you may like a lot more than your first!). Set aside specific times each week to be at your desk, working on your script, producing pages. Of course, that means actually writing during the times you've set aside, not straightening your desk or responding to e-mail, or organizing your iTunes. Would you blow off your regular job to play a video game? Okay, stupid question, but please don't also do it with your second job.

So where do you find the time for this second job? The key is to be realistic in setting a schedule, *but then stick to it.*

If you're working full-time, try scheduling a three-hour block two nights a week, plus at least one afternoon per weekend. That's ten hours a week, minimum. If you're more ambitious, add a third night. That's what I did when I started, writing twelve hours or more a week while also working my day job as a prosecutor with the Los Angeles County district attorney's office. If it worked for me, it can work for you.

Raising a family? Set your alarm early five days a week and squeeze in an hour or two of writing before the kids wake up. That's five to ten hours a week. And/or schedule your writing for after the kids fall asleep, à la *Twilight* author and mom Stephenie Meyer. Two hours a night, five nights a week, means ten hours a week devoted to your script.

In addition, whenever possible, grab any free time you can. J. K. Rowling famously started *Harry Potter and the Sorcerer's Stone* while riding the train to work. Then, after her first child was born, she'd dash off a paragraph or two whenever her daughter napped. Fifteen minutes here, twenty minutes there—this "found time" can really add up.

The bottom line: Set a schedule and stick to it, and the pages will soon start stacking up. Now, for some balance, here are two things you *don't* want to do as you gear up to write your first draft.

Don't Allow Research to Slow Your First Draft Down

Hey, I love facts just as much as the next guy. ("You're more likely to be killed by a donkey than in a plane"; "There are no clocks visible in Vegas casinos"; "Albert Einstein never wore socks.") Nonetheless, in my experience, the main purpose of much of the research done by beginning screenwriters is to give themselves an excuse not to write.

Harsh? Perhaps. But also true.

Look, I'm not saying research doesn't play a part in screenwriting. With a *CSI*-style mystery, for example, the entire plot hangs on scientific minutiae, so you'd better know your stuff. But, few exceptions aside, you're almost always better off just diving into your script rather than spending weeks researching first.

To begin with, you already know a lot about a lot of things. Take submarines. You may not know what to call those round monitors with the blips that you've seen in every movie about submarines ever made, but you sure as hell know that submarines have them, and five minutes on the Internet will give you the name. (A search for the phrase *submarine terminology* resulted in 967,000 hits, the first of which informed me that those blippy things are called "sonar screens.")

And if the answer doesn't come so fast? No worries—it's your first draft, remember? Rather than interrupt your forward momentum to conduct research, just drop in a note as a placeholder (something like "[*Name of round monitor with blips?*]") and move on, knowing that you'll be able to fill in the blank later. Don't let research—or anything else—stand in the way of your forging ahead with your script.

Don't Wait for Inspiration to Strike

There's a notion (hope?) that writing is somehow magical, with brilliant ideas floating hither and yon, just waiting to land upon some lucky scribe to inspire him or her to greatness.

Sadly, that's not the way it works. There are no floating ideas, magical writing fairies, or ready-for-hire muses out there. Screenwriters can't rely on inspiration to carry them through a script because that script would never be finished.

Sure, there will be moments when a fantastic idea will come effortlessly, when the perfect speech or scene will flow from pen to page as if by magic. (Believe me, you'll treasure those moments.) But, more often than not, brilliance will remain elusive, replaced by a lot of "not so bad"s and "this'll do for now"s.

The truth is, screenwriting is work. The best work in the world, but, still, work. And, like other types of work, results come from effort. So, instead of waiting for lightning to strike, make your own lightning.

Transform those "not so bads" and "this'll do for nows" of your first draft into the "hey, that's better than I thoughts" and "wow, that's actually pretty goods" of your later drafts. And, always, always, *keep moving forward*. Your steady progress will serve as its own form of inspiration.

Writing the First Draft

Okay, enough with the backseat writing. It's time to start your first draft (at last!). The following are some things to keep in mind while you write.

Don't Feel Tethered to Your Outline

Here's another screenwriting truth: *Scripts evolve.*

More times than not, what you set out to write isn't what you end up with. And that's a *good* thing. Writing a script is a conversation, not a monologue. Sure, you're dictating events and telling your characters how to act and react. But at the same time your script is also "talking" to you, leading you to unexpected places, urging you to find the deeper truths. You've just got to be willing to listen.

Often, it's only after you're knee-deep into your first draft that the *real* heart of your story begins to reveal itself. You'll be making discoveries, stumbling on new directions, and when these opportunities arise (and they will), you'll need to be open to deviating from your outline.

Remember, your outline is meant to establish the *general* parameters of your plot, characters, emotional through-line, theme, and overall structure. Within those parameters, however, there's *lots* of room for discovery, exploration, and experimentation.

How much room? In my experience, the "macro" elements of my outline (premise, theme, and plot) tend to carry over pretty directly to my first draft, while the "micro" elements (specific details) may change significantly. That's why I avoid getting into too much detail in my outline, since details can obscure the bigger picture of what I'm trying to create. There's truth in that old saying "You can't see the forest for the trees." Getting bogged down in detail ("the trees") too early in the process may prevent you from nailing down the broader and more significant elements of your script ("the forest").

So use your first draft as an opportunity to discover and explore within the broad parameters of your outline, and avoid getting too locked into specifics too early.

Write for "the Suits"

Ultimately, there's one, and only one, goal for screenwriters: to get their scripts made into movies. But before that can happen, before your scripts can reach directors and actors, they have to pass through a group of people who serve as filters of material: agents and managers, studio readers and executives, producers and production executives. Collectively, these folks are referred to as "suits," and, more times than not, they determine whether your script lives or dies.

So what are the suits looking for in a script (besides the potential to make lots and lots of money)? Pretty much the same thing any reader is looking for: a fast read that's well written, with a strong narrative and a story that's emotionally compelling.

"A fast read," as in a page-turner, is one where the reader's eyes seem to fly down the page. That's why, in general, you want to avoid big blocks of type that slow the read. Instead, keep your stage descriptions and dialogue tight, communicating as clearly and concisely as possible. Break up long paragraphs. Eliminate extraneous words and phrases. Remember, "brevity is the soul of wit" (or, as *The Simpsons* put it, "Brevity is . . . wit").

"Well written" means a script presented in a professional manner, with no errors in grammar, punctuation, spelling, and formatting. (While presentation is well worth keeping in mind while writing your first draft, it becomes more vital as you make your final passes through the script.) It also means writing with style and flair, taking the time to find a way to say something interesting in an interesting way.

Finally, and most importantly, the suits are looking for a strong narrative that pulls them into a script and a compelling emotional throughline that keeps them there. This is no different from what any reader wants. As Anthony Lane of *The New Yorker* put it in a review of *Anvil: The Story of Anvil:* "the emotion that swept the cinema, at the climax, seemed unanimous, binding, and true: pretty much all that we ask of a movie, when you think about it."

Note that, unlike actors, who are specifically trained to focus on the emotional subtext of scripts, suits tend to appreciate guidance in tracking the emotional flow of your story. That's why it's often a good idea to specify key emotional moments with stage descriptions like "Ted is devastated" and "Jane is astounded." Doing so facilitates a quick read, since the suits won't have to wonder or guess about the most important element of your script, the emotion. It'll all be right there, on the page.

Avoid "Directing" in Your Script

Making a movie today involves the efforts of hundreds, if not thousands, of professionals, all of whom influence the final film. But the screenwriter is first on the job. And, at least for a time, he or she is in complete control.

That can be heady stuff, control—especially since a screenwriter knows that, soon enough, his or her influence over the movie will be greatly reduced, if not outright eliminated. So there's a temptation while writing to impose control over the script as much as possible while we still can.

And how do we seek to impose control? By becoming beret-wearing *auteurs,* seeking to dictate each and every detail of the film in advance. Instead of writing, "Mary's ring was lovely," we write, "Mary wore a brilliant fancy-cut diamond with nary a blemish, set amid a flourish of baguettes, marquises, and pears, in steely-white platinum—and it was lovely." We predetermine the details to make damn sure that Mary's ring is exactly how *we* see it and not subject to the whim and judgment of others.

Now, if Mary's ring is a vital element in your story (say, serving as the crucial clue to solving a string of murders), well, then, by all means, go to town. Otherwise, you'd be much better off describing the ring as concisely as possible, thereby saving your energies (and those of your readers) for more important matters.

The same holds true for dictating camera movements. For some reason, we can't resist writing SWOOP DOWN and ZOOM IN and ANGLE ON and PULL WIDE. Sure, sometimes it's necessary to "direct" in a script. If you're hiding the identity of a killer, for example, you'll need to write something like "CLOSE ON a HAND as it opens a door, its lovely ring glistening." Otherwise, I suggest you be *very* judicious with specific camera movements in your script, and avoid all unnecessary PULL BACKs and WIDE SHOTs and ZOOM INs.

Why are these efforts to hold on to control a problem? Two reasons: They don't work, and they're self-defeating.

They don't work because no one involved in the making of the movie will feel bound to follow such specific details. Instead, the director and his or her production crew will modify and adjust the script as necessary to serve the overall needs of the film. And while the screenplay will certainly factor into those decisions, it's the premise, theme, and tone of the script that matter, not any specific detail in a stage description.

More significantly, such efforts to maintain control are self-defeating because they'll lead you to write in a manner that makes it less likely your script will be made. Too many details and camera directions result in a cumbersome read, all those specifics diverting attention from what *really* matters in your script (plot, character, and theme). So, focus on *those* elements, and leave the directing (and the beret) to others.

Don't Worry About Page Count . . . *Yet*

As noted earlier, knowing that you're going to rewrite gives you tremendous freedom in how you approach your first draft. You can let yourself go, give in to intuition and impulse, and follow your imagination where it leads you (within the general parameters established in your outline). If you go overboard, it's okay—you can always pull things back in your rewrite.

The same holds true for page length. For aspiring screenwriters, your goal should be a final draft somewhere between 95 and 115 pages long; anything more than that and you're in dangerous waters. In the words of an experienced script reader:

> A screenplay that is over 125 pages is usually an automatic pass just on general principle. [And] please don't recite James Cameron's screenplay page lengths to me as your defense for writing your 178-page magnum opus. . . . James Cameron overwrites his screenplays because he knows he's going to edit out huge chunks of the story in post. Plus, he's James Cameron.

Note, however, that these page limits apply to *final drafts,* not *first drafts.* The time to worry about overall length is when you design your script via your outline and then while rewriting—*not* in the middle of writing your first draft. When it comes to your first draft, it's okay to write long. Better that than to cap your creativity and limit your chances for discovery. Sure, eventually, cuts will have to be made, but you'll end up with a leaner and meaner final draft in the process.

If, on the other hand, you try to cut length while in the midst of your first draft, there's a real danger you'll throw off your script's balance. Let's say that you're sixty pages into your first draft, but, according to your outline, you should only be on page twenty. At that point, there's a real temptation to slash elements of your upcoming story so that the completed draft will come in at less than 115 pages—but *don't do it!* You'll be left with a way-too-fat act 1 and way-too-thin acts 2 and 3.

Instead, forge ahead, writing the rest of your story as you originally intended. Then, and only then, should you go back and address the real problem: your too-fat act 1.

Don't Sweat the Small Stuff . . . *Yet*

When I first started writing screenplays, I agonized over particular lines of dialogue and stage descriptions in my first draft, only to cut those same lines and descriptions while rewriting. What a waste of time and energy!

Twenty years of experience has taught me not to fret over the minor details of my script (dialogue and specific beats) until I've *first* nailed down the bigger elements (premise, plot, theme, emotional through-line, structure, and main characters). Remember, you don't *really* know your story until *after* you've completed your first draft. So don't let details derail you early in the process. Unsure about a particular speech on page 30? Just write a rough draft of the speech, and/or drop in a note or two about the subtext; then move on, knowing that when you tackle the speech later in your rewrite, you'll be better equipped to get it right. Nail down the core of your script before you start worrying about specific details.

Keep Moving Forward!

My approach to first drafts is simple: Begin at the beginning and plow through to the end. I start by referring to my outline ("What's the next scene?"), brainstorm for a while ("What am I trying to accomplish here, and what's the most compelling, interesting, and visual way to get there?"), then jot down any ideas, notes, and exchanges that come my way. After that, I dive right in and write a rough draft of the scene.

Once the first pass is done, I'll often rework the scene again, adding a beat or two here, trimming a line there, and maybe doing a third or fourth pass as well.

Even then, the scene is probably still too long, with my sentence construction off and the whole thing a little light on inspiration. But it's *close,* and that's all I'm looking for in a first draft. So I'll return to my outline and move on to the next scene.

And that's how I suggest you convert your own outline into a first draft: moving forward one step at a time, getting each scene "close enough" before continuing on to the next, and always progressing.

Now, along the way, you'll inevitably stumble upon some important realization or discovery that you didn't anticipate while working on your outline. And/or you'll run into some big story or character problem that you didn't foresee. (As noted earlier, that's exactly what you *want* to have happen, since the main goal in writing your first draft is to explore and learn all you can about your story.) Also inevitably, these realizations and discoveries will create in you an overwhelming desire to go back and modify the pages you've already written to incorporate the changes.

If these changes are small and specific ("Phil should be from Wisconsin, not Minnesota"), sure—take a minute or two and go back to fix the particular line or stage description. But for anything more involved, my advice is simple:

Don't do it!

The urge to rewrite while in the middle of your first draft is normal, natural, and understandable. It's also a massive mistake that may very well derail your entire script.

First of all, you'll be in a much better position to make any and all changes *after* you complete your first draft, rather than midway through it. It's only then that you'll really know your characters, your theme, and the best way to tell your tale. So why not wait to make the changes? Save your rewriting for the rewrite stage.

Second, you'll no doubt be making even more realizations and discoveries as you march through the first draft. And, as before, you'll want to go back and immediately make the changes. *Each and every time.* So wouldn't it make more sense to wait and handle all the changes at once? (Especially since it's quite possible that some of the later changes will negate the earlier ones?)

Finally, and most significantly, by giving in to the impulse to go backward, *you may never finish your first draft.* I've seen the pattern too many times to count: A screenwriter embarks on a script and reaches page 20, then decides to go back and make some changes . . . after which he or she continues on, this time reaching page 30 before again hitting the wall and going back . . . once again moving forward, maybe getting to page 40 before—you guessed it—he or she again hits a snag and decides to go back.

Lather. Rinse. Repeat.

And what does the writer end up with after this constant looping back? An amazingly polished first fifty pages of an otherwise never-completed script.

So, don't go backward! Instead, when you're struck by a new idea or direction while writing your first draft, just follow these three steps:

1. Drop a note regarding the change wherever you currently are in the draft.

2. Review your outline to consider the implications of the change and modify your outline accordingly.

3. Resume your first draft at the point where you left off, writing the new pages as if you've already incorporated the change.

Then, *after* you've finished the first draft (*and only then*), go back and modify the earlier pages to reflect the change (at the same time you're making all the other changes as part of your overall rewrite).

Of all the advice I give my students, "Keep moving forward" is the most important. Following this approach will save you tons of time and effort and may just be the difference between finishing your script and not.

Write Fast!

When it comes to the first draft, *just go for it*! As Andrew Stanton, the genius behind *WALL-E,* said about first drafts, "Write it wrong as fast as you can." Remember, the faster you write your first draft, the more time you'll have on the back end to rewrite your script to perfection.

Finishing the First Draft

The biggest difference between professional screenwriters and amateurs? *Pros finish scripts.* Here are some suggestions to help you reach the finish line.

Writing Through Blocks

Screenwriting is a marathon. And, as with any marathon, there's a real chance you may "hit the wall" midway—you may lose your momentum, run out of energy, and want to quit altogether.

The first thing you need to know? That's normal. Not only normal—*usual.* Professional screenwriters hit the wall, too, but they work through it. They don't give up, and neither can you.

For example, there will undoubtedly be times when you'll suffer from the dreaded "writer's block," when, suddenly, *no* idea is forthcoming. Nothing. Nada. Zilch. What do you do then?

Simply write through the block.

Write the horrible version of the scene, the one that would prompt hara-kiri if anyone saw it. Sure, most of the results will be utter garbage, but buried within is likely to be a glimmer of something worthwhile. A clue as to how to proceed. A key to unlocking the block. (At a minimum, you'll know how *not* to write the scene.) And then move on, comfortable in the knowledge that you'll be better equipped to tackle the scene in your rewrite, after you've finished your first draft.

Also, note that there's something about the physical act of writing (whether typing on a keyboard or scribbling on paper) that helps unleash the imagination. Maybe the activity accesses a particular part of the brain or maybe it's sense memory—I don't really know. All I can say is that writing something—*anything*—can often break a block.

Remember, writing a screenplay is a long-term proposition, with inevitable ups and downs. The key is to keep moving forward until you reach the finish line (and then reward yourself with a muffin).

And now, the big, big question.

How Long Should It Take to Finish a First Draft?

The short answer: It takes as long as it takes.

The longer answer? Studios and producers often give professional screenwriters three months or so to turn in a "draft." But, note, what the suits call a draft is most likely the screenwriter's fourth, fifth, or more pass through the script. Which means that screenwriters usually try to complete a first pass within a month or two (in order to give themselves a chance to go through the script several more times before the due date).

Of course, you're not a professional (*yet*), and, more likely than not, you're also juggling a day job, a full schedule of classes, and/or a bevy of kids. So what's a more realistic time frame for you?

Well, if you were able to set aside ten to fifteen hours of writing per week and stuck to that schedule, there's no reason you couldn't complete a first pass of your script in three months or less.

Do the math: Ten hours a week, averaging one page an hour, adds up to one hundred twenty pages in twelve weeks. If you managed to work a few more hours per week, and/or upped your average output to, say, two pages per hour, well, then, you'd be looking at a finished first draft in as little as six weeks.

I know it can be done. My advanced feature film writing students at the UCLA Extension Writers' Program (most of whom also hold down full-time jobs) complete a first pass in eight weeks.

Think about it: Two or three months from now, you could have a finished first draft of your screenplay. It's just a matter of setting the goal and seeing it through to the end.

Speaking of the end . . .

One Last Thing

I have a confession to make. At the beginning of this chapter, I said your first draft was going to be "bad."

That was a lie.

The truth is, it depends on how you define *bad*.

For a first draft, "bad" would mean failing to explore fully your premise and theme. Failing to learn all you could about your characters, to take chances, to try new things. "Bad" would be a first draft agonized over for a year or more . . . and then never finished because you got discouraged and gave up.

And what would a "good" first draft be? One where you really let yourself go, gaining real insight into your plot, theme, and characters. One you wrote quickly, without second-guessing yourself and without restraint. One where you put yourself in a position to rewrite and polish your script into something truly terrific. *One you finished!*

So, write *that* first draft, the "good" one. Fun and fast and filled with discovery, the first step on the road to writing a *great* final draft.

CHAPTER 8

The Who, What, Where, When, Why (and How!) of Writing a Scene

by Dan Vining

How do you keep going?

It's a question I'm asked all the time by beginning writers, especially when the hour is late and beer is involved. Not "How do I get an agent?" or "How long should the first act be?" or "What the hell is the pathetic fallacy?"

How do you keep going? The answer is: *the scene*. You write scenes. And after a while, with a little luck, you get good at it and one thing leads to another and you find yourself at the end of a screenplay with a big grin on your face. (Your first goal is to entertain yourself.)

I've been a writer my whole life, and a working (paid) writer for all but the first few years when it was just me and my journal. My first paying job as a writer was as a newspaper reporter, which will explain the "who, what, where, when, and why" organization of this chapter. I've written features and television movies and miniseries and now mystery books. I have six produced movies with my name on them, and like every other writer, I wrote ten drafts on the way to the shooting script. For every produced screenplay, there were six or seven that were commissioned but never used. (Never mind all of the poor, sad, orphaned spec scripts and novels, written but unloved, at least by the people who sign checks.) I'm a writer, so I wrote.

For the first eight years of my screenwriting career, I made deals, sold pitches, wrote and rewrote screenplays, was paid to adapt books and re-write other people's scripts, but nothing made it to the screen. I bought a house and a Porsche, got a beagle with papers, put my kids into tony private schools. But nothing got made. My parents assumed I was a criminal of some kind. How else could you explain it? What kind of business pays for work and then doesn't use it?

Hollywood.

But I kept going. How? Scenes. From a young age, I liked scenes—scenes in real life, scenes in books, in comic books, in great movies, in good movies, in bad movies, in good and bad television shows. I liked scenes and so I learned how to write them. Like Chauncey Gardiner in *Being There,* I like watching people doing things, and so I started writing scenes of people doing things. Then I discovered that I *really* like watching people that *I* made up *doing* things that I made up.

Scenes are discoveries, *your* discoveries. They're the little movies you get to watch before anyone else. They are yours, yet minute by minute, line by line, they're surprising you too, along with the audience. (Surprise should always be your writing partner.) In a well-written scene, you're tapping into something, unlocking secret chambers. You're in bedrooms or offices or inside people's heads or out on battlefields or baseball diamonds or craters on the moon—and human beings (and sometimes aliens and animals and demons and robots) are there and they're talking and moving!

How do you keep going? Scenes keep you going—*your* scenes!

Just the Facts, Ma'am

When I teach at UCLA Extension, I figure my job is to demystify screenwriting—and then remystify it. I spend the first three or four classes working at getting beginning writers to see the component parts of movies, to look at them stripped down, naked. (The components, not the students.) Then slowly, so as not to scare anybody, together we start examining the *mysterious* elements in a good screenplay, the *extra*-ordinary components that make a screenplay come to life, come off the page, and walk around. It's like *Frankenstein*. Get the basic pieces you need however you can (yes, mostly in the dead of night), stitch them together, and then breathe (or shock) life into the beast. *It's alive!*

Scenes are just people doing things and saying things, sometime, someplace, for a reason.

Let's start looking at those elements.

As I said, I started out as a newspaper reporter, just a kid, seventeen. I was terrorized by a crusty city editor with the wonderful name of Charlie LaPoint who humiliated me on a daily basis in front of a room full of adults—and taught me to write a news story. The method? The Five W's. How do you write the lead paragraph of a news story? You answer five questions: Who? What? Where? When? And (sometimes) why? Usually in that order. As in . . .

An eighteen-year-old Central High School senior, Darrell Porter, was shot and killed by a convenience store clerk during an apparent robbery attempt at a Kwik-E-Mart on Miller Road in Westphalia Friday afternoon. Distraught family members said Porter wanted money to buy a class ring.

A writer's job is to find order in chaos. Or to *impose* order. The Five W's make the seeming chaos of a real-life event into a tellable story. Who? Darrell. What? Shot and killed by a clerk during a robbery attempt. Where? At a convenience store in Westphalia. When? Friday afternoon. Why? He wanted a class ring.

We're going to use the Five W's to break down writing scenes. I'll give you my overview of the general structure of scenes, and then we'll get specific and talk about what each W needs to do to serve you and advance the story. Along the way I'll offer tips about how to make your scenes not only useful but also entertaining. (The *useful* is what *you* need. The *entertaining* is what the *audience* needs.)

And then we'll look at these ideas in relation to an early, pivotal scene in *The King's Speech*.

Nuts and bolts. (We'll also get to the more mysterious stuff.)

A Quick Overview of Scene Structure

Structure keeps your story from killing you. That's why we writers like structure, why we talk about it so much, why so many books have been published about structure, why Robert McKee is rich. Structure helps tame the beast. Structure is a cage for the story. Structure is strong. Structure is antichaos. (Structure *isn't* mysterious.) Structure's a little obvious and not terribly imaginative but it's dependable, like the guys and girls your parents want you to marry.

Beginning, Middle, and End: Scene Structure Mirrors Screenplay Structure

The structure of a scene is just like the structure of the screenplay at large. I think of screenplay structure (and teach it) not in terms of acts, but in the looser terms of the Beginning, the Middle, and the End. (Me and Aristotle.) It makes more sense to me as a writer. I rebel against hard-and-fast rules when it comes to something as *lively* as a good story. Not thinking about acts and act breaks also can keep you from getting hung up on counting pages and hitting arbitrary marks.

Here's another bonus: Aristotle said the B/M/E form is organic (natural, from nature), so that when your story or scene has a clear beginning, middle, and end, the audience thinks it's right and true, that some higher authority has made or decreed it. All of us writers like to imagine ourselves as gods on Mount Olympus—the gods of story—making and decreeing the truth, so that's a bonus on top of a bonus.

A scene's structure is as simple as 1-2-3. The beginning of a scene, like the beginning of a screenplay, draws us in, presents a problem, and shows us how characters respond to the problem. The middle of the scene deals with the consequences of those responses—action leads to reaction, which leads to new action—at the same time we are led toward an (inevitable?) conclusion to the scene. The End.

Of course, scenes in a screenplay don't *end* end, unless it's the last scene of the movie. But a good scene *does* come to a conclusion, even if it's just a *Huh?* look on a character's face. The end of a scene concludes a piece of action in such a way that there are implications, repercussions. This is so important I'll repeat it: *The end of a scene concludes a piece of action in such a way that there are implications, repercussions.* It's not the end of the scene if it doesn't have implications. We're not sure what will happen now, but we know *something* will happen, something that wouldn't have happened without the action and talk we've just witnessed.

The end of a scene should make us ask, "And now what?" You've built a little machine that makes things happen. If we don't care what happens as a result of the scene, you're in deep dramatic peril. You may have inadvertently written a terminal scene, a movie killer! Maybe you can get a pass from the audience for one or two dead-end scenes, but after that, we'll be looking at our watches, wondering if we have time to jump over to whatever is playing next door in the multiplex.

I once wrote a thriller. Here's how it came into being: I was working on a script, and on the short drive to my office, an idea for another movie popped into my head. When I got to my desk, I tried to write down the new idea in a few sentences but it wasn't working. I thought, *What the heck, I know the first scene. I'll just write it.* It was three pages. It took me an hour. Now here's the cool part. Because I was writing fast, not planning ahead, the three-page scene ended sharply, abruptly, with a line of dialogue that was like a big flashing neon arrow pointing to the next scene. So I wrote the next scene. For some reason, the second scene also ended with a neon arrow pointing to the next scene.

Before I knew it, I had written fifteen pages, there were two parking tickets on my car, I had blown off a lunch date, and my wife was mad at me—something about the dog and the vet. Eight days later, I typed FADE OUT. My first thought was, *I finally figured out how to do this.* Of course, my next screenplay took four months, but still—I had cracked the combination to the safe! The beginning of a scene just answers the question that the last scene posed. The middle of the scene is a reaction to what the beginning of the scene set in motion. The end of the scene reacts to the back-and-forth in the middle of the scene and heads toward a question that leads us to the next scene.

The eight-day thriller was optioned twice but never got made. However, it was my hot number one writing sample for a year or two.

General Goals, Specific Actions: Scene Structure Operates on Two Levels

Before we can get to the specifics of the Five W's, we also need to talk about general versus specific. You need to be thinking about your scenes and your overall story in two ways, at two levels: the general and the specific. This is true for all of the components—who, what, where, when, and why—but it is particularly true in the why, which explains what the scene is supposed to do in your screenplay. Movies are about people who want things, and about other people or forces that stand in their way. What do your characters want specifically, right now, and what do they want generally, long-term?

Another way to think of general versus specific is soft versus hard, or maybe ephemeral versus physical. Some examples: In *Saving Private Ryan,* Tom Hanks's Captain Miller wants to get his physical body back home. Physically. He literally wants to sit on his porch. In softer, ephemeral terms, what does he want? To find peace. To get back to the way he felt before the war, before it changed him. Bruce Willis as John McClane in *Die Hard* physically wants to retake the high-rise he's in that has been seized by very bad men. He moves physically, violently, room by room, floor by floor, scene by scene, goal by goal, through setback after setback, but what he *really* wants is to make his estranged wife (who is also in the building) love him again.

Jon Heder's Napoleon in *Napoleon Dynamite* wants a girlfriend and a job and to be left alone, but generally he wants to find acceptance—oddball that he is—in the ordinary world. The same can be said of Robert De Niro's Travis Bickle in *Taxi Driver*. The guys in *The Hangover* physically want to find their missing friend, but they all also want to find out who they are and what they mean to each other. The two characters in *Lost in Translation* aren't at all sure what they want (from each other, from their spouses, from life), but . . . they want to dress up and go sing karaoke together.

The specifics in your scenes should always be in service to the general. You write scenes that deal with general goals (hard and soft) by dramatizing specific actions that will give your characters half a chance to achieve those goals. The poet in you (who wants to make people see the truth) loves the general goals. The crafty storyteller (who first wants to engage the audience) loves the specifics.

Let's look at those five W's.

The *Who* of a Scene

Who should be in the scene?

Generally? Human beings, even if they're vampires or ghosts. If not human beings, animals, aliens, demons, robots, or in the case of *Cars* . . . cars. (Remember: The more humanized nonhuman characters are, the better. Always.) Specifically, who should be in the scene? Start with the people who are in the most vivid conflict with each other (or with nature), people who strongly, clearly represent positions that are in opposition.

Most scenes are centered on a conflict between two people. Maybe three. Why? Because most drama deals with conflicts that have two sides. (It's just one of the many ways movies oversimplify life.) Even if your story is about the Nazis and the Allies in World War II, you'll probably find yourself writing scene after scene with pairs of people in conflict with each other.

Rambo tends to face his opponents one at a time. Rocky is in the ring with one fighter at a time. In *Kramer vs. Kramer,* Dustin Hoffman's Mr. Kramer is versus Meryl Streep's Mrs. Kramer. Juno in *Juno* is up against the judgment of society but the scenes are mostly Juno confronting a person who represents some aspect of judgmental society, scenes designed to comment on or further reveal her plight. *Napoleon Dynamite*? Same thing. Seth and Evan (okay, and maybe McLovin) cruise around arguing about how to score some booze in *Superbad.* Jerry Maguire gets fired by his boss in a restaurant full of Boston ferns at lunch. The room is crowded with other people but the scene is really just between the two of them.

There are almost always other people in the background or in support positions (often best friends or kids). But don't clutter up (and defuse) your scenes by adding speaking characters who really have nothing to say about or do about the central conflict, even if they're your pals and you promised them they could be in some scenes, *especially* if they're hanging around from an earlier draft you just can't let go of.

One more thing. We want two people with a problem who *matter.* People with an interesting problem who are ready to engage the problem. Right now. Don't get in your characters' way. Let them go to work. I read screenplays from beginning writers in which the main characters don't make an appearance for two or three (or four or five or six) pages. I call it "deadly setup." Every writer has been on the hot seat with development executives or producers who say things like, "Why isn't Jack on the first page? Where the hell *is* he?" And then they start flipping and ripping—pages, that is.

Here's a way to keep yourself on the straight and narrow when it comes to introducing, and then using, your main characters: Imagine dream casting. Think of the actor you'd most like to play the part. *Voilà! They're in your movie.* It's the first day of shooting and you're on set. Where's Jack? (Brad? Leo?) Where's Jill? (Jen? JLo?) Your actor is in his or her trailer, waiting to go to work—three days from now!—and it's your fault. Think like the audience. Who do they want to see? Jack! When do they want to see him? Now! All the time!

What do they want to see him doing? Getting in trouble and trying to get out of it. Which brings us to . . .

The *What* of a Scene

What's in a scene? Action and talk. Movement and dialogue. *Focused* movement and *focused* dialogue. What do your characters *do* in the scene? You as the bifurcated screenwriter might be hard at work on your long-term goals— what your screenplay is *really* about—but the audience doesn't give a damn about your dreams. They want craft before art, unless this is France during a three-year period in the early 1960s and your name is Jean-Luc Godard. They want specifics. Your characters aren't acting generally. They're acting specifically. (Again, remember that speaking words is a form of action.)

Every scene is a struggle to make the internal photographable. I think it's the single hardest thing about screenwriting. A man can't just be frustrated, fed up. You can't leave it at that. James Cagney in *The Public Enemy* has to pick up that grapefruit and shove it in Mae Clarke's face. A specific grapefruit and a specific face. Dustin Hoffman in *The Graduate* is desperate to stop his girlfriend from getting married, but you can't just tell us that. You have to find an action, make him pound his specific fists on the specific glass as he shouts a specific word—"Elaine!"—and then stick a specific cross through the handles of the church door.

A screenplay is ten thousand decisions. A specific action is yet another choice the writer has to make. The great writer and teacher Frank Pierson (*Cat Ballou, Dog Day Afternoon, Cool Hand Luke, Presumed Innocent*) would tell young writers and directors, "We're photographing moments of decision." Your character decides something (after you do), and then he or she *acts* upon that decision, does something, says something. Right here, right now, with the camera going. Conflict leads (eventually) to decision. Your characters had better be in conflict, large or small, one way or another. Again, general conflict and specific conflict. Then they'll be primed to act.

How? Here's how I start to write a scene. I begin with "the three-by-five-card version," a handful of words that describe where I *think* I'm headed, the action of a scene. Sometimes the card is a literal card and I literally stick it on the literal wall in front of me. Usually I've lived with that scene card for a few weeks or months or years, so it's covered with scribbled ideas (baked and half-baked), a possible order of things, bits of dialogue, coffee stains. There's a headline. The three-by-five card is there in front of me mostly to ground me, to keep me on task, to give me a goal, to yank me back when I start to drift.

> Start with an explosion. And build!
> —Samuel Fuller, writer and director of *The Big Red One,*
> *Shock Corridor,* and *Pickup on South Street*

When I write the headline on the card, it's a simple declarative sentence. Subject. Verb. Object. *Tom robs a bank.* The subject? Ask yourself: Whose scene is it? Who is most significantly acting or being acted upon? *Tom.* The verb? Ask yourself: What is going to happen in general terms? *Robbing.* Here's a tip: For your scene cards, always think in terms of verbs that convey action: *Tom robs a bank*—not *Tom becomes overwhelmed by his situation,* which is more internal and unphotographable. That's great in a *New Yorker* short story but death for a screenplay. If your verb suggests visuals, all the better. One more tip: If your verb suggests visuals *and* conflict, even better. *Mary confronts Joe* is way better than *Mary talks with Joe.* The object? Ask yourself: What is the action pointed toward—what gets acted upon?

If the action in your scene isn't completed or can't be completed, that's all right too. Just modify the verb on your scene card. *Tom* tries *to rob a bank. Mary* tries *to confront Joe. Todd* almost *gets fired.* Often failure makes for an interesting (and very lifelike) scene. Failure is drama. Serial failures only make more dramatic the eventual success or completion.

Here's a scene for you. A circus performer's act is to balance chairs, one on top of another, and then eventually balance the whole tower of chairs on his nose. He starts out, gets one chair on top of another, and then a third. They start to wobble. They fall. The audience is embarrassed for the poor sap. But he's a persistent sap and tries again, gets the three chairs up again, and then an unsteady fourth. He reaches for a fifth chair, but disaster strikes once more, and the whole thing comes tumbling down around him. He's thinking of running for the dark beyond the spotlight. But . . . he sucks it up and tries again. (Would you?) The audience is right there with him. One chair, two chairs, three chairs . . . four chairs . . . five chairs. Steady, steady. He lifts the whole tower of chairs onto his nose. It wobbles back and forth but then steadies. He's done it! He lets the chairs drop and the audience goes nuts.

Could he have balanced the five chairs on his nose the first time out? Yeah. Balancing chairs is what he does for a living. I call this *intentional failure,* intentional on your part as the one who is plotting things. Serial failure makes photographable the strength of will, the sense of purpose that is inside your character.

Incidentally, can you spot the beginning, middle, and end of that little scene?

> Try again. Fail again. Fail better.
>
> —Samuel Beckett

Conflicts big and small. Action met with resistance. I think that some people are too nice to be screenwriters. God bless 'em, some people just don't like to see other people struggle and confront problems and fail, particularly when people fail spectacularly, which is what the rest of us *bad* people like to see when we go to the movies.

Purposeful conflict. With a beginning, a middle, and an end. That's what's *what*.

The *Where* of a Scene

INT. or EXT.—_____—____. What goes in the first blank?

Where should you set your scene?

Let's make more of those ten thousand decisions. Where are we generally? The United States. France. Alabama. Lyon. Düsseldorf. Outer space. Daytona Beach.

Anytown? I come out of a Southern tradition of storytelling, so I never dismiss the general location of my story as insignificant. I would never write a screenplay set in "a small town somewhere" or "New York or Chicago" or "a city" or even "a planet far away." The writers I admire most believed place is as important as plot or character. Ask Mr. Faulkner. *Where* matters. The Bronx is not Tucumcari, New Mexico. The people native to those places are wildly different from each other. Place changes things. Place changes people. And gives you story! If you don't believe it, take your main character out of the Bronx and plop him down in Tucumcari. Or vice versa. Watch what happens. Oh, and write it down.

Specifically, where should your scene be set? Just as the more artful screenplays don't start a scene with a blunt, direct approach to the business at hand, when it comes to a location for your scene, it's probably not the best idea to go with the first location that pops into your head. It probably popped *out* of one of the movies or television shows you've seen. When you pick an obvious, *expected* location, your audience knows exactly where this is headed. Or they will assume they do.

It's what I call *the fast-forward problem*. I used to watch my young son watch movies on television. A scene would begin and he'd stick with it just long enough to figure out where it was going, and then he'd hit the fast-forward button. *Paris. Eiffel Tower. Sidewalk café. Berets. Young lovers.* Got it. What's next? When he watched *Mad Max 2: The Road Warrior* the first time, he put down the remote. There was no way he could be two steps ahead of the writers, so he surrendered himself to the movie. Just what we all want.

Some scenes have to be set where they have to be set. (The judge never moves a trial out of the stuffy courtroom and onto the grassy plaza so everyone can chill out.) But when you're picking a location, at least *consider* a setting that might stand in contrast to the business at hand, the action of the scene. Your scene card reads: *Jack and Jill argue and break up.* Where do you set it? A marriage counselor's office? Only if you don't mind Johnny Vining burning rubber out of your scene. A dinner table at home? *Where's that remote?* A restaurant? *Seen that one a bunch.* How about a picnic? *Better.* A picnic probably means at least one of the two people didn't know that today was the day they were going to break up.

How about a baseball game?

The United States. Los Angeles. Dodger Stadium. High in the cheap seats. Everyone else is having a great time. The sun is shining. It's the middle of the sixth inning. The score is tied, but it's a lazy day. We're kicking back . . . but not Mr. and Mrs. Doe, neither one of whom knew today was the day their relationship would fall apart. They find themselves saying things they've been holding in for a long time, right there in the cheap seats, surrounded by strangers. It's angry and then it's sad and then it's angry again. The people around them start to notice, until along comes the crack of a shot to left field. Everybody jumps up, everybody except one man and one woman who just stare at each other, knowing that something is torn and can't be put back together.

"You want me to rent a *baseball stadium* for the breakup scene?" your producer says.

"Think about how great it will be," you say. "How relatable, how unexpected, how nakedly emotional."

A movie is a magic trick. Your audience has been exposed to thousands of screen stories, thousands of breakups and robberies and trials and murders and crashes and crying jags and doin'-shots-in-a-bar scenes. They've been there, done that. Your job is to blast past cliché.

The *When* of a Scene

So . . . EXT. DODGER STADIUM—CHEAP SEATS—DAY.

Or is it . . . NIGHT?

When?

Generally . . . Now. The present. Today. This year or fairly recently. Of course, the common exception to this is when your story is set in the future or the remote past. The trick with period pieces (set in the past) or altered-reality movies (set in the future or somehow out of our space-time continuum) is to make your story seem as if it is taking place *in the today of the characters*. Your job is to put us there and make us believe that this is a day in that reality. Today on Tatooine.

As for a *specific* when, start by asking yourself some fundamental questions, the kind only writers (and maybe painters) ask: What does day mean? What does night mean? What does dusk mean? Dawn? Noon? High noon? Decide for yourself what a time of day means, and pick the time of day that supports or even heightens the drama of your scene. Is your main character lonely? Nights are usually thought of as lonelier than days. Is that what *you* think, or is it another cliché? Thinking about these things is what a writer does for work.

Now I get to answer the (unasked) question about the pathetic fallacy. The term originated with nineteenth-century poet, artist, and critic John Ruskin and it refers to writers and artists treating things (inanimate objects) as if they had human feelings, as if things can have intentions. The term *pathetic* isn't negative; it relates to pathos or empathy. In this context, a sky is sympathetic or unsympathetic to a person: "the merciless sky . . ." Of course, a real sky doesn't think about you, doesn't make judgments about you or your situation one way or another; but the sky in a drama or a painting might. The term *fallacy* refers to the fact that this concept, however poetic or interesting or engaging, is at its heart false.

But here's the thing: While the term *is* something of a pejorative as a device in a literary work or fine art—a lowbrow cheat, a somewhat cheesy appeal to base emotion in the reader or viewer—we're writing *screenplays*! Even artful, ambitious, *literary* screenplays are at heart a little (or a lot) melodramatic. Things are heightened, writ large, boldfaced.

> There is no point in bothering to see films that are not sensational!
>
> —Peter Bogdanovich

So how does the pathetic fallacy relate to screenwriting in general and specifically to the when of your story? Consider this. Maybe your scene doesn't take place on just any night, but the night of a thunderstorm. A stormy night. In *Basic Instinct*, a woman is attacked in her home during an explosive night storm, almost as if the sky is commenting on the violence. Or supplementing it. As if the sky too has purpose, is taking part in the story, *is* the story. In my breakup-at-the-ballgame scene, I'd make it a day that is as hot as hell, the heat yet another component of the scene, one more thing that makes the couple wish they were anywhere but there.

For the classic, unforgettable funeral scene in *Shane,* it's a spring day, flowers blooming, colts frisky, and kids happy, in stark contrast to the dark grief and fear in the adults gathered around that hump of dirt. But when Alan Ladd rides into town to face Jack Palance in the scene that is the climax of the story, thunder rumbles and the sky is purple, like a bruise. The sky cares. This day is an important one. The Fates care. Even God is watching.

There's also something else I call *the special when*: choosing a very specific date or time for a story, a specificity that adds additional import to the events depicted. In *Jaws,* the shark strikes for the first time one night just before a big holiday weekend in the beach resort town. *The Hangover* takes place the day before the wedding. In *Independence Day,* everything leads to a climax on . . . Independence Day, July 4! John McClane in *Die Hard* (literally, wonderfully) walks barefoot across broken glass to save his wife on Christmas Eve. The ticking clock ticks toward high noon in *High Noon*. Notice how the changing of the seasons is used to add or shade meaning in *A Beautiful Mind*.

That's who, what, where, and when.

Why does something happen in your scene?

The *Why* of a Scene

I (and my then writing partner) once cowrote a script for Michael Keaton. In it, Keaton plays (or would have played if it had been made) a world-weary New York cop who's ready to quit. At the end of a bad day, he comes home to his empty apartment, throws his keys on the dresser, sits on the bed, looks at the red zero on his answering machine, takes off one shoe, pauses . . . and puts his head in his hands. In an early script meeting, Keaton said, "What does this mean? Why am I doing this?" I thought it was obvious and said, "He's world-weary. Today he saw a guy killed, up close. He's all alone, alienated. Today he reached the end." Keaton said, "Okay, I just thought he was tired."

The why of the scene: We hadn't written the scene right, hadn't made clear what *we* knew about the internal workings of our character. The why of the action: Only you know why your characters are behaving the way they are behaving, why they are saying the things they are saying. You know—or are discovering as you write—the why.

I admit that sounds a little mysterious, but this is when the real writing starts. This is when writing gets challenging—and becomes something not everyone can do. And very satisfying.

Here's a secret: No one really cares about plot. We care about *story*. Plot is what happens. Story is plot plus emotion. Story is plot plus why. We follow plot. Story follows us, follows us home, stays with us. Story is humanity. No executive or producer ever bought a screenplay because it was perfectly formed and formatted, had three clearly defined acts, and hit all the marks. Nobody ever made a movie because there was nothing wrong with it.

Scripts get bought and movies get made because somehow *life* gets onto the page. Humanity. Scenes are what we use to uncover *life* along the way as the main characters get what they want (comedy) or find out they can't (tragedy). What is it about scenes that makes them valuable? What keeps us watching, listening, reading? The place in the scene where action expresses meaning. The why. The emerging *humanity* in a scene, unfolding like something blooming, is what draws us closer, makes us give in to the story. The humanity in a scene moves it past plot to story.

It's your job to make the actions of your characters make sense. Maybe not immediately, in the moment, but in time, before FADE OUT. If not, you get the walking-to-the-car problem. Some girl more or less enjoyed the movie but now, as she is walking from the theater to her car, she thinks (or says out loud), "Wait a minute . . . Why did she do that? If she loved him all along, why did she . . . ?"

Why did this happen this way? What's the meaning behind it? Sometimes *you* know but you keep it to yourself for a beat or two to make the story more interesting, more dramatic. Motive should be clear to you, even if you're not yet revealing it to the audience. You try for clarity, moment by moment—yes, even in *Inception*—but what we do is not reportage; it's drama. Can there be a surprising, even out-of-the-blue why? You bet. The why of a scene presents the writer with another opportunity to surprise us and make a larger point or even just a different point than the one we thought he or she was going to make.

How can you as a writer learn to have your scenes mean more? Start by watching people more closely. Observe human behavior. What does a person *do* when he gets bad news? When you write, try to blast past the clichés. What does a person *do* when she sees something that brings her sudden, unexpected joy? What do people *do* when they're seething inside, when they snap? Blast past more clichés. When you find the perfect actions and the perfect lines that express the all-too-human stuff all of us have inside, your scenes will be rich.

Rich with why.

Let's test all this by looking at a very good scene.

Oh Yeah? Prove It.

The general situation of *The King's Speech* is that King George VI of Britain (Bertie) stutters. His nation needs him to lead. With his voice. His wife (Elizabeth) hears of an oddball speech therapist (Lionel Logue) who may hold the answer.

Let's pretend we're David Seidler. ("Get your hands off my Oscar!") How do we start? Where do we start? What are we trying to do? What's on our three-by-five card for this scene? What will be the specific situation of our scene?

Bertie meets Lionel. All right, let's get Bertie and Lionel together.

A "scene-let" precedes the big scene of the two men meeting. Elizabeth and Bertie enter the empty reception room. Elizabeth tells an apprehensive Bertie there's no receptionist and then loudly announces their arrival, using a fake name. Lionel yells from the other room that he's busy with someone else. Elizabeth tries to reassure her husband but concedes that Lionel Logue is an odd duck. A patient/client comes out of the inner sanctum, a stammering young woman who immediately recognizes the king and queen. She haltingly tells them Dr. Logue said they'll have to wait, then yells to Lionel in the inner room, asks if that was all right. Lionel yells back that it was bloody marvelous. Lionel has not yet been seen but we (and Bertie) certainly have a sense of him. (The beginning.) They wait. The apprehension builds. (The middle.) Then, after letting the king and queen of England cool their heels, Lionel calls, "Mr. 'Johnson,' do come in." (The end.)

That's a page and a half, page 19 and half of page 20, in Seidler's screenplay. It's lean, tight, purposeful, efficient, every little piece of it. It's no longer than a minute, yet it has a clear beginning, middle, and end. The parts work together to set up the next scene. Nothing is superfluous or self-indulgent on the writer's part. That's how screenplays work. Nothing can lie around. Nothing lazy can stay on the page. Everything has to *work*.

You have to be able to justify everything you put in each scene you write—the who, what, where, when, and why. Nothing drives this point home like getting something produced. Imagine leaving your motel in Wilmington, North Carolina, at dawn, driving in your rented car out to a two-lane road in the middle of nowhere where twelve big white trucks and trailers are parked in a vacant lot that had to be rented. Fifty people are working: unloading cop cars, rigging camera mounts, brewing coffee, hauling lights, wrapping up stuff with duct tape, and putting paint on Nic Cage's face while the helicopter with the director and assistant director and director of photography takes off—all because a couple of years ago you wrote, "Cal guns it when a cop tries to pull him over on a lonely stretch of road." Everything on the page has to be intentional, focused on the job at hand.

Now we have Bertie entering Lionel's inner sanctum and we're ready to jump into what by Mr. Seidler's hand will be a seven-and-a-half-page scene. It's a big scene. It's crucial, a microcosm of the whole movie, the first meeting of the two stars whose faces will be on the poster. It's daunting, maybe even paralyzing. How do you as the writer tackle all of the big and little tasks ahead? How do you advance the story and at the same time make it engaging and entertaining and revealing and . . . unassailable?

You calm down. You start making decisions. You start answering questions. You already have your who and where and when and you're in pretty good shape on why. All you need is the what of the scene.

So Bertie-the-king comes in. The screenplay takes a few lines to describe the room, gives details that tell us about Lionel Logue. As the writer, you should have tons of details in your head about every location, every character. All of that won't (and shouldn't) go into your script, but your scenes should be rich in detail in your mind's eye. You have to *see* a movie before you write it. Seidler's brief description of the room ends with "The walls are pearl grey and smoky blue."

"My wife's favorite colours," Bertie says, stuttering, the first line of dialogue.

Next there's some "settling in" talk of model airplanes that Lionel's boys built and a line or two about the woman who just left. Don't think it's just casual chitchat. It's full of purpose. It's working. Why do the two talk about the previous patient? Because this is the beginning. It needs to draw us in, establish who's there and why, and then begin to tell us what we should think about these characters and this situation. The beginning prepares us for what comes next: directly tackling the problem that brought the characters together and, at the same time, put them at odds with each other. The beginning also needs to create atmosphere, make the world of the story seem real. The beginning's first job is to entertain. Like children, we need to be constantly entertained. The beginning of a scene jingles keys in front of us, as if we're bored babies.

The first half page of talk between the two men quickly produces a conflict, presents a question. It's about proprieties: How close does a commoner stand to royalty? How does one properly speak to a king? Lionel is forceful, demanding. Bertie is anxious and embarrassed at being there, but his anxiety and embarrassment rapidly give way to anger when his authority is questioned. (Progression!) It quickly comes to a head, a direct confrontation presented in a pair of lines: "Aren't you interested in treating me?" the king says. "Only if you're interested in being cured," Lionel says. "More silence," the script tells us in the next line of description. Now we know the men in the scene in a way that we didn't a minute ago—literally one minute ago, one page. Now we know why we're here and that this isn't going to be easy. The line about the men falling silent tells us Bertie isn't going to quit, isn't going to walk out. Not yet.

Now comes the five-page section of the scene that is the middle. (And the middle has its own beginning, middle, and end. Are you beginning to see how this works?) The two men discuss what Lionel should call the king. Bertie insists upon one of his formal names. Lionel balks at that, asks what the queen calls him. *Bertie.* Bertie tries to smoke. Lionel stops him. The rules are being laid out, the men dancing around each other. These are the implications, the repercussions of the beginning of the scene we just lived through. If Bertie isn't going to leave, he's going to face the rules of the man whose room this is.

"My physicians say it [smoking] is good for stuttering, relaxes the throat," Bertie says.

"They're idiots," Lionel says.

"They've all been knighted," Bertie rejoins.

"Makes it official then," Lionel says.

Now the scene has also become entertaining. We're entertained and engaged as each new conflict raises the stakes. These two men are in trouble, and the trouble is deepening. We half expect one or the other to bolt from the room.

Then Lionel asks if Bertie stutters when he talks to himself. (The middle of the middle, a turning point.) The king thinks it is foolishness and says so. Lionel bets Bertie "a bob" that the stuttering king can read some text flawlessly, right here, right now. You're on, Bertie says.

Now comes the best part of the scene, a deft, graceful combination of talk and action that restates the central problem in a surprising and entertaining way and then illustrates again how difficult it will be to solve it. Lionel hands Bertie a book and tells him to read. Bertie reads some of the most famous lines ever written, "To be or not to be . . . ," and reads them badly, stuttering, the worst stuttering we've yet heard. This is the principle of rising action, the idea of dramatic acceleration, being put into play. Each beat in the story is an escalation, each event bigger or more intense than what preceded it.

Bertie thinks his stuttering performance has proven his point and won the bet for him. Not so fast, Lionel says. He hands Bertie headphones and turns on a record player with loud music, and turns on another machine to record Bertie's voice. Bertie reads aloud the famous lines again but *we* can't hear what he's saying, can't tell if he's stuttering. All we can hear is what Bertie hears, the music.

Bertie snatches off the headphones when he finishes. "I was terrible," he says. It's the hero's all-is-lost moment. Bertie heads for the door—and the middle of the scene gives way to the end. Six pages and six minutes of talk and action have pointed us toward what *has* to happen now, the end of the scene. My first writing teacher, Smith Kirkpatrick, probably quoting *his* first writing teacher, Eudora Welty, used to say, "The end of a story should be the only thing that could have happened and yet still be surprising." (Welty probably got the idea from our friend Aristotle.) Apply Welty's test to the end of each of your own scenes.

Let's see if Seidler's scene passes Welty's test. Here's the end. Bertie heads for the door, never to return, or so he vows. He now realizes that his problem can't be solved this way, not this easily. It's hopeless. (This early in a movie, the hero's plight should always seem hopeless—or nearly so. The more hopeless it looks now, the more satisfying and entertaining it will be when he or she triumphs.) Lionel stops Bertie, hands him the recording, a disk in a paper sleeve. The screenplay tells us, "Bertie glances at the record. POV—THE LABEL: His Master's Voice." Inevitable and yet surprising? I say yes. What surprised me about the end of the scene—and the scene as a whole—is how brutal it is, how painful for Bertie, how angry this made him and how little his anger accomplished, how powerless he is, how soundly the door has been slammed in his face. A *king's* face! "His Master's Voice" indeed.

How could anyone not want to know what happens next?

Let's break down the scene. . . .

Who is in it? Bertie and Lionel. Reluctant patient and overbearing therapist. Lion and lion tamer. King and commoner. Yin and yang. Two sides of the central argument. Why isn't Elizabeth invited into the consultation room? Because the scene is not about her. Because she would give comfort to Bertie if she were there and thus diminish the conflict, reduce the pain of the problem for Bertie just when the writer is trying to increase it. The nice screenwriter who doesn't like to see people suffer would put her in that scene. Don't be that guy.

What is in the scene? Actions and words that present the central question of the story—can the king of England be cured of his debilitating stutter by Lionel Logue? The what of the scene? Two men fight. A series of small battles test and reveal the men as we're pushed toward the inevitable climactic battle of wills, the recording of Bertie's voice. Believing he has been beaten, the main character leaves the battlefield.

Where does the scene take place? The battlefield. The consultation room. On Lionel's home turf. (Imagine the difference in the scene if Lionel Logue had been made to come to Buckingham Palace.) The consultation room isn't just any room. It's shabby, unprofessional. It suggests a place of last resort.

When does the action take place? An ordinary day. Probably midweek. Possibly in the afternoon. It's just another day, business as usual for Dr. Logue, the opposite of what the day is in the king's life, which strengthens Lionel's position and puts Bertie at a disadvantage.

Why? What does the scene *mean*? Why is it in the screenplay? Could it be cut? No! Why not? Because of what it tells us about the two main characters, generally and specifically, externally and internally. Because it makes perfectly clear that a king, underneath all the trappings, is a man like other men. Because of what it tells us about the seriousness of the central problem. Because it shows us that there will be large obstacles to overcome. Because, skillfully, mysteriously, it makes us care.

The Who, What, Where, When, and Why of You

Now the time has come to ask yourself the five questions about your own scene. Write that sucker. Rewrite it. Fail better. Then test it—and yourself—with a whole bunch of new questions: What was it about these characters and these situations that made you think of them in the first place? Would these people (and animals and aliens, robots and cars) really have done and said what you just had them do and say? Who are they down deep? Where are they from? Where are they *really* from? Who are they in relation to you? What do they want, short-term and long-term? What do they *really* want? Ask yourself if your scene addresses those goals:

Does your scene keep us in the story?

Does it advance the story?

Does it deepen the story and deepen our sense of the characters?

Does your scene have clear implications and likely repercussions?

What in the scene is visually interesting?

Is the scene entertaining?

Be hard on yourself. Poet and teacher John Ciardi said, "The minimum requirement for a good poem is a miracle." Can your scene pass Ciardi's test for a poem? Did you somehow in your scene make a place for a miracle to occur? Did you present a dilemma so real and so clear and so human that the audience (or the reader) identified with your characters and their plight and was drawn in to try to tackle it too? If you did, that's a miracle! If you didn't, keep trying. Test each scene.

Then, when you've finished your screenplay, for fun and to make yourself feel good, put a big asterisk beside the one scene you think they'll use for the Oscar show. That asterisked scene can tell you something very important: what it is about writing that makes you want to do it, whether or not anyone else gets you and your work. That scene is you. Ultimately your very best scenes will not only be a microcosm of the script as a whole; they'll be a microcosm of you.

And you are the only original thing you have to offer.

CHAPTER 9

Pictures in Motion:
Scenes and the Movement They Create

by Chrysanthy Balis

A body in motion stays in motion, and a body at rest stays at rest. New-ton's First Law of Motion is scene-craft law, as well. A script in motion stays in motion, and a script at rest stays at the bottom of the trash can. To tap into the true art and power of scene writing, you must master what I call the *principle of movement,* both in how you choose and place your scenes and in how you construct each individual scene. Think of your screenplay as a selection of scenes that involve your reader emotion-ally, that continuously reveal moments of dramatic tension in the lives of your characters, and that push your story along its arc, culminating in a satisfying conclusion.

I learned the importance of the principle of movement early and painfully in my career. In my fifteen years as a professional screenwriter, I've written a feature film released by Paramount, a pilot for HBO, and numerous scripts for the studios and TV networks. I've even written for the pleasure of doing it. However, there was one script that caused me physical distress: a road movie, which quickly earned the moniker *The Ulcer*.

This peptic disaster was a massive collection of grandly conceived scenes—so many, in fact, that it was a bloated 160 pages long. I had originally set out to tell the story of five friends who go across the country to retrace their dead friend's steps in the hope of finding out why he committed suicide. However, during the development process, the producer got sidetracked by his own poetic imagery and I lost track of the fact that a collection of scenes alone does not a screenplay make. Ultimately, *The Ulcer*'s demise was nobody's fault but mine. I was a new writer and that's about all I can say in my defense. It was only a couple of years and a few more assignments later that I was able to figure out what would have saved the script:

Movement.

I know what you're thinking. It was a road movie! The characters literally moved across the country! True, but while they traveled physically, the story itself lacked dramatic movement. Despite a host of themes, a cast of eccentric characters, funny moments, and clever banter, the scenes existed largely independently of one another. The moments I had been so enamored of were actually isolated anecdotes in which the characters talked about how much fun college was, how it sucked when their van broke down, and how they wanted to visit this or that obscure roadside attraction.

Occasionally, a clue to the suicide would bubble up and the friends would ruminate on it a bit, but the scene would quickly lead to a hashing-out of the issues they had with one another. The result was a script bereft of rising dramatic action, made up of stagnant scenes with no arc, so that while the van's engine was speeding these friends along America's roads, the story engine of their pursuit was missing. It was a road movie that went nowhere.

This chapter is intended to save you from a similar fate by delving deeply into how scenes work to embody the principle of movement in dramatic storytelling. In the previous chapter, you learned the general structure of scenes and received masterful guidance on the "who, what, where, when, why, and how" of writing them. Now we'll make sure that your choice of scenes and the order in which you have placed them create dramatic movement—a must in the revision process. We'll cover the "must-have" scenes and explore how they can work together to contribute to a sense of movement in your script. Lastly, we'll review a few tools that are essential to creating movement within each scene. Our goal will be to ensure that your script becomes a true "picture in motion."

The Principle of Movement at Work in Scenes
Arrangement of Scenes

The principle of movement pertains, first of all, to the script's overall arrangement of scenes. They start in one place and end in another, often arcing from one end to its opposite. For a great model of how this principle works, take a look at *Jaws*. The story's movement can be easily tracked, scene by scene, along a path of rising action, starting with the shark's first attack on a swimmer, which leads to an investigation, which leads to the closing of beaches in the tourist season. A series of attacks, ever more frightening and with ever-bigger risks, drives the story forward and culminates in a final showdown between man and beast. In this way, *Jaws* arcs from one place to its opposite: In its beginning scenes, the shark is alive and killing. At the end, it is blown to smithereens.

Simultaneously, the hero's objective, to pursue and kill the shark, moves forward along this path of rising action and dramatic tension, informing the engine of the story and every scene. With each shark encounter, the story and its hero travel along an escalating path of dramatic tension, higher than the last.

Be aware, as you map out your scenes, that rising action doesn't mean placing a higher-tension moment after a high-tension moment, in a straight line, from start to finish. If you write your script this way, you'll exhaust your audience and lose their interest long before the movie ends. Instead, your story should have a roller-coaster effect, so that a series of scenes reaches a crescendo of dramatic tension, followed by a low-tension scene that begins a new climb, until dramatic tension reaches a new and even greater crescendo.

In *Jaws,* the opening scene sequence ends on a crescendo of tension with the shark horribly finishing off its first victim. The next scene is low-tension: The hero gets ready to face the day as if it were any other day, unaware of what has transpired. From there, a new escalation begins as he learns of the attack and takes action in response to it, and a new opportunity to explore deeper layers, greater complications and obstacles, bigger risks, and higher stakes opens up.

The Individual Scene

The principle of movement is also at work inside each individual scene in a movie. In *Jaws,* the climactic scene starts with the hero facing off against the shark, which throughout the movie has gotten the better of him, his companions, and his sinking boat. However, the movie ends with the hero defeating the shark by shoving an oxygen tank in its gaping maw and then shooting the tank so that it explodes, killing the shark.

So whether you are looking at your story as a whole or at one scene in particular, like a shark, it has to keep moving to stay alive.

Placement and Choice of Scenes Along the Story Thread

A movie is a tapestry of story threads, which are woven tightly together to create a complex fabric. Each story thread can be pulled out and looked at on its own, and as the writer, you want to make sure that the scenes you put along each of these threads function to move your narrative forward. Like caffeine and deadlines, scene placement and choice go hand in hand.

Placement of Scenes

Placement refers to the order in which you arrange your scenes along a story thread and is how you tell the story. Regardless of the genre you are writing in, it's vital to place scenes in an order that creates dramatic movement. In the thriller *Seven,* for example, the main story thread is of two detectives pursuing a serial killer who begins an opus of murders based on the Seven Deadly Sins. Each discovery of a new victim is more complex and more shocking than the last, right up to the final chilling discovery in the climax scene wherein the final victim is revealed as the rookie detective is handed his wife's head in a box.

This order can be achieved either by stringing scenes together chronologically or by jumping around in time. Just remember that the goal is to construct a path of rising action dictated by your character's journey. As Matt Bird put it perfectly in his blog *Cockeyed Caravan,* "The next scene should be the next step in the escalation or solution of a problem. We follow the path of the hero's problem, not the hero's life."

One common way to create this sense of movement along the path of your hero's problem is to place scenes that revisit an identical or similar scenario but change in some key way each time. In *The Wrestler,* screenwriter Robert D. Siegel presents a grocery store scenario four times throughout the script, thus creating a thread that reflects the hero's growth from has-been to warrior. In the first grocery store scene, Randy the Ram, a washed-up wrestler, asks his jerky manager for extra shifts and gets them but endures humiliating treatment. A bit later, the grocery store is revisited to show us that Randy has been promoted to the deli counter but struggles to handle impatient customers. A third scene shows confident Randy charming customers as he works the meat slicer. This new life without wrestling just might work out!

But in the last scene of this thread, Randy is in a dark emotional place due to events that occurred in other threads woven around this one. Compounding his mood are nagging customers and a critical boss who, together, bring his temper to the boiling point. He intentionally cuts himself on the meat slicer, smears blood over his face, and unleashes the warrior within. Randy will go on to wrestle one more time so that he can die on the field of battle.

Choice of Scenes

The next step is to test the scenes you have planned to see how they work. It's not uncommon to realize that a scene you thought would work feels inadequate now that you're actually writing the script. Imagine you are Peter Benchley and Carl Gottlieb writing the climactic scene in *Jaws,* and you first choose a scene in which the hero has his final encounter with the shark but lets it get away forever. You put that scene where it belongs in act 3, sit back, and look at how it works. Hmmm. Not very satisfying in light of the journey your hero is on and what's at stake if he fails, is it?

So you remove that scene and write a new one in which the hero has his final encounter with the man-eater, but this time stuffs an oxygen tank into the shark's mouth, shoots the tank, and—*boom!*—no more shark. You then replace the previous scene choice with this one, sit back, and have a look at how it services the story as a whole. Much better, don't you think? So this choice of scene stays.

As you consider the best possible scenes to include, strive to choose ones that "show" rather than "tell" the big dramatic moments. For example, a common pitfall is to use phone conversation scenes in which one character tells another about the horrible/wonderful/life-changing event that happened to her. Often, a better choice is a scene that shows the event as it happens, in all its dramatic, comedic, and emotional glory. Choose scenes that go for life, concentrated: make us laugh, make us cry, make us crap our pants.

Scene Sequences

There are occasions where it might take two or more scenes—a sequence—to accomplish the overall intended effect. Consider the opening sequence of *A Single Man,* in which George prepares to take his own life. The first scene shows George choosing a dapper outfit for his corpse. The next one shows a gun and bullets laid out beside paperwork comprising his final affairs as he lies down beside it on the bed and sticks the gun in his mouth. After a beat, he gets up to go to the bathroom.

In the next scene, George is in the shower, reasoning that it would be a cleaner location for suicide, but can't bring himself to do it there, either. In the final scene of this sequence, George returns to the bedroom with a sleeping bag, lies inside it on the bed, and puts the gun to his mouth— but this time, the phone rings. He tells his friend that he won't forget the gin and will see her in ten minutes. End of sequence. Several scenes are required to complete this story beat and connect them to a single mini-objective—for George to kill himself.

Placement and Choice of Events Within a Scene

The placement and choice of events within an individual scene are also key because they, too, create a sense of narrative movement and rising action.

Placement of Events Within a Scene

The placement of events within a scene is determined by the need to start it in one place and end it in another. In *Hotel Rwanda,* hotel manager Paul Rusesabagina and his wife, in the midst of terrible violence, share a quiet romantic moment alone on a rooftop terrace. By candlelight, they reminisce about their courtship to reveal a wider version of their lives. We see them not just as victims caught up in genocidal chaos, but as a married couple still very much in love. This moment is interrupted by the staccato of gunfire. Murderous gangs have infiltrated their neighborhood and they need to flee. The viewer's emotions jump from warm mirth to tingling fear within a single scene, thanks to screenwriters Keir Pearson and Terry George's placement of events.

The Single-Purpose Scene

Keep in mind that an individual scene can have either a single or double purpose in moving the story forward. When you are writing a single-purpose scene, you place events so that the purpose is reached at the scene's end. In *The Town,* a scene set in a Laundromat begins with Doug, a bank robber, encountering Claire, the woman he temporarily kidnapped during his most recent robbery getaway. Claire doesn't recognize Doug minus his mask, and so she innocently makes small talk. By the end of the scene, Doug has grown emboldened enough to ask her out on a date, which she accepts—a simple climax to the scene's arc that reflects the scene's purpose in pushing their romance thread a step forward.

The Double-Purpose Scene

When an individual scene has two purposes, the events in the first part push one story thread forward, while events in the second part push another story thread forward. Writer-director Tony Gilroy takes us through a stunning two-purpose scene in *Michael Clayton,* whose protagonist is a lawyer who cleans up his clients' messes but can't seem to clean up his own.

To capture the slow and silent boiling up of Michael's emotional turmoil in the first part of the scene, Gilroy shows Michael leaving a client's house and driving his Mercedes through winding roads in the pre-dawn light. As he reaches an open pasture, Michael pulls to a stop just as the sun is rising and stares at three horses poised in the fog like ghosts. He leaves the engine running and approaches the horses, compelled to be a part of their peace, and just as he connects with the horses—*boom!*—his car explodes.

With Michael's internal story arc pushed forward, the scene jumps to its second purpose: to set up the external arc story thread, which is the mystery of who wants Michael Clayton dead. This shift can occur at any point within a scene and is entirely up to the writer's sensibility.

Start Late, Get Out Early: Choice of Events Within a Scene

Where do you start your scene? You start at the end. You'll hear that a lot in creative meetings with development execs: "Can we start this scene closer to the end?" So enter a scene as late as you can while still leaving room for a buildup toward that scene's purpose(s) and end the scene as soon as the final purpose is complete. Move to the final purpose too quickly, and the scene will feel like a cheat. Take too long and your scene will drag. Trust the revision process to eventually hit the sweet spot.

Find those compelling events that open the scene and close it, as well as the beats that take the scene along its arc from one end to its opposite. In the above example, Michael doesn't connect with the horses and then have his car explode behind him. Instead, the writer builds a rising tension within the scene, starting just far enough back to reach a crescendo by showing Michael choosing this place to stop while on a drive, building his connection with the horses, and giving the explosion a chance to shock us in jarring contrast to the peace.

Once Michael's car explodes, anticipation is set in motion for the audience: What will Michael's next action be in response to the discovery that someone is trying to kill him, and will it help him find the peace he seeks? Once you've reached the final purpose of your scene, end it on a note that strikes a chord of tension in order to create a sense of anticipation. If you do this for every scene, your reader won't be able to put down your script.

Connectivity Between Scenes

Connectivity between your scenes also contributes to their sense of movement. Look for opportunities to create connective tissue by linking how you end one scene with how you open the next. Look for an image, object, line of dialogue, or sound that can be matched to some degree at the end of one scene and the beginning of the other. For example, in *Slumdog Millionaire,* a scene in the police station ends with "we close in on the TV screen where Prem is smiling his crocodile smile and find ourselves . . . INT. STUDIO—NIGHT as Prem asks the first question." The image of a smiling Prem carries us from one scene to the next—first on a TV screen and then to the real Prem in his studio.

Consider, too, the power of contrast. You might end one scene on a dark image and open the next one on a light one, or end on a moment of high tension and open on a moment of low tension. Whether it's through dialogue, action, or a single image, look for organic opportunities to connect your scene to the one that will follow it.

Scene Types

As you work on scene placement and choice along your story threads and within individual scenes, you also want to consider the array of scene types you have at your disposal. For the most part, there isn't an "industry-standard terminology" by which all scene types are identified, so in some instances, I have invented names that convey the essence of a particular scene's purpose. This list of scenes isn't all-inclusive, but it does provide the basics, the must-haves, and a few of the most commonly used optional scenes available to you.

The Pillar Scenes

A script's structure is composed of six key pillar scenes as well as the scenes that fill in the spaces between them. Whether you want to write a seemingly iconoclastic script like a *Babel* or a *Slumdog Millionaire,* or a successfully formulaic script like *Bridesmaids,* a strong grasp of how story pillar scenes work allows you to embrace the larger spirit of storytelling they represent. Done well, story pillars satisfy basic stages of progression in storytelling and mark key turning points within a story filled with twists and turns, regardless of whether you divide a script into six acts rather than three or use the term *plot point one* instead of *first turning point.*

Pillar Scene #1: The Opening Scene

The opening scene establishes the tone of your movie and hints at the story to come without giving anything away just yet. Its main purpose is to tantalize and hook the audience—often with an event that ends with a twist or "hook." Imagine that you are telling a story around a campfire, using your voice to mesmerize the listener—that's the approach to take when writing your opening scene. You may also want to precede the opening scene with an establishing scene, which sets up the where and when of your story—the Manhattan skyline, for example, or a small village in the Himalayas. Either way, you must draw your reader into your story from the very first image.

In *Bridesmaids,* the opening consists first of an establishing scene outside a bachelor's home as Annie and Ted exchange dialogue in a voice-over. Then we move inside the home and realize that the conversation is taking place during a session of vigorous sex. This opener ends on a funny and shocking twist as Ted, postcoitally, asks Annie to skedaddle. The scene's purpose is to illustrate, in an entertaining but cringe-worthy way, how the hero is in a place in her life where she's willing to settle for less.

Pillar Scene #2: The Catalyst Scene

This scene is the bomb dropped on the status quo of your story and sets it in motion. Without it, there would be no story. In *Bridesmaids,* the catalyst scene occurs when Lillian tells Annie she's getting married and asks her to be her maid of honor.

Pillar Scene #3: The First Turning Point Scene

The events in this scene transition the story from act 1 to act 2 by providing a specific focus for the story. After the catalyst scene, your hero will likely have spent some time dealing with its immediate aftereffects. While he may have taken preliminary action in response, Fate (the writer) barrels him ever forward to his date with Destiny, as eventually manifested in the first turning point scene. This scene gives the hero an objective to pursue and, as a result, asks the central question of the story.

In *Bridesmaids,* the first turning point scene is the engagement party scene, where Annie and Helen sing "That's What Friends Are For" in an effort to outdo each other as Lillian's true best friend. At that moment, the competition is on! The movie now has a specific focus for the hero's journey—to win the "best friend" award—so the central question of the story is "Will Annie beat Helen out for the role of Lillian's best friend?"

Pillar Scene #4: The Midpoint Scene

This scene effectively cuts the movie into two halves. Stakes are raised, difficulty is elevated, and the movie shoots off into a new and heightened direction. If the hero spent the first half of the movie being an arrogant jerk, he spends the second half learning to unjerk. If he had the help of the police in the first half, he has to go it alone in the second. If he was previously able to keep his crumbling life together, he now finds it increasingly impossible to stop it from collapsing.

In the first half of *Bridesmaids,* Annie is Lillian's best friend, but in the second half, she's the increasingly estranged friend. The midpoint scene that creates this pivot takes place on the flight to Las Vegas, during which Annie's flying phobia causes her to accept both the antagonist's offer of an anxiety pill and her suggestion to wash it down with a cocktail. Annie gets lit like a firecracker and creates a huge midair spectacle, which compels Lillian to ask her to step down from the responsibilities of being maid of honor. Now the game has changed as the hero is further than ever from reaching her goal and must work harder, against greater obstacles, to achieve the final victory of being Lillian's best friend.

Pillar Scene #5: The Second Turning Point Scene

This scene brings the story to its darkest moment: What your characters have been pursuing now seems out of reach for good. This is the story's transition from act 2 into act 3 and is most commonly referred to as the "all hope is lost" moment. While you want to craft many scenes in which your hero encounters obstacles and complications that risk overwhelming him, you really pile it on here.

Movement boils down to common sense: The deeper the trench from which he begins to climb, the more dramatically satisfying it is once he reaches the top. In *Bridesmaids,* this scene plays out at the bridal shower as Annie's paltry wedding gift is trumped by Helen's gift of a trip to Paris. Annie finally snaps, unleashing all her emotions. Surely, all hope seems lost after behavior like that. Annie's not only no longer maid of honor but probably no longer Lillian's best friend.

Pillar #6: The Climax Scene

This is the payoff scene that the audience is waiting to see: the big show-down in which the hero is challenged one last time. In its strictest version, everything ends happily, but the focus here is not so much on creating a happy ending as on finding that ending that is, as Aristotle described it, both surprising and inevitable. This climax scene must answer the central question raised at the first turning point: Will Annie earn her role as best friend and maid of honor? Yes, she will. Everything wraps up nicely as Annie talks Lillian out of having cold feet. Annie regains her best friend status on firmer ground, having at last done something selflessly for Lillian as a true friend.

One of the biggest pitfalls for student writers is a climax scene that doesn't satisfy the theme and message of the story that were set up (ideally) in act 1. My UCLA Extension Writers' Program screenwriting students will sometimes kill off their hero just to avoid writing a "hokey Hollywood ending." I tell them that they are welcome to kill their hero (*American Beauty*), or have him lose the prizefight (*Rocky*), or deliver his wife's head to him in a box (*Seven*), as long as the chosen ending is one that satisfies the theme and message of their movie.

Between the Pillars

In addition to the major pillar scenes that prop up your story, scene choice is about finding those moments of obstacles, complications, changes, and discoveries that propel the story from one pillar to the next. It's important to note that there is a measure of crossover regarding choices of scenes. An obstacle scene can also be a midpoint scene, for example. However, in order to pinpoint each type of scene's specific narrative intentions, I cover each separately.

The Expository Scene

As your story begins, you'll need a few scenes that establish and explain the status quo of your world and the characters in it. That way, the reader can appreciate the changes that are about to come. Even though you're painting a world as it exists before an event occurs to set your specific story into motion, keep in mind that there must still be narrative movement hurling the hero forward toward the catalyst.

For example, a series of heavily expository scenes from *Up in the Air* is triggered when Ryan's boss informs him that he will no longer be required to travel for work. Through these scenes we learn that that his home is a hotel, he can only handle friendships that are casual encounters like the ones on a plane, and he prefers to cruise through life at an altitude that keeps him safe from the messiness of real, long-term human interaction. Writers Jason Reitman and Sheldon Turner don't give us every detail about Ryan's life, but we learn enough to appreciate the weight of the catalyst— his becoming enamored of a woman with the same philosophy (and fears) who lives like he does. Now that we've been given vital information, we can eagerly anticipate the potential for conflict and drama.

The Signature Scene

This is a type of expository scene that illustrates who a character is in a nutshell and often comes early in a script. In *The Cooler,* Bernie explains what it is he does as a Vegas "cooler" by stepping up to a hot craps table and cooling it. As he plays a few rounds, the house wins back all its money and then some. This signature scene captures who Bernie is when we first meet him: a professional loser.

The Setup Scene and the Payoff Scene

If you set something in motion in one scene, you need to see it through in a later scene. In *The Silence of the Lambs,* Dr. Chilton unwittingly drops a pen inside Lecter's cell in one scene so that, in a later scene, Lecter can use it to pick the lock of his handcuffs. Between these two scenes, we wait on pins and needles knowing that there has to be a payoff scene in which Lecter will use the pen to his advantage—and to our perverse satisfaction. Without a proper payoff scene, the story will feel directionless and without dramatic movement. Conversely, without a proper setup scene, the subsequent events will appear as arbitrary choices of convenience.

The Obstacle and Complication Scenes

The obstacle scene places something before a character that threatens to prevent him from reaching a goal. The complication scene is a result of that obstacle or obstacles and takes some time to come to full effect later in the story. Ideally, you will have plenty of both along your story threads. A character can't simply embark on a journey, attain his objective, and call it a day—movies would be one minute long! Instead, obstacles and complications must litter his path, challenge his pursuits, and throw multiple wrenches into his best-laid plans.

In *Training Day,* David Ayer wrote a terrifying obstacle scene in which Jake, a rookie cop on his training day on the streets of L.A. with veteran cop Alonzo, discovers that he has been purposefully left behind by his mentor in a gangbanger's apartment. Deep in enemy territory, alone and surrounded by gangbangers whom Alonzo has instructed to kill him, Jake comes up against his biggest obstacle yet.

The Victory Scene

When confronting obstacles and complications, the character either overcomes or is temporarily set back by them. This can occur within the obstacle scene, or the dramatic tension can be stretched out a bit further and culminate in a separate victory scene. The victories you chart for your hero show his growth, even as they help him get ever closer to attaining his overall goal. In *Hotel Rwanda,* Paul faces the captain of a gang of Hutus preparing to slaughter his family along with a group of Tutsis. Paul finds a way around this terrible obstacle by appealing to the killers' vulnerability to bribes, handing over watches, cash, and jewelry belonging to the frightened group and him as well—and for the moment, everyone is saved.

The Setback Scene

Here the hero attempts to overcome an obstacle or complication, but instead of gaining victory, he experiences a setback—a temporary failure along his journey to complete his central objective. A powerful scene sequence in *American Beauty* shows Carolyn, desperate to become a successful Realtor, come up against an obstacle in the form of a crappy house she has been given to sell. Despite her best efforts to overcome it by cleaning the house herself and painting a rosy view of it to prospective buyers, no one makes an offer. Her cheery façade cracks and she breaks into tears.

The Discovery Scene

In this type of scene, your character discovers a new piece of vital information. What he finds out will spur him to make a decision and in turn spur him to action at some point in the story. Put enough discovery scenes in your script, and you'll lead your character through the unraveling of a mystery as he fulfills his quest.

In *Moneyball,* Billy is the general manager of the Oakland A's baseball team, and his task for the upcoming season is to put together a team that doesn't suck but costs very little money. When an Ivy League numbers cruncher explains how mathematics can be applied to pick players who get runs but whom managers don't want for other reasons, it's a huge discovery for Billy. Now he can go after cheap players and still stand a chance at creating a winning team—an unheard-of combination in professional baseball. *Moneyball's* discovery scene provides Billy with a way out of a dire situation and moves him a step closer to achieving his overall objective of creating a winning team.

The Inspiration Scene

The inspiration scene is a more spiritual type of discovery scene, in that a character discovers something within himself that often inspires him to make some kind of change in his life. Such moments of discovery and inspiration may serve to make a character rethink his choices, his philosophy, and his treatment of others, and these changes, in turn, create a sense of movement through the story.

In *The Wrestler,* Randy has sabotaged his last chance to make amends with his daughter by standing her up on their "date." In an inspiration scene, he tries to get Stephanie to forgive him, but this time she cuts him out of her life for good. The brutal finality of it is the last straw for this hero. It's a moment that inspires him to change from the broken Randy, who sought to embrace a life without wrestling, to a warrior with nothing left to live for and who is unafraid to die.

Decision-in-Action Scene

The result of a discovery or inspiration scene, this type of scene is where a character puts his decision into action, thereby advancing the plot. In *The Wrestler,* Randy the Ram decides to cut his thumb and smear blood over himself to renounce the tame life he has been trying to lead and instead be a warrior, ready for one last fight in the ring. Sometimes a writer will combine a discovery scene and a decision-in-action scene into one.

Transition Scene

This is a short scene that is also short on dramatic content. It's used simply to create a natural transition between very different locations or time periods, or when jumping from one story thread to another. The decision of when to use it is often instinctive. In *Bridesmaids,* a scene ends with Lillian telling Annie that she needs to step down from her responsibilities as maid of honor. Immediately following is a transition scene, in which a saddened Annie drives home from her meeting with Lillian and spots Officer Rhodes's car parked at its usual spot. She asks him if he wants to hang out, and the transition from "best friend thread" to "romance thread" is complete.

Dazzler Scene

This is a scene in which the magic of the cinematic medium is used to full effect, often at a point of transition. It can be a fantastical journey, a trip toward a new planet, or a chase through the streets of Baltimore. Such scenes delight us, as they afford an opportunity to see things from a perspective only film can deliver. They can be comprised of a series of incredible obstacles to be overcome or they can be a series of wondrous images.

In *Up*, Carl's transition from being an elderly man facing a move to a retirement home to being a man starting a new life as an adventurer occurs in a sequence of dazzler scenes. Just as the nursing home representatives come for him, Carl takes off—or rather, *up*—in a house elevated by a cluster of balloons and headed for South America. He floats down the street, to the wonderment of all, and then rises higher up among the clouds. A knock on the door shocks him and he finds Russell, the overeager Boy Scout, hanging on for dear life. Hoping to get rid of the pesky kid, Carl dangles him off a rope in an effort to dislodge him atop a passing roof. These are impossible things in real life, but what the cinematic medium can make possible is dazzling.

Optional Scenes

Montage: This is a series of short scenes or images. It's a helpful device when you need to show a transition over time without putting a lot of narrative focus on it. For instance, a media montage in *Ghostbusters* chronicles the Ghostbusters' rise from being nobodies to being famous celebrities in compressed time. Since we don't need long, ponderous scenes to track this progression, a montage comes in handy. But be wary, friends: Don't go montage-happy. When I read a script with five or six montages, I know that the story is covering too much material over too long a span of time, giving us more information than we require, or skimming over story beats that require more focus. Aim for one or two montages in a given script, if at all.

Flashback Scene: A flashback scene takes place in the past in relation to the time period of your movie. This device is used most successfully when it creates its own mini-narrative thread, complete with dramatic tension and a question that it seeks to answer. In *Moneyball,* we flash back to a series of scenes showing Billy as a promising young ball player in the 1980s, thus generating a sense of mystery that we want to see solved: Was Billy really that good a player? If so, why is he now a GM and not a star player? These questions don't get answered until act 3, so these flashback scenes create a nice side thread of tension to illuminate Billy's character.

Unfortunately, flashback scenes are often misused as a story crutch. Sometimes a writer fills in the past with a flashback instead of doing the harder work of weaving backstory information naturally into present-day scenes. Another pitfall of an overreliance on flashbacks is that it suggests that a writer doesn't trust the power of his present-day scenes. And if he doesn't trust them, why should anyone else?

Because a flashback takes an audience out of a real-time thread and cuts into the overall sense of rising action and anticipation, you need to be sure that your flashbacks convey backstory without losing a sense of narrative movement. A flashback scene cut from the final version of *Unforgiven* (David Webb Peoples) showed William Munny in his old identity of murderous outlaw, whipping his tormented horse in a blind rage. However, at the point at which this scene occurred, the audience has already been told in present-day scenes that Munny used to be a very bad man and a killer of women and children, but his dear departed wife changed his heart. When in doubt, take out the flashback.

Dream and Fantasy Scenes: Dream and fantasy scenes can serve to create their own sense of a mystery unfolding by providing symbolism and a glimpse into the subconscious of a character. The trick is to make sure that the symbolism is clear enough for an audience to appreciate yet inventive enough to offer something they haven't seen before. When such a scene is misused, it's reminiscent of those excruciating conversations you have with that friend who insists on recounting to you the details of "the weirdest dream" he had last night.

A movie that uses dream and fantasy scenes to powerful effect is *The Diving Bell and the Butterfly*. The hero, Jean-Do, is a quadriplegic, and since the only action he can perform in the present-day narrative is to blink his left eye, screenwriter Ronald Harwood relies on flashbacks and dreams to reveal information about him in a dramatic way. In one dream scene, Jean-Do sits inside a diving bell bubbling down through a murky green sea. He panics, wildly banging at the porthole. A female voice calls out, awakening him from his reverie. Through scenes like this one, the writer communicates what it feels like to be trapped in your body and how the only working part of you left—your mind—tries to cope.

Scene Types in Action: *Ratatouille*

Let's look at act 1 of the screenplay for *Ratatouille* to see how these different types of scenes are used in a successful movie. Notice, too, how once you gain an understanding for what each scene type's purpose is, you can meld them together to great effect.

Opening Scene: A black-and-white documentary clip sets up Chef Gusteau, the story's message ("Anyone can cook"), and the larger theme that stems from it—the importance of being true to yourself. The scene ends with a challenge to that notion by Paris's top food critic, Anton Ego.

Establishing Scene: A farmhouse in the French country-side.

Obstacle Scene: Our hero, Remy the rat, is in midchase as an old lady hurls a cookbook at him and shatters a window. How did he get into this mess?

Flashback Scenes as Expository Scenes: Remy explains his dilemma: He lives a rat's hard life but is endowed with a refined sense of smell and a passion for cooking. Here we see short scenes from his status quo existence, stealing food and cooking in secret, as well as moments that illustrate his relationship with the other characters in his life. As a rat, he's forced to eat garbage, steal, and hate humans, but as we learn, these circumstances go against his true nature. These scenes reveal the movie's larger theme—the importance of being true to yourself. Remy finds his inspiration in the famous Chef Gusteau, whose cookbook title assures him that "anyone can cook."

Discovery Scene: A bolt of lightning transforms the piece of cheese and mushroom Remy is holding into a delicious melted morsel, which inspires him to build on its flavor by adding some saffron. Saffron, however, is to be found in the old lady's kitchen.

Decision-in-Action Scene: Remy rummages through the farmhouse kitchen for saffron as his brother nervously looks on.

Catalyst Scene: On the old lady's TV is a report that Chef Gusteau has died. Just then, she confronts the rats with a shotgun. They run.

Dazzler Scene Sequence Presented in the Form of Obstacles: We're back to the present-day chase. A sequence of high-octane scenes ensues as Remy and his brother, Emile, dodge shotgun blasts around the farmhouse. Coming to the rescue, the rat colony drops into the chaotic mix and they scramble out of the farmhouse and into a stream. Remy, the last to make it out of the farmhouse and unable to catch up to the drifting colony, gets separated from his tribe for good.

Victory Scene: In the tunnels of the sewer system, Remy braves the dangerous waters to make it to safety atop the floating cookbook.

Inspiration Scene: Alone in the sewer and without any direction, Remy witnesses the image of Gusteau from the cookbook beneath his feet come to life. It is a manifestation of his conscience, which tells him that he has a chance at a new chapter in life. It's time for Remy to reinvent himself from rat to chef.

Transition Sequence: Remy scuttles past images of life in a big city before surfacing in central Paris next to Gusteau's restaurant.

Decision-in-Action Scene: Inspired by Gusteau's words, Remy decides to enter the famed restaurant as a first step in pursuing his dream of becoming a chef.

Discovery Scene: When Remy notices the dishwasher Linguini ruining the soup, he's horrified.

Dazzler and Obstacles Scene Sequence: Suddenly, the skylight Remy's on gives way and he drops into the chaos of the kitchen. He dodges death at every turn as he narrowly avoids being immolated by a series of flaming burners, run over by a dining cart, and cooked in an oven. But when he sees that he has a chance to fix the soup, he can't resist doing so.

Victory Scene That Quickly Transitions to an Obstacle Scene: Remy manages to doctor the soup to his tastes before Linguini spots him and captures him under a colander.

Victory Scene: The soup is whisked out to the patrons before Linguini can stop it, and they rave about its flavor.

Discovery Scene: Chef Skinner and the other kitchen workers mistakenly "discover" that Linguini is a great chef—anyone can cook!

Decision-in-Action Scene: Remy tries to make his escape from the kitchen.

Obstacle Scene: While in the process of offering Linguini the opportunity to move up to being a chef, Skinner spots Remy midescape and shouts, "Rat!" Linguini captures Remy in a jar. Skinner tells him to kill the rat outside.

Discovery Scene: Linguini confronts Remy and realizes that the soup was great because of what this rat did to it. He also discovers that Remy understands him when he speaks. Linguini makes the decision to pair up with Remy: "This could work!"

At this point, act 2 begins. Every scene for act 1 addressed the character's pursuit of an objective in some way. The hero moved physically from life in the country to life in the city, and intellectually from frustrated wannabe chef to newbie chef who has made his first successful dish. After a series of scenes reaches a high-tension climax, it's followed by a low-tension scene that begins the next climb of dramatic tension. All of this points to the principle of movement at work.

That's a Wrap

Now it's your turn to put your script in motion through the creation, placement, choice, and types of scenes that propel your characters and their story arcs forward, until the very end, when the story threads you first set into motion unfurl and intertwine and come to rest at last. With the principle of movement at work in your scenes, you will have taken your reader on a marvelous ride.

SECTION III

Rewriting Your Feature Screenplay

CHAPTER 10

Taking the Script to the Next Level:
The Rewrite Process Begins

by Quinton Peeples

Your script is *sick*. And I don't mean in the cool sk8r-boy way. I mean it as a medical diagnosis. If you're honest, you know I'm telling the truth. As you read back through the draft, there were places where you were excited, proud, and a little surprised at yourself. But there were also passages that made you feel queasy, uneasy, and a little worried. Don't despair. It happens to the best of us. I'm going to give you a prescription for a rewrite. Don't take it on an empty stomach.

Party On!

Before you begin your revision, I want to stop here and ask, "Did you celebrate?" Did you throw yourself a First-Draft Fiesta? Because if you didn't, you need to put this book down, call your friends, and load up on junk food, libations, and loud music. Why? Because you've already done something most people only dream about. You put your butt in the chair, day in and day out, and you persevered. No matter what happens from here on in, you set a goal and achieved it. It's hard work and deserves some celebration when you finish.

Soak in the fact that you created something out of nothing, bring your friends in on that, take as many toasts and slaps on the back as you can. Renew and revitalize the vision you have of yourself as a creative powerhouse. Recharge your engine. Because now the revision process *begins*. You'll notice I emphasized the word *begins*. Revision is an ongoing process. One of the most common questions I get in my UCLA Extension Writers' Program classroom is "How many drafts is this going to take before it's right?" If I knew the answer to that, I would be a prophet and not a screenwriter. It will take as many drafts as it takes. I hate to be the one to break it to you, but you need to know this from the top, and I'll also let you know that my firmest belief is . . .

Writing Is Rewriting

This cliché is nothing but truth on a stick, and it will beat you down until you accept it as your master. Sorry. I know that first draft was tough. I know what it was like to stare at that blank page and be terrified. But here's the good news: That day is over. There's something new ahead.

The skill of rewriting is the most important one you can acquire as a professional screenwriter. It is essential to going forward and becoming a success because no one, and I mean *no one,* gets it right the first time. I've made a long career of rewriting scripts in all sorts of formats: independent features, studio features, television movies, one-hour dramas. I've rewritten other writers. I've been rewritten. I've been fired, rewritten, and then rehired to rewrite the guy who replaced me. On a script that I cowrote with Billy Crystal called *Have a Nice Day,* we did twenty-two revisions before sending our "first" draft to the studio. Then we got their notes and started all over again.

That's the game. I don't make the rules. I just love to play. I want to emphasize it again: This is a process. You must find a way to enjoy the act of revision or else you are going to be miserable.

My Foolproof Rewrite Process

In this chapter, I'm going to tell you how I revise my screenplays. I guarantee you that this rewrite process works for me every time. By following this formula regardless of the specific project, I keep myself focused and avoid working on things in the script that are minor, don't really need fixing, and might even disappear in the final draft. I recommend sticking to these steps and undertaking them in this order.

1. **Diagnose Your Draft.** You are going to begin your rewrite process by getting feedback from other people and by doing your own assessment of your script's weaknesses. It's very important to get notes from people you trust, learn how to listen, sort out helpful from unhelpful comments, and use the notes to your best advantage to improve your script.

2. **Put Your Draft Aside and Daydream Ways to Improve It.** After you have accumulated all of your notes, take some time to think and daydream about all the ways you might make your script better. You may be tempted to start writing right away or even give up altogether. Don't. Be still and let the best ideas come forward.

3. **Apply the Feedback.** Using the techniques and tricks I share in this chapter, you begin to shape new approaches to your script's story, structure, and character issues; make sure your writing is clear; and test out the authenticity of your characters and the specific universe they inhabit. In the end, if you take this step seriously, you will be solid and confident in your solutions, and your rewrite process will be faster, better, and more enjoyable.

4. **Write the Next Draft.** Once you commence rewriting your draft, don't look back. Keep your forward momentum going all the way until the end. This won't be the last time you touch these pages, so don't waste time hovering over and polishing things you may need to change later anyway.

5. **Put Your Revision Away.** This may be the hardest advice for you to follow, but here it is: Once you finish the revision, put it in a drawer for two weeks (at least), and don't look at it. You will need this time to freshly appraise the work you did.

6. **Repeat as Needed.** You get the picture. Repeat step 1. It's a process.

Now let's get to the specifics of just how to execute each step of this rewrite process.

Step 1: Diagnose Your Draft

How to Get Script Notes That Really Help You

The first step is to figure out what's really going on with your draft. This process is one of the most difficult for writers because it means being open, humble, and vulnerable—three qualities found in short supply in the population at large, not to mention artists in particular. It also means that you are going to have to admit that you fell short of your original goal. The way around these potential emotional roadblocks is to see that the problems you will learn to identify in this chapter aren't "mistakes." They are simply flags planted all over the screenplay that show you where you need to improve your work. The sooner you address them, the sooner your script will be healed.

The most surprising discovery for me, as my career progressed, was that the best notes I got on first drafts did not come from people in "the industry." In fact, some of the worst notes I have ever received have come from professionals. Here's an example: "There really are no such things as villains. Just misguided people." If you want boring drama, try taking that note seriously.

When choosing who you want to read your first draft, keep in mind a couple of fundamental rules:

1. Give first drafts to readers who are there for you on a regular basis, share the vision of your being a paid screenwriter, and root for your success. (This may or may not include your mother, as the case may be.)

2. Your readers should also be people with shared tastes who enjoy and avoid the same kinds of films you do. That way, you have a shorthand for what's quality and what's not, and that's invaluable as you take in their feedback.

3. Your contact in the movie business likely will not be the best choice as a reader during the rewrite process. The truth is that you're probably going to need that industry person's very real help when your script is the best that it can be. Now is not the time to play that card.

With these things in mind, turn over the draft to two or three people who meet the above criteria, and then prepare for what they have to say. If you are very, very lucky, they will be brutally honest.

How to Listen to What Your Readers Are *Really* Saying

Whether the notes come from your roommate or the head of the studio, your job is to get down to the essence of what they mean. Most people won't say, "On page seventy-five you have failed to escalate the tension to the degree required." Instead, you'll more likely get comments such as, "I thought she was funny." Or "I was kind of bored in that part." Or "I didn't get this one thing." This is where you need to pull out your stethoscope and start thumping on their backs. You must ask your readers a series of probing questions, read between the lines, and in general, be a very good listener. Being a good listener requires two things that you will have to practice: silence and humility.

By silence, I don't mean you sit there and say absolutely nothing. I mean that you wait until those from whom you've requested feedback put a period at the end of their sentences. We rarely do this, because we assume we know the point of what other people are saying before they are finished. In reality, they may not get to the point until the very last moment, and you are doing them, and yourself, a great disservice by interrupting. Very often, what you think is a period is actually a comma. Wait. Listen. And then respond with humility.

Humility does not mean being a doormat. It simply means that you are prepared for the possibility that someone else might have a better handle on this one particular thing than you do. If you can take notes without it being an exercise in who's right/who's wrong, you'll get a lot further a lot faster. If you are truly going to fix what is wrong with the script, you must put the defensive part of your personality away. You asked for your trusted readers' help and they are doing their best, so take their feedback in the spirit in which it is given: as a gift.

Ouch, That Hurt: Sorting Out Helpful Versus Unhelpful (Possibly Destructive) Feedback

Let's not kid ourselves; not every note is helpful. And many will set us spinning off in the wrong direction. How do you know the difference? You are going to use the two most powerful allies you have: your gut and your mind.

Let's begin with your gut, or more accurately, your creative instinct.

It's that tingly sensation you get when you know you are onto something good. It also works in the other direction—that queasy feeling you get when something's not right. When it comes to discerning the value of notes, it's always best to focus on the tingly sensation. Not the nausea. Now, this can be tricky, because often we will hear a note that makes us uneasy because we know it's true and we don't have a solution to the problem that is being pointed out. I often pull a Scarlett O'Hara on those notes—"I'll think about that tomorrow"—and file those in the back of my mind. The solution comes to me later, and then I feel excited.

But there are many notes that I can't reconcile no matter how hard I try. I have this powerful feeling that they aren't right for the story I am telling. Those are the notes I reject, even if they are coming from an "expert" or from someone I admire. When it comes to my story, I get to be the final word. I often have to remind myself of this, so you should practice it frequently.

There is a whole class of notes that fall into the "ambivalent" category. What to do about the notes that you don't have a strong feeling about one way or the other? This is where your mind comes in. Use some simple math: If you've gotten a note more than once, take it seriously, no matter how you "feel" about it. Your gut may be misleading you here. (It happens. We've all been on a date like that, right?)

If people who read your work point to something again and again, you've got a problem, but if you hear a note only once, it may just be a matter of taste. If this random note confirms something you had an inkling was a problem, then take it on. If it's off the mark, and this is the first and only time you've heard it, then it doesn't pass the criteria for serious consideration. Move on.

How to Understand the Notes

Once you have received all of your notes, you will need to "decode" their meaning. I have found that most notes fall into one of three categories:

pacing problems, lack of clarity, and lack of authenticity. They usually indicate specific problems with the script's structure, story, or character, or some combination of all three.

Pacing Problems

Your readers may experience boredom and use a variety of terms to express that reaction in an effort to be gentle. They may say the script was "slow" in some parts, or that you could "do without" some scenes. You need to go after this kind of note with great gusto, because it indicates that your script has a structural problem, which is most likely related to your script's pacing. Most first drafts suffer from this malady, and that's why it tops my list.

Lack of Clarity

When readers say, "I didn't get this one part," or "That didn't pay off," you are being told that what you wrote wasn't clear enough. To get at the heart of this note, you begin by asking them to identify which scene or action puzzled them and why. You then explain what you were going for, at which point your readers might say, "Huh. I didn't get that." Or even better, your explanation might enable them to pinpoint exactly where you went astray. Either way, these notes show you the places you need to be clearer, so flag these spots in your script.

Lack of Authenticity

When you get the note "I don't buy it," or "I don't think she would do a thing like that," or "That didn't seem very realistic," it usually means that you have failed to represent your characters' life and/or the world they inhabit in a way that's consistent with who and what they are.

Step 2: Put Your Draft Aside and Daydream Ways to Improve It

At this point, you've gone home with your notes, and you are sitting on your couch wondering why you ever thought you could do this in the first place. What happened to that awesome feeling you had at your First-Draft Fiesta? Maybe you should just abandon your script and try a different idea, because this one seems dead in the water.

Don't. I'm begging you. Don't. Do. That.

You've already given an extraordinary amount of time and energy to this project. It's been a huge investment on your part. Abandoning a script at this stage is a common mistake and it is shortsighted. The note-taking process hurts—believe me, I know. In the hours following a notes session, I am a bear—a cursing, wounded, intolerant grizzly. *I do no writing during this time.* I wait for the emotions to subside. They always do. Sometimes it takes days. That's all right.

But as my feelings retreat, usually some answers start to make their way into my pea brain and I start to see my way forward. I realize that a lot of what my readers pointed out, I already knew. That's encouraging. Then I start to get a little excited about how much better the script will be once I start solving these problems. Looks like I just might live after all.

Step 3: Apply the Feedback

Now that you've gotten your full set of notes and figured out how to interpret them, it's time to apply all that feedback and dig into improving your script. Remember, before you start rewriting your draft, you need to come up with a number of solid solutions to three main problem areas that plague every first draft: structure (often as indicated by pacing), clarity, and authenticity. This is the critical third step of the rewrite process, and I've organized my fixes to these three problems in the order of their importance.

Remember, to apply each of these fixes, you may want to focus on each individually, which means going through your draft *three separate and distinct times*—what I'm calling "passes." It sounds like a lot of work, and it is, but: 1) This method prevents you from being overwhelmed by all the work you need to do, 2) it helps you approach your script from multiple angles, and 3) it's effective—you *will* rewrite your script.

The other method to use is to go through the draft now, making notes in the margins about what specifics need to change in each scene or section. I will often do this using different-colored pens, one for each category: red for story, blue for structure, green for character work. This is dorky but colorful, and at this point, I need some things to keep me entertained. This is hard work, so injecting some fun here is important.

Maybe you don't feel as passionately as I do about colored ink, but you can see my point—it gets the job done and helps keep my spirits high. You can adapt this to suit your own tastes. I teach these exact techniques in my Writers' Program course "The Rewrite Toolbox." They've worked for my students for years, and they will work for you. Since you started out wanting to tell a story, let's begin there.

Pass #1: Fixing Your Script's Structure

Decide on Your Story

Nine times out of ten, no matter how well you have constructed your screenplay, it will still have structure problems. Let's begin with structure's most basic component, story, which I define as a *unique* protagonist facing a *compelling* conflict that leads to an *inevitable* end. (Story is not to be confused with plot, which is all the twists and turns *inside* the story that lead us to the end.)

First, boil down your story to its essence. Here's an example: Orphaned farm boy leads a group of rebels against a powerful empire and is victorious. Sound familiar? It should. It's the story of *Star Wars*. You are probably saying to yourself, "Wait! There's so much other cool stuff you left out!" And you would be right. That's not the point. The point is you need to get to the core: Who is your unique protagonist, what is the compelling conflict, and what is the inevitable end?

Second, ask yourself, "Is this the story I set out to tell, or is it now something different?" It's common for beginning writers to start out with a great premise but lose sight of it and drift toward another story altogether. As a result, you may end up with two distinct stories warring against each other inside your script, pulling your main story off its spine. Decide what story you want to tell, and then organize all your efforts around supporting it. Describe this story in one or two sentences, jot it down on a three-by-five note card, and keep it where you can see it throughout your entire rewrite process.

Third, get four sets of colored note cards. You will use them to get a better look at the structure you currently have and make visible problems you can't see. It doesn't matter by what method you laid out your draft (note cards, beat sheet, or outline) or what structural form you used. The technique I'm going to share with you—based on the classic three-act structure—works equally well with all and keeps things clear and easy to follow. The goal is to give you a powerful tool to get a grip on basic structure problems that you can use for any feature film script you write.

The first thing to do is assign specific colors to each act—red for act 1, blue for act 2, green for act 3—your choice. The remaining fourth color, which I will discuss shortly, will be for places in which you foresee major changes occurring. Now go through your entire script, and for each scene, put its essential information on its own card. It should look something like this:

INT. FOUR SEASONS HOTEL — DAY
Joan leads Tom into the room with the promise
of sex. Instead, she kills him. We learn here
that Joan is actually a man.

Very simple—just the basic scene information. As you move through this process, you will change card colors at each of the three act breaks. Once you have finished creating cards for each and every scene in your script, look for a very big room or hallway, lay out all your cards, and examine them as a whole. This is the timeline of your film.

Just by looking at the colors, some things should be readily apparent. Using the standard percentage for a feature film, 25 percent of your cards should be in act 1, 50 percent of your cards should be in act 2, and the final 25 percent in act 3. If they are not (for instance, if you have a larger percentage in act 1), it may reveal why your reader said, "It took a long time for the movie to get going." If you heard, "It kind of drags in the middle," you may have too many cards in act 2. If your notes reveal that your movie has two endings, take a look at the cards in act 3.

Weed Out Repetition

Once you've identified your script's overall problem areas through the color coding, the next step is to focus on solutions for the content in each troubled zone. The number one thing to look for is all the places you repeat the same piece of information. This is the screenwriter's most common mistake, and you have to trust that the audience is smart enough to get it the first time. If you have two cards in a row or close to each other that say similar things, one of them has to go. Let's use the example above. Say the next card in the sequence says,

```
INT. FOUR SEASONS HOTEL — DAY
We see that Joan is actually Jim. He dresses in
a nice suit and leaves the hotel in a Mercedes.
```

Take a close look at the information in this scene. You could easily fold it into the previous scene—or even better, pick up Jim in the next location, *doing something* that sheds new light on him and drives the story forward.

Here's a quick test to gauge the effectiveness of each scene as it appears on your cards. Ask yourself, "What new information is revealed about this character that I didn't know before?" and/or, "What new information is revealed here that drives my story forward?" If you can reveal new information about the character *and* drive the story forward with a fresh plot development in every scene, you're golden. It's not always possible to achieve both, but it's worth striving for. Let's take a look at what that next card might say that would accomplish this goal.

```
INT. HOSPITAL — DAY
Joan/Jim arrives at work dressed in a suit. He
is a Medical Examiner. He takes Tom's body
parts and stores them in a secret locker for
future use.
```

We now see that Joan/Jim has a job that helps cover her/his dark secret, *and* we get a sense that something else is afoot to be explained later. The story is now moving along and we are getting tons of info on Joan/Jim in only a few lines.

Balance Internal and External Struggles

As you look at the cards in act 2, identify where the obstacles arise to keep your protagonist from his/her goal, and then indicate which of two categories these obstacles fall into: personal challenges and plot challenges, or alternatively, internal struggles and external struggles. You want to have a balance of both. If only external forces are working on your protagonist, your script will be a Warner Bros. cartoon version of drama: Anvil falls on head. Bomb explodes while character tries to light it.

The internal struggles revolve around what the protagonist fears most, and when he/she meets this fear in your screenplay, that struggle should be tremendous. In *The Social Network,* Mark Zuckerberg's greatest fear is that what his girlfriend says about him at the end of the opening scene is true: Girls won't dislike him because he's a computer nerd. They will dislike him because he's a jerk. Zuckerberg struggles beneath the weight of her indictment for the entire film and is crushed by it in the end, when its truth extends beyond the male/female relationship and infiltrates his entire life. This internal struggle is externalized as we watch Mark in multiple scenes manipulate, dodge, badger, and lie to friends and acquaintances while launching Facebook. His actions illustrate his internal character, and Aaron Sorkin's script is peppered with them. Zuckerberg is a jerk. He might struggle against it, but that's who he is, and sadly so.

Escalate the Tension

Once you've achieved a good balance of internal and external struggles in act 2, consider how they escalate across the timeline of your cards. Do these struggles get increasingly more difficult? Do they force the protagonist to go deeper, stretch further? Act 2 should feel like a ride in a convertible Porsche with a teenager: accelerator all the way to the floor and never let up until you are freaking out.

In *The Town,* Ben Affleck portrays Doug MacRay, a small-time criminal who gets romantically involved with the manager of a bank he and his gang have previously robbed. Every time Doug has to lie to his new girlfriend, we know it will come back to haunt him. Then when he plans new heists with higher risk, we want to jump out of our seats and rescue him because of his growing commitment to his love interest. This dramatic tension between good impulses in a character and bad impulses keeps us riveted. Will Doug overcome his darker tendencies or is this a doomed love story? You have to watch all the way to the end to find out, and this is just what we want as a viewer—and what we aspire to as writers.

Resolve the Action

With act 3, the main structural issue you have to assess is whether you have an ending or a resolution. An ending feels forced, as if you are simply going through the motions, making sure you've tied up every loose end for every single character we've experienced in the movie. "Oh, look! The barista at the Starbucks got a boyfriend too!" Avoid this temptation at all costs. I don't care about the barista. I'm following the protagonist. As soon as the protagonist achieves or is defeated in his or her quest, that's the resolution and the clock is ticking. You can show me a scene of a wedding, or an apology, or some tiny bit of appropriate action after this, but if you go too far I will resent it.

Can you find the card in act 3 that shows the protagonist achieving the goal? How many cards after that? Uh-huh. Lose those excess cards. If you find that you have placed some very important action after the resolution (this usually involves secondary characters or some subplot), move those scenes to a spot before the protagonist's goal is reached.

Replace Some Old Ideas with Better Ones

You are probably getting a sense of what that fourth-color card is for. As you've addressed structural issues throughout your screenplay, you have discovered that you want to replace some existing scenes and ideas with new ones you're generating. Remove the old card and put a replacement-color card in, indicating what change you would like to make. Chances are you will find that there are new cards in all three acts. No cause for alarm—that's the way it's supposed to be. All three acts are interrelated and must work as a unit. A lot of new cards in your timeline means you have a ton of exciting writing ahead.

Pass #2: Improving Your Script's Clarity

Now that we've conquered the biggest beast of script structure, it's time to return to act 1 and confront the "clarity" issues in your draft. In your notes session, your readers gave you feedback on where they experienced confusion, and that led you to figure out particular plot points or character actions you need to sharpen. Here are two important concepts to keep firmly in mind as you tackle those areas; they will help you to solve most "lack of clarity" notes you might receive.

Show, Don't Tell

I want a piece of candy.

You don't want me to have it.

We fight until one of us is victorious.

Simple, right? Not necessarily.

The way in which I go about getting the candy from you reveals my character and makes watching me fun. The viewer needs to see an action and reaction: an exchange between characters, and then a subsequent action that reveals how each character has been affected, either positively or negatively. Moreover, as I progress from one interesting action to another, these actions must conform to some logic that you have set up to *show* the audience who I am. You can try *telling* them, but they won't really retain it:

"But didn't you see where his girlfriend said he was a jerk?"

"Yeah, but he walked his dog in the pouring rain, kept that baby from being hit by a bus, and then took his blind neighbor to church."

If a character changes direction and becomes something different from what you've already set up in the screenplay, we need to *see* why. What made him or her change? Just having a character "decide" isn't enough, because that is primarily an internal motion that cannot be photographed.

Here's a tool my students find helpful when dealing with a "show, don't tell" clarity note. Look at those cards again. If you have a character or story question, ask yourself, "What made him or her change? Where is the scene in which I set this situation up? Where is the scene where I complicated it? Where is the scene where I make it pay off?" Look at any well-written character drama for help in this area.

In *The Kids Are All Right,* the very first time we see the entire family together having a meal, it is painfully clear that Annette Bening's character doesn't really take her life partner, Julianne Moore, very seriously. This is the setup. When Mark Ruffalo, the sperm donor for their children, reenters their lives, he causes problems for a lot of reasons, but one of the primary ones is that he listens to Julianne Moore and takes her seriously. This is beautifully played out in another meal scene around an outdoor table where he offers her a job. This is the complication. Julianne likes the attention. She's attracted to it, and so strongly that they end up in bed together. Perfect. You can track how this was set up, complicated, and then made to pay off across the landscape of the film. No one is surprised when Ruffalo and Moore begin their affair because we have seen exactly how it came about.

Be Specific

The more precise you are, the better the writing. When you indicate that Johnny has a gun and stop there, I'm left wondering, *What kind of gun?*

A machine gun? A pistol? A deer rifle? You don't need to go over the top with your description, but do make sure that you give readers the key details they need to follow your story and gain insight into your characters. The reason people choose one thing over another indicates what their character is like. You only need look to Javier Bardem's character Chigurh in *No Country for Old Men*. The guy is nuts. Just look at his haircut and his choice of weapons. A compressed-air-fired bolt through the head? Bad mojo. That's the flavor that specific details can give you.

Pass #3: Making Your Script Authentic

Now we come to the final area of concern, and in my experience, the toughest. The challenge is how to imbue your script with emotional reality—or to put it another way, how to make your characters and their universe authentic. It may take several drafts to master, so don't despair.

Let's start with your characters. Here's a formula that will help to resolve a number of authenticity problems your characters might suffer from: The protagonist takes an action that leads to a conflict. We watch him or her change because of that conflict. The protagonist prevails or is defeated because of what he or she learned or didn't. In the *Toy Story* movies, Woody's pride is always his downfall. He is a great leader, but whenever Buzz Lightyear steps into the limelight, Woody inevitably behaves badly, suffers for it, and then spends the rest of the film paying for his behavior through acts of self-sacrifice. At the end of each *Toy Story* film, Woody becomes a better friend and leader. The key here is that your characters' actions must be true to who they are from FADE IN to FADE OUT, even as they change through the conflicts they face and eventually overcome (or not) throughout.

Now consider the rules you created for your universe. Do you have a firm grip on them? They are the gravity holding everything in place. No matter how simple or complex your script is, it should constitute a universe with its own set of rules and realities—and conform to them. In *The Dark Knight,* Batman is the suave billionaire Bruce Wayne by day, but by night he dons his trademark vigilante costume and protects Gotham City from the criminal underworld. In the dark and fully realized world of director Christopher Nolan's film, Batman's skintight black suit, pointy bat ears, and mask represent vengeance, ferocity, justice over evil. If the filmmaker even hinted that Batman's iconic outfit was laughable, he would violate the rules of *The Dark Knight*'s universe, and its authenticity would be undermined.

Here are two quick remedies for an inauthentic world. First, if you are writing way outside your realm of experience—for example, if you're a molecular biologist writing a buddy cop movie—there's a big chance your script may feel inauthentic. To fill in this experiential gap, go on a few ride-alongs. If you're writing a fantasy movie, keep the rules to the world simple and clear, add vivid detail, and drop hints about bits of backstory. When Obi-Wan Kenobi tells Luke Skywalker that he fought with his father in the Clone Wars and says, "I was once a Jedi, the same as your father," this makes the audience feel like there's a real world that exists.

Still feeling shaky about how to inject emotional truth into your script? Consider the following additional strategies.

Write from Your Own Experience

As you look at the emotional content of the scene in question, ask yourself, "How do I know this to be true?" Generally, the authenticity of a scene comes from the author's ability to illustrate accurately a reality the audience can recognize, which is rooted in the simple phrase "Write what you know." I'll use the chase scene to illustrate what I mean.

Very often chase scenes read as simple descriptions of where cars go, fences that get jumped, or alleys that get raced down. This is a missed opportunity. As a writer, you want to convey emotional content that grabs readers in their gut, and in order to do that, you must delve into your own experience and remember a time when you were chased.

What was it like to make the decision to flee? Did you try to make a plan on the run? How did it feel when you realized you were going to be caught? These common feelings will hook the reader in a way that a mere description of what the stuntmen should be doing won't. Rely on this skill of transposing your own experience to bring your script's scenes to life, especially important when faced with scenes that are cliché traps: weddings, funerals, first kisses, proms.

Write from What You Observe

Sometimes, of course, you will lack direct life experience, and acquiring it is difficult, if not impossible. This is when you can use your powers as an observer of the human condition. For example, you know that not everyone screams when angry; some people get very quiet and withdrawn. Say you've written a scene in which a boss gets angry and yells at his assistant, and you get the note, "I don't buy this."

Look at what you've already told us about the boss: He lives alone, he has no friends, and he's generally shut off from the world. The reason that the reader "didn't buy" your character's aggressive behavior may be because it wasn't true to your overall portrayal of the boss, and on a larger level, you had him do something that was counter to a reality that we generally see with people who are withdrawn.

Be Unpredictable, but Not Random

As you can see, consistency is essential to achieving both clarity and authenticity in your script. Now, you may be asking, "Does it have to be so rigid? Can't the characters or story just go off and do something unpredictable every once in a while? Won't that keep things interesting?" Yes—if their actions are truly unpredictable and not random. Randomness comes out of nowhere, and while it exists in real life, it has no place in screenwriting. However, an unpredictable action can work to good effect when it conforms to the internal logic of the character or story you've laid out. In *Raiders of the Lost Ark,* when Indy takes out a gun and shoots the sword master instead of using his whip, that's unpredictable. If he'd broken out into a show tune when faced with his sword-wielding adversary, that would have been random.

Step 4: Write the Next Draft

Wow. That's a lot of notes. At this point you could be in one of two places—either totally overwhelmed with what needs to be done, or boiling over with ideas and ready to jump in. I hope it's the latter, but if not, let me encourage you.

It can be done. This is the spot everyone gets themselves into—tons of sticky notes, colored cards, marks on a whiteboard, script pages folded over. It can be intimidating. Remember this one thing, though: You're in charge. Here's some advice to get you off on the right foot.

Work from your strengths, not your weaknesses. In order to teach this process and write this chapter, I've had to organize things in a linear manner. But the truth of writing is that it is often an instinctual process. Use your instincts now and discern where you are most likely to encounter some early success and start there. This is how you build momentum. Rewrite a couple of jokes that you thought were great when you were working your way through the draft. Go to the section where you had a fantastic idea for a character detail and weave that in first. This reminder that you have great ideas and creative solutions to problems will build your confidence so you can set out boldly into sections where you may struggle.

No one laces up a pair of Nikes on the day of a marathon and decides to run for the first time. We build up to it. We start small and make our way forward, and somehow, some way, we end up crossing the finish line. You can do this. You have everything you need. Now write.

Step 5: Put Your Revision Away

Someday you're going to type FADE OUT for the last time, I promise, but for now, put the revision away. Hit SAVE. Back it up and then call your friends. Time for the Second-Draft Fiesta. Enjoy it—you've just done some very hard work. Forget about the script—two weeks, minimum. Walk your dog, take up tennis, do anything else you can think of, but resist the temptation to read the script. You need clarity that only time can bring.

Step 6: Repeat as Needed

Remember what I tell my students when they ask me how many drafts they'll need to write? As many as it takes to make your script the absolute best it can be.

Feeling Better?

If not, I've got three more tools you can take along with you. These things will help you out of almost any jam you get yourself into.

Research

If you haven't already made a list of films similar to the one you are writing, do it now. If you are stuck on a problem and a solution is not coming to you, go and watch how others solved the dilemma you are encountering. You don't need to reinvent the wheel; someone, somewhere solved the problem you are having. I'm not saying that you are going to copy that exact solution, but it may inspire you in a direction that you would not come up with on your own.

Accountability

This is something every writer needs. For a professional, the accountability is required by people who hire and write the checks. I must turn in those pages because people are depending on me. They have put their trust in my talents, and I don't want to let them down. Plus, I want to eat. For the independent writer who is writing on spec, this accountability has to come from somewhere else. If you choose to rely on yourself, you will have to be extremely self-disciplined and motivated. Most of us have a much more difficult time with this.

That's why it is always good to find a friend or family member to hold us accountable. Simply tell them what you are working on, and ask them to ask occasionally how it's going. This little voice will pop up at unexpected moments and goose you into action. When you are rationalizing about how you don't have time or you're stuck, the fear of your best friend asking you about your script may be just enough to get your butt back in the chair.

Community

The students in my classes at UCLA Extension have an instant community. They politely endure my ranting, listen to notes from one another, and participate in and contribute to one another's work, all of which binds them together as brothers and sisters in the great screenwriting conspiracy. Friendships and alliances are formed that continue long after the class is over. Every. Writer. Needs. This.

Writing can be a lonely endeavor. Unless you have a writing partner, you are in solitary confinement, writing down a conversation you are having with yourself. It can get a little weird. The best antidote for all of that is to gather a group of like-minded individuals with whom you can exchange pages, discuss ideas, and generally bitch and moan to. If you don't take classes or have access to this kind of writer's community, then use your friends. Ask them to come along on this journey with you. You may even inspire them to write something of their own. Being a writer dedicated to your craft has that effect on people.

Throw Down Those Crutches and Walk!

Your script has been healed! Well, kind of. Your commitment to rewrite your screenplay has taken you to the next level. When you read over those new pages, I'm certain you will get something you really need: a growing sense of confidence. Your story will be clearer, your characters more compelling, your jokes funnier, and your drama more intense. All of this will combine into a revelation that you actually are a writer with something to say. It should also reveal to you that this process of revision has real value. I hope you will put a high priority on that value, because as good as your script is right now, it can be better.

You've got to get back in that chair and churn up some magic. There is a point of diminishing returns, but after one full revision, you probably aren't there yet. But here's an encouraging thought: You have less and less to work on in each pass. The script is getting better every time, and you are the one with the power to heal. Keep going. We all need better movies, and you are just the one to give them to us.

CHAPTER 11

The Art and Craft of Dialogue Writing

by Karl Iglesias

Writers love to write it. Readers love to read it. Actors love to say it. Audiences love to hear it. And if you're reading this chapter, chances are you want to improve it. Great dialogue makes your characters leap off the page. It reveals their views, attitudes, and flaws. When spoken by actors projected on a giant screen, it can move an audience to laugh, cry, and sit at the edge of their seats. Equally important from a marketing point of view, dialogue attracts talent to your script. Agents and producers sell "packaged" scripts—scripts with actors already attached to them—and what attracts those actors to a script more than anything is the dialogue. They all want to say cool lines.

How do you write great dialogue? Here's the secret: You don't really write it. You rewrite it. As three-time Academy Award–winning screenwriter Paddy Chayefsky put it, "I'm not a great writer, I'm a great rewriter." Rare is the dialogue that comes out fully formed in the first draft. Most writers rewrite their dialogue until it's as lean and edgy as it can be. It's why this chapter is in the rewriting section, because you should never worry about crafting great dialogue when you are writing your first draft. In fact, you should just assume that your characters' speeches will be flat, stilted, bloated, too expository, and too on-the-nose on your first pass.

But once you've written and rewritten your first draft, you're ready to learn how to make your dialogue actor bait. For the past twenty years, I've studied dialogue, become skilled at writing and rewriting it, and been hired to doctor other writers' dialogue. Eventually I started sharing what I know about crafting it in my book *Writing for Emotional Impact* and through teaching on-site and online workshops at the UCLA Extension Writers' Program. And now I'm going to give you the step-by-step process I've developed for crafting compelling dialogue, which has worked for hundreds of my Writers' Program students. While every step is important, you can undertake them in any order that works for you:

Step 1: Is my dialogue active?

Step 2: Is my dialogue as lean as it can be?

Step 3: Is my dialogue realistic?

Step 4: Is my dialogue individual to each character?

Step 5: Does my dialogue reveal exposition "invisibly"?

Step 6: Is my dialogue emotionally impactful?

Step 7: Does my dialogue have subtext?

Step 8: Is my dialogue error-free?

Step 9: Does my dialogue sound good when read out loud?

Step 10: Can I learn more from the masters of dialogue?

Step 1: Is My Dialogue Active?

I always start with this key question: "Why are the characters talking to each other?" You must understand the real purpose of dialogue in a scene.

Beginning writers often learn that dialogue exists to advance the plot through exposition, to reveal character, to create conflict, and at times to be funny. Sure, these functions are all valid, but they're secondary to dialogue's main purpose, which is to be the *active means* by which a character gets what she wants in the scene, be it by threatening, insulting, blackmailing, charming, or asking to be loved.

When we workshop a scene in class and a line doesn't work, I ask, "Why did you put that line there?" The answer is usually focused on the *student's* objective: "I want to show this character's trait here," or "I want to reveal this piece of information here," or "I want to have this joke here." Professional writers, on the other hand, always think about the *character's* objective: "At this moment, the character wants X and this is what stands in his way, so he says Y to get it."

So when you reread your dialogue, ask yourself of every line, "Why is the character saying that line? What does the character want from the other character, and is she saying a line designed to get it?" Or put another way, "How is what the character says, including delivering information, *actively* connected to his desire?" For example, if a character's objective in the scene is to get an interviewer to offer him a job, his actions throughout the scene may be, through dialogue, to charm, to convince, to assure, to impress, to humor, to manipulate, to persuade, or to inspire. Keep in mind that it's never a character's main goal to give information to the audience, unless he's a politician running for office or a professor lecturing students, so edit out lines that exist solely to reveal information to the reader.

If you truly grasp that dialogue is action, not just conversation, and make sure all your lines are active, your dialogue will be 80 percent improved. To tackle the other 20 percent, you need to fix common dialogue mistakes that all writers, including the pros, make. The trick is to spot them and correct them before anyone reads your draft. This is when I take out my red pen.

Step 2: Is My Dialogue as Lean as It Can Be?

Line Length

The second step is to trim the script's "fat." As I flip through my script, do I see mostly one-, two-, or three-liners? If so, that's good. On the other hand, if I see huge blocks of text, that probably indicates my characters are speaking more words than necessary. This may sound weird, but contrary to popular belief, actors hate long speeches. Director John Lee Hancock once said, "Good actors want fewer words, and bad actors want more words." Always strive to trim down, to make every word count. While exceptions in great scripts do exist, the reality is that most great dialogue is short and clear.

Repetition

Next, I look at multiple sentences within a speech to check for repetition. For example, if a character says, "I can't do it without you. I need your help," he's actually repeating the same thought. Often, the first sentence is enough, though sometimes the second sentence might convey the meaning better or more poetically. So I read each sentence and pick the best one, depending on the context. In the example above, the first sentence implies the desire. It's more subtextual. The second "explains" the thought and is therefore more direct. If the dialogue is between a married couple, I'd pick the first sentence. If they're buddies, I'd pick the second.

Repeated First Names

"Look, Tara . . ." "Don't tell me what to do, Bob!" "Listen to me, Laurie!" Sometimes names are necessary to balance the rhythm of a line or indicate a specific recipient when there are more than two characters in the scene. But repeating names can become a problem when done too often. If we can see Bob is talking to Tara, you don't have to mention their names. It also makes the dialogue stiff and unrealistic, because real people don't add names after each line of dialogue. So I read each version of a line, with and without the names. Nine times out of ten, I delete them.

Fillers or Handles

These include words and phrases such as *nevertheless, I mean, well, so, look, you know, by the way, still, anyhow, the point is, as I see it,* etc. Just like first names, they seem natural when I write them, and sometimes they're useful for the rhythm of the dialogue. But when I reread the line with and without these fillers, deleting them usually makes the line leaner and crisper.

Chitchat

Routine exchanges of ordinary conversations, like "Hello . . . How are you? . . . Fine," are often found at the start of scenes but don't usually contribute anything unless there's a dramatic reason. If not, delete them.

Step 3: Is My Dialogue Realistic?

My third step is to look for dialogue that sounds artificial, mechanical, and forced, which generally happens when a character speaks with a formal vocabulary, complete sentences, proper grammar, and no contractions—"I do not know," as opposed to "I don't know." Unless this style of speaking is part of a character's personality, status, or background, it should be avoided. Writing stilted dialogue is a habit many of us acquired from our early training in writing school compositions, but we don't want our characters to speak as if they're reading from an essay! Here's a purposely stilted version I made up of a speech given by hot-rodder John Milner (Paul Le Mat) in *American Graffiti* (written by George Lucas, Gloria Katz, and Willard Huyck):

```
                    JOHN
I believe that is Freddy Benson's Corvette.
He was involved in a collision with an
inebriated driver. He never had a chance.
It is a shame because he was also such a good
driver. What a tragedy when a human being
dies and it is not even their fault.
```

Now, compare it with the original:

```
                    JOHN
That's Freddy Benson's Vette . . . Got his
head on with some drunk. Never had a chance.
Damn good driver, too. What a waste when
somebody gets it and it ain't even their fault.
```

Note where sentences are fragmented instead of complete, where slang and casual words replace formal vocabulary, where contractions are used and words are dropped, as when John says, "Damn good driver," instead of "*He was a* damn good driver." The result is a filtered-to-its-essence version of real-life speech, minus the redundancies, the tangents, the non sequiturs, the ramblings, the *ums* and *uhs* and *likes*, and other fillers. Just as director Alfred Hitchcock said, "Drama is life with the dull bits cut out," so is dialogue real-life speech with all the unnecessary words cut out.

Step 4: Is My Dialogue Individual to Each Character?
Uniqueness of Voice

Personality, Feelings, Values, and More
The fourth step to creating great dialogue is to make sure that each character speaks in a unique voice. Every line of dialogue is an opportunity to

reveal your characters' distinctive personalities and attitudes, and to express their particular feelings, fears, hopes, values, and social background.
In fact, you should know who's speaking just by hearing a line—or if
you're reading the dialogue in a script, you should be able to cover all the
characters' names and still know who is talking. (Try out this exercise on
your own script. If you find that your characters all speak in the same
voice, with the same speech pattern, vocabulary, and cadence, it means
you haven't developed your characters fully and that you need to go back
and work on their dimensionality.)

In the following scene from *Crazy, Stupid, Love* (Dan Fogelman), the
main characters reveal, through dialogue, an enormous amount about
themselves and their relationship. Emily (Julianne Moore) tries to apologize to her husband, Cal (Steve Carell), for cheating on him, as he's moving out of the house:

```
                    EMILY
     I think I'm having a mid-life crisis maybe.
     Can women have mid-life crises?


                    CAL
          (avoiding engagement)
     Make sure the lawn gets enough water.


                    EMILY
     In the movies it's always men having them
     and buying ridiculous yellow Porsches, but
     I'm not a man and I really don't want a
     yellow Porsche.


                    CAL
     You have to fertilize once a month. Not
     twice a month, not once every two months.

She takes a deep breath, finding her balance.
```

                    EMILY

We got married so young, Cal. And I'm forty-one.
And that's so much older than I thought I'd be.

                    CAL

The sprinklers turn off behind you.

                    EMILY

And I got really upset with an umpire at
Molly's T-ball game last month-like really
upset, like I screamed at him and wished he
would die--and I started feeling like the person I promised I wouldn't turn into, you know?

                    CAL

If it rains a lot, you need to shut off the
automatic setting.

                    EMILY

And we haven't been us, not for a long time.
And I don't know when you and I stopped being
"us" but...I mean, do you?

Cal finally turns and looks at her.

                    CAL

I think it was when you screwed David Lindhagen.

Ouch. Emily's face registers the blow, but
she nods: she also understands it.

                    CAL

Make sure my azaleas get enough sun.

This scene works on several levels as it clearly individualizes the two characters. First, at the gender level, it captures, at least stereotypically, the way men and women often speak. Emily communicates openly, emotionally, using long speeches, while Cal is more terse and direct and stubbornly focuses on his hobby, the plants. There's also a clear contrast at the emotional level. Emily tries to apologize, to mend the severed bond between them by being vulnerable and justifying her unforgivable action. Cal, who's been betrayed and is heartbroken, disengages emotionally and puts up a wall between them. This is also a good example of avoiding a painful subject, which is another useful technique for subtext.

The scene is also a great example of another way skilled writers use dialogue to create a clear contrast between their characters—they have them focused on a particular topic from start to finish. Throughout almost all of their exchange, Emily and Cal are completely oblivious to each other. Instead of listening and reacting to each other, they are in their own worlds, Emily in the self-justifying grip of a T-ball mom middle-age crisis, and Cal in his shut-down world of pain and rejection. It isn't until the scene reaches the climax that Cal finally confronts Emily with the blunt truth that she broke their marriage when she slept with another man.

Word Choice

Vocabulary is key to defining who each character is, even in the potentially most mundane lines. For instance, when writer-director Quentin Tarantino had his small-time criminal Mr. Pink (Steve Buscemi) in *Reservoir Dogs* say, "Where's the commode in this dungeon? I gotta take a squirt." he injected new life into "I have to pee, where's the bathroom?" Take a look at this exchange from *Juno* between sixteen-year-old pregnant Juno MacGuff (Ellen Page) and Rollo (Rainn Wilson), the clerk who has sold her three pregnancy tests in one day, to see how screenwriter Diablo Cody individualizes her characters through word choice:

```
                    ROLLO
So what's the prognosis, Fertile Myrtle?
Minus or plus?


                    JUNO
      (examining pregnancy test stick)
I don't know. It's not...seasoned yet.
Wait. Huh. Yeah, there's that pink plus sign
again. God, it's unholy.


She shakes the stick desperately in an
attempt to skew the results. Shake.
Shake. Nothing.


                    ROLLO
That ain't no Etch-a-Sketch. This is one
doodle that can't be undid, homeskillet.
```

Rollo clearly stands out through his dialogue, starting with the use of the word *prognosis* instead of *result,* which contrasts with the vocabulary you'd expect from a store clerk. Rollo also uses metaphoric nicknames, like *Fertile Myrtle* and *homeskillet,* which are perfect for the situation in which Juno finds herself, a common technique I'll discuss next. Then there is the use of metaphor, comparing the stick Juno shakes to an Etch A Sketch that can't be erased—subtext for "You can't erase the problem; you've got to take responsibility." This is poetry, and when you can incorporate it into the lines of a character, that character is sure to stand out among the others.

Favorite Expressions

As I just mentioned, I always ask myself if a character would be further individualized by a speaking quirk, like Rollo's habit of addressing other characters by descriptive nicknames in *Juno,* or using a favorite phrase, buzzword, or tagline. For instance, fast-talking con artist Leo Getz (Joe Pesci) in *Lethal Weapon 2* often starts his rapid-fire speeches with "Okay, okay, okay . . ." Retro-hipster Trent (Vince Vaughn) in *Swingers*'s tagline is "You're so money."

Consistency of Voice

Now that I have established a distinct voice for each character, I want to make sure that voice remains consistent throughout the script. One common technique is to pick a trait or attitude and "translate" it into dialogue, reflecting it through word choice or manner of speaking, in different contexts throughout the script. The concept is simple, though the execution must be creative. For example, if your character is frugal, you may reveal this trait when he says to his wife, "Hope you didn't throw away the coupons," or to the waiter when he's out to lunch with business colleagues, "Separate checks, please." To double-check your characters' consistency, read one character's lines from start to finish, and then repeat this process with each important character.

Step 5: Does My Dialogue Reveal Exposition "Invisibly"?

Exposition's Biggest Don't and Biggest Do

Now we come to one of the most challenging areas in dialogue: exposition, or how to communicate important information about the story and characters without being awkward and obvious, which is often labeled "on-the-nose." The biggest don't is to have your characters explain what they already know: "As you are aware, Chris, I'm your father."

The biggest do is to remember that exposition must be as active and purposeful as the rest of your dialogue, always a part of a character's agenda. It should have a reason for being uttered, and it should have emotional edge. In this exchange from *Duplicity* (Tony Gilroy), corporate spy Ray Koval (Clive Owen) has just discovered that the mole he's working with is Claire Stenwick (Julia Roberts), the woman who, years earlier, seduced him at a party in Dubai and stole top secret documents from him.

                        CLAIRE
          How did you get this job?

                        RAY
          I've got news for you, okay? The day
          I left MI6, I had fifteen *major* companies
          begging for my services.

                        CLAIRE
          Well, I guess you picked wrong. But you
          must be used to that.

                        RAY
          Where's the drop? Hand it over.

                        CLAIRE
          Forget it. I'm not working with you.

                        RAY
          Excuse me?

                        CLAIRE
          You think I'm gonna let you be my contact
          officer? This is way over your head.

<pre>
                    RAY
     Over my head? Lady, I worked Yemen,
     Athens, and Cairo. I've been promoted and
     decorated in every place I served.

                  CLAIRE
     Tell Duke to send someone else.
</pre>

Note how Ray's exposition about his past has purpose—to prove he's competent enough for the job. It's active information because he needs to convince Claire that he's experienced and not the easy mark he was in Dubai.

Emotional Glazing

The key to handling exposition is to misdirect the reader's attention by presenting the information in a way that emotionally impacts the reader. In the example above, Gilroy accomplishes his dramatic setup of a spy duped professionally and sexually by the very person he is now partnered with by creating expository dialogue drenched in tension. There are a number of storytelling emotions a writer can use to coat exposition, including conflict, humor, anticipation, curiosity, surprise, and urgency. I call this technique emotional glazing.

Conflict

One of the easiest ways to coat exposition is to surround it with conflict. Think of the information you absorb through fights, arguments, and life-or-death situations. The more tense the conflict, the more invisible the exposition becomes. We saw how this worked in the *Duplicity* scene.

Another good example is in *The Terminator* (James Cameron and Gale Anne Hurd), where Reese (Michael Biehn) has just saved Sarah Connor (Linda Hamilton) from the Terminator, who is pursuing them, along with the cops. Throughout a wild car chase, Reese is laying out the exposition about where he comes from, what the Terminator is, and all the foreshadowing. It's a twelve-minute sequence of pure exposition, and yet it doesn't feel like it because of the conflict, tension, and excitement generated by the chase. Can you imagine what this exposition would have felt like if it were presented in a twelve-minute restaurant scene without any conflict surrounding it?

Curiosity

Curiosity is another effective way to glaze exposition. If you set up the emotional need to find out something, the reader won't feel bombarded with facts; instead, she will feel relief when she finally gets her curiosity satisfied. In the *Terminator* example, by the time Reese delivers the bulk of the exposition during the car chase, we are eager to know who the Terminator is, why he has chosen Sarah for termination, who Reese is, where he's from, and whether he's a good or bad guy, or simply crazy, as Sarah initially believes.

Tension and Anticipation

A powerful ingredient in the exposition glaze is the reader's superior position, which creates tension and anticipation by giving the reader information that one or more of the characters themselves don't have. Writer-director Alexander Payne and screenwriters Nat Faxon and Jim Rash use this technique skillfully in *The Descendants*, in which Matt King (George Clooney) is a lawyer who must deal with going from "backup parent" to full-time parent to two spirited daughters when his wife, Elizabeth, goes into a coma after being critically injured in a boat race. As an audience, we're given two major pieces of information that give us a reader's superior position to everyone close to Elizabeth besides Matt. The first is when Matt is told by her doctor that she will never recover, she should be removed from life support, and her friends and family informed of the decision. In the next scene, Matt enters his wife's room and discovers her best friends, Kai and Mark Mitchell (Mary Birdsong and Rob Huebel), playing music for Elizabeth on a mini boom box while Kai applies makeup to Liz's face, explaining that Liz has been looking a little pale lately all cooped up in her room.

The entire scene is a casual interaction among friends, but from the reader's superior position, it's clear that Matt knows Liz is about to die, so the issue becomes, how will he respond to the questions about Liz's condition? He lies to protect Kai and Mitchell (and himself) from the painful news, and from this point on, all the exposition about Liz is coated with tension, as we wonder how Matt will act with his daughters. Will he hide or tell them the truth?

The second instance comes when Matt discovers that Liz was having an affair with a real estate agent named Brian Speer (Matthew Lillard) and that she had planned to ask Matt for a divorce. This revelation sets Matt off on a search for Speer, to confront him and to let him know that Liz is dying. When he tracks him down to a vacation home in Kauai, Matt discovers Speer is happily married with two kids.

In one of the tensest scenes in the film, Matt runs into Speer's wife, Julie (Judy Greer), and their two boys at the beach. The scene is pure exposition, simple getting-to-know-you questions and answers. But because of the reader's superior position (knowing something Julie doesn't—that Brian was having an affair with Liz and that Julie is now chatting with Liz's husband, who knows everything), the exposition is glazed with potent tension. We wonder how much Matt will reveal in this scene and what his actions will be now that he's befriended Julie.

"Hiding" the Exposition

Here's one last effective technique that actually makes the reader an active participant in the scene: You "hide" the exposition by implying it instead of stating it outright, thereby forcing the reader to figure out the meaning of the line. Check out how screenwriters Hampton Fancher and David Webb Peoples do it in the science fiction classic *Blade Runner,* in which genetically engineered robots called "replicants" have escaped from off-world colonies and returned to Earth. In this scene, retired replicant-hunter Rick

Deckard (Harrison Ford) is being recruited by his former supervisor on the police force Bryant (M. Emmet Walsh):

>   BRYANT
>   You're gonna spot 'em an' you're gonna
>   air 'em out.
>
>   DECKARD
>   Not me, Bryant. I won't work for you anymore.
>   Give it to Holden, he's good.
>
>   BRYANT
>   I did.
>
>   DECKARD
>   And?
>
>   BRYANT
>   He can breathe okay...as long as nobody
>   unplugs him.

Note how the last line alludes to the fact that Deckard's colleague Holden has been shot and is now at the hospital on life support. What we will soon learn is that Holden has been mortally wounded by Leon, an escaped replicant, which ups the stakes for Deckard.

For more on how to handle exposition masterfully, study Aaron Sorkin's script for *The Social Network,* which won the 2010 Academy Award for Best Adapted Screenplay. Sorkin's script delivers tons of information, mostly through conflict-drenched deposition scenes in which Facebook creator Mark Zuckerberg (Jesse Eisenberg) is being accused of stealing the social media concept from Harvard classmates. In addition to the conflict between the plaintiffs and the defendant, who is facing loss of fortune, loss of reputation, and prosecution, Sorkin uses the emotional glazing of curiosity, tension, and anticipation as we witness the unfolding of how Zuckerberg betrays his only friend and Facebook cofounder Eduardo Saverin (Andrew Garfield).

Step 6: Is My Dialogue Emotionally Impactful?

This next step is about creating dialogue that entertains, that makes us laugh, gasp, appreciate a witty zinger, or look forward to the next beat. It's at the heart of why people love great dialogue. Not every line, of course, but a few here and there to make them pop off the page. This effect is especially important at the end of a scene. We call these lines *buttons,* as in they button, or close out, a scene in a memorable way.

Weed Out Predictable Lines

There are several proven ways to increase the emotional impact of your dialogue, beginning with highlighting all the predictable lines and replacing them with surprising ones. For instance, when a character says, "I love you," the expected response is, "I love you, too." Consider, however, these classic responses: "Snap out of it" (*Moonstruck*), "I know" (*The Empire Strikes Back*), and "What do you expect me to answer?" (*When Harry Met Sally . . .*). Other predictable lines include "Yes" and "No" answers to questions. Sometimes a straight yes or no can carry an emotional punch, but more often than not, it generates repetitive and easily predictable dialogue. So I look for alternatives, as in the following examples:

Terms of Endearment (James L. Brooks):

> AURORA
> Would you like to come in?

> GARRETT
> I'd rather stick needles in my eyes.

City Slickers (Lowell Ganz & Babaloo Mandel):

> MITCH
> Hi, Curly, kill anyone today?

> CURLY
> Day ain't over yet.

Sideways (Alexander Payne & Jim Taylor):

> JACK
> Been checking your messages?

> MILES
> Obsessively.

Create "Verbal Shrapnel"

Second, I look for opportunities to transform a flat line into an emotional weapon—a comeback zinger, sarcasm, or any line designed to provoke, insult, or put down. I call this "push-button dialogue," and we often see it in buddy films and romantic comedies where two people dislike and constantly insult one another using dialogue that's verbal shrapnel:

Aliens (James Cameron):

> HUDSON
> Hey, Vasquez, have you ever been
> mistaken for a man?

> VASQUEZ
> No, have you?

CUT TO THE CHASE

Miller's Crossing (Joel Coen & Ethan Coen):

> VERNA
>
> Where're you going?

> TOM
>
> Out.

> VERNA
>
> Don't let on more than you have to.

Use Metaphors and Similes

Third, I consider using figures of speech, especially metaphors and similes, which paint a vivid picture by making unexpected and original comparisons:

Almost Famous (Cameron Crowe):

> Mom drives William to the San Diego Sports Arena.
> She looks out the window at the adrenalized
> concert-goers.

> ELAINE
>
> Look at this. An entire generation of
> Cinderellas and there's no slipper coming.

Brokeback Mountain (Larry McMurtry and Diana Ossana):

> JACK
>
> You should see Lureen, punchin' numbers into
> her adding machine, huntin' for extra zeros,
> her eyes gettin' smaller and smaller, it's like

```
watchin' a rabbit tryin' to squeeze into a
snake hole with a coyote on its tail.
```

Austin Powers: The Spy Who Shagged Me (Mike Myers & Michael McCullers):

```
                    DR. EVIL
You're not quite evil enough. You're semi-evil.
You're quasi-evil. You're the margarine of
evil. You're the Diet Coke of evil, just one
calorie, not evil enough.
```

Step 7: Does My Dialogue Have Subtext?

Now we come to the most challenging step for most writers: to create *subtext*. Subtext is the meaning *beneath* the lines, what characters imply instead of stating outright. There is no doubt that writing dialogue that conveys what's *not* being said is not easy. One reason is that in screenplays, as in real life, emotions are often difficult to express outright because they may have negative consequences; therefore, a character has to reveal emotions indirectly. As writer-director Robert Towne once said in an interview, "The more it means to the character, the more difficult it is to say. If there's no restraint, no inhibitions, no guilt, no shame, there's no drama."

In this scene from *Michael Clayton* (Tony Gilroy), Karen Crowder (Tilda Swinton), a lawyer for an agricultural conglomerate named in a multibillion-dollar class-action suit, is indirectly exploring with agent Mr. Verne (Robert Prescott) the possibility of murdering Arthur Edens (Tom Wilkinson). Edens has been U-North's top litigator but has cracked under the pressure of the case and is threatening to expose his client's guilt:

```
                    KAREN
You have to contain this.
```

                         VERNE
Contain?

                         KAREN
Right. That's my question. What's the
option that we're looking at...along
those lines?

                         VERNE
You're talking about the paper? The data?

                         KAREN
Well, I'm wondering if there is some
other option. I mean, something I'm not
thinking of.

                         VERNE
We deal in absolutes.

                         KAREN
Okay. I understand that. I do.

                         VERNE
The materials, I'm not a lawyer, we try.
We do what we can.

                         KAREN
And the other way?

                         VERNE
Is the other way.

Heavy pause. Life passing all around them.

                    VERNE
Maybe you want to bring Don in on this.

                    KAREN
No.
        (on that she's sure)
This has nothing to do with Don. He's busy.
This has nothing to do with Don.
        (a pause)
Do you think it's doable?

                    VERNE
We have some good ideas. You say move,
we move. The ideas don't look so good, we
back off, reassess.

                    KAREN
Okay.

                    VERNE
Is that okay, you understand? Or okay, proceed?

Clearly, there's a lot at stake here. Karen can't just blurt out, "We need to kill Arthur," so most of the dialogue is subtext, as Karen carefully navigates through her options. The reader's knowledge of just how high the emotional stakes are grows as indirect reference upon indirect reference to committing a murder builds in a powerful crescendo, and is brought to a stark climax when Mr. Verne asks if it is "okay" to "proceed."

Turning Verbal Response into Action

I use a variety of techniques to create subtext, including checking to see if I can turn a response to a question into a physical action instead of a direct line of dialogue. For example, if one character says, "I love you," and the object of his affection responds by slapping him instead of saying, "I hate you," the slap would be communicating subtext. Imagine other physical actions as responses to "I love you"—crying, leaving the room, staring at the person for a long beat, or going back to reading the newspaper. Each of these specific actions speaks volumes without a character uttering a single word. Here's a great example from *Network* (Paddy Chayefsky):

                         MAX
        Listen, if we can get back for a moment to
        that gypsy who predicted all that about
        emotional involvements and middle-aged men,
        what're you doing for dinner tonight?

        DIANA pauses in the doorway, and then moves
        back briskly to the desk, picks up the
        telephone receiver, taps out a telephone
        number, waits for a moment--

                        DIANA
               (on the phone)
        I can't make it tonight, luv, call me tomorrow.

    She returns the receiver to its cradle,
    looks at MAX; their eyes lock.

Double Meaning

Sometimes I like to use a line that has a double meaning—the first meaning being direct, while the second is the implied emotion, as in this flirtation bit from *Something's Gotta Give* (Nancy Meyers). Harry Sanborn (Jack Nicholson) is a successful record mogul in his sixties who's proud to have never dated anyone over thirty, including his latest girlfriend, Marin (Amanda Peet). While spending the weekend at the Hamptons home of Marin's divorced mother, Erica Barry (Diane Keaton), Harry suffers a heart attack and is ordered to convalesce nearby, forcing Harry to spend time with Erica, who has given up on romance. She despises Harry for his womanizing habits and yet finds herself attracted to him:

> HARRY
> What's with the turtlenecks? It's the middle
> of summer.

> ERICA
> Now seriously, why do you care what I wear?

> HARRY
> Just curious.

> ERICA
> I like them. I've always liked them. I'm a
> turtleneck kinda gal.

> HARRY
> You never get hot?

> ERICA
> No.

> HARRY
> Never?

> ERICA
> Not lately.

Emotional Masks

When we experience negative emotions like embarrassment, fear, frustration, or anger, we often try to hide them by putting up an artificial front of strength and pride. As Oscar Wilde once said, "Man is least himself when he talks in his own person. Give him a mask, and he will tell you the truth." For example, if a teenage boy asked a girl out and she turned him down, the boy would cover his shame by saying something like, "No biggie, I had some stuff to do anyway." This deceptive front—tough on the outside, hurt on the inside—is a great way to create subtext in a dialogue exchange. Here's this technique in action in dialogue from *Unforgiven* (David Webb Peoples), as retired outlaw and killer William Munny (Clint Eastwood) turns down sexual favors from Delilah (Anna Levine), a saloon prostitute whose face has been mutilated by a customer:

>   DELILAH
>   (shy, timid)
>   You want...a free one?
>
>   MUNNY
>   (embarrassed)
>   Me? No. No, I guess not.
>
>   DELILAH
>   (covering her hurt)
>   I didn't mean...with me. Alice and Silky,
>   they'll give you one...if you want.

Use of Figurative Language

Another effective way to create subtext is to use figures of speech like metaphors and similes. Albert Brooks and Monica Mcgowan Johnson in

The Muse capture a downtrodden screenwriter's sense of despair and impotence with this amusing but sad comparison:

> PHILLIPS
> Being a screenwriter in Hollywood is a
> lot like being a eunuch in an orgy. The only
> difference is the eunuchs get to watch and
> I'm not even invited to the set.

The Power of Silence

One last technique in my subtext toolbox follows the "Less is more" principle of screenwriting to its logical end: silence. Whether the silence is involuntary due to overwhelming emotion or calculated to ignore a comment or question, it can effectively imply a character's emotional state, as in these examples from *Brokeback Mountain,* which chronicles the tragic romance between two cowboys in the American West from 1963 to 1983. It's important to know that prior to this bit, there's a brief shot of Joe Aguirre, Jack and Ennis's boss, spying on them through his binoculars as they play and joke around with their shirts off (another example of the reader's superior position—we know something Jack and Ennis don't). So when they return to town with the sheep, Joe's disappointment at the sheep count and at them carries some extra weight:

> JOE AGUIRRE
> (comes over)
> Some of these [the sheep] never went
> up there with you.
> (pause, hard look)
> The count ain't what I'd hoped for, neither.
> You ranch stiffs ain't never no good...

The boys shift uncomfortably. No response.

The subtext is even clearer when Jack returns a year later to ask for work, as Aguirre looks at him with contempt:

```
                    JOE AGUIRRE
          You boys sure found a way to make the time
          pass up there.

Jack gives him a look.

                    JOE AGUIRRE (CONT'D)
          Twist, you guys wasn't gettin' paid to
          leave the dogs baby-sit the sheep while
          you stemmed the rose.
                    (pause, looks hard at Jack)
          Get the hell out of my trailer.

Without a word, Jack steps out of the trailer.
```

The silence in both scenes communicates Jack and Ennis's embarrassment at not having done a good job, but also Jack's anxiety, especially in the second example, at having been found out, a fact that could have had tragic consequences at that time.

Step 8: Is My Dialogue Error-Free?

Okay, almost done! Now I review my dialogue one more time for typos, spelling errors, missing commas, redundancies, or extra spaces. Why do I bother? Because I'm aware of what it feels like to read something, to get lost in it when it's good, and conversely, have errors break the spell and remind me I'm just reading a script. Want to know the impact of a missing comma? Compare these two examples: "Let's eat, Grandma!" and "Let's eat Grandma!" Yes, a comma can save a life.

Step 9: Does My Dialogue Sound Good When Read Out Loud?

All kidding aside, I always discover missing commas or missing words when I read my dialogue out loud. Like the error checking, most aspiring writers neglect this step. When my students read their scenes aloud in class, they are amazed at the difference between silently reading dialogue and actually hearing it. They learn that when they can't say a line, if it's awkward, or painful to hear, they need to cut it or make it simpler to say.

Step 10: Can I Learn More from the Masters of Dialogue?

If you want to become a great dialogue writer, you have to study the greats. Isaac Newton once said, "If I have seen further, it is by standing on the shoulders of giants." This is how I learned all the techniques I've shared with you in this chapter—by reading the screenwriting giants' scripts.

Here's my list to get you started, which is by no means inclusive: Paddy Chayefsky, Billy Wilder, David Mamet, Robert Towne, Aaron Sorkin, William Goldman, Quentin Tarantino, Joel and Ethan Coen, Diablo Cody, James L. Brooks, Nora Ephron, Shane Black, Joe Eszterhas, Robert Riskin, Preston Sturges, Woody Allen, Elmore Leonard, and Neil Simon. That should keep you busy, but if you read any script and you love the dialogue, take the time to analyze why you love it so much. Chances are the writer went through the dialogue-rewriting steps you've just learned.

Parting Words

There you have it. Ten steps to rewrite your dialogue to excellence. Effective dialogue is developed through trial and error and lots of rewriting, so don't get discouraged. Think of yourself as a painter on the page and the dialogue techniques as the colors on your palette. Get to know them, like a painter knows the power of each color on the spectrum, and apply them to your dialogue in every rewrite of your scripts. I guarantee that if you do, your dialogue will grow brighter, more vivid, and more emotionally impactful and will bring you closer to creating great lines actors will want to say.

CHAPTER 12

"Show, Don't Tell": Visual Screenwriting

by Philip Eisner

In his memoir *Adventures in the Screen Trade*, legendary scrwwwwwenwriter William Goldman[1] famously wrote, "Nobody knows anything." This makes my position quite curious; if an Academy Award–winning writer like Goldman confesses to know nothing about writing movies, then you have every right to ask why you should value my advice.

My answer: Two years after graduating from Stanford, I sold the second screenplay I'd ever written. I've made a living writing screenplays ever since.[2] I've had the good fortune to have three projects produced as of writing these words.[3] Since 2006, it's been my pleasure to serve as an

---

[1] *Butch Cassidy and the Sundance Kid, Marathon Man, The Princess Bride,* and a whole lot more.

[2] Writing for Sony Pictures, Universal, Walt Disney, Paramount, with producers like Kevin Spacey's Trigger Street, Robert De Niro's Tribeca, the Jim Henson Company, Edward R. Pressman, Gale Anne Hurd, Scott Rudin, Sean Daniel, and Larry Gordon.

[3] As of 2012: *Event Horizon* (Paramount); *Firestarter 2: Rekindled* (Syfy/Universal); *Mutant Chronicles* (Magnet).

instructor in the UCLA Extension Writers' Program. I don't argue with Goldman—in fact, I agree with him entirely—but I do suggest that, while I know nothing, I've had enough experience writing in the industry trenches to know a lot of it.

The Visual Medium

In 1878, Eadweard Muybridge created the first motion picture to settle a bet. He used a twenty-four-camera array to capture the motion of a galloping horse, proving that all four hooves did indeed leave the ground, and as a by-product, invented motion pictures. Ten years later, Louis Le Prince made the first narrative film. His 1888 opus, *Roundhay Garden Scene,* was two seconds long.

Hardly auspicious beginnings, but by 1927—when Warner Bros. released *The Jazz Singer*[4] and effectively ended the silent era—movies had become the most popular form of storytelling in the world. Strong demand led to the creation of studios like Warner Bros., 20th Century Fox, and Paramount. The movie stars of the silent era—Charlie Chaplin, Rudolph Valentino, Lillian Gish—were every bit as famous as their contemporary counterparts Tom Cruise and Angelina Jolie.

The filmmakers of the silent era created complete worlds and told compelling stories, and they did it all without dialogue. *They did it all with pictures.*

We have more tools at our disposal nowadays, but the language of film hasn't changed. The pictures tell the story, not the dialogue. Pictures are quick and efficient; they convey character and context at a glance. But while they are worth a thousand words, the words still have to come first, and the screenwriter has considerably less than a thousand to devote to each image. The task facing us is this: What is the best image to communicate each event in our screenplay, and what is the most direct and

---

[4] Adapted by Alfred A. Cohn from Samson Raphaelson's play.

compelling way to translate that image into words? How do we show our audience our story and not tell it?

The answer is, on the surface, simple: *Imagine the complete movie in your mind, and write down what you see and hear.* Sometimes this process is easy. When I imagine stories, many scenes are inherently visual: fighting in a giant battle, or escaping from exploding spaceships, or hiding from a killer. But other scenes aren't: Brad and Janet plan their wedding, the doctor tells Carol the cancer has spread to her lungs, Paul tries to confess his love to Billie and fails. I love that last one: How do you film someone *not doing something*? How do you make two people having a conversation visually interesting?

This chapter explores a range of ways to maximize your story's visual quality, emotional impact, and relevance, which I break down into three major categories. In the "Wide Shot" sections, if you'll pardon the analogy, we examine the general principles of visual writing. These topics have less to do with your style of writing or your ability to create an image for your reader, and everything to do with making choices that ensure your story will make a good movie. After all, there are plenty of great stories that don't translate to the screen—think of how often you have found yourself disappointed by the movie adaptation of a good novel. Conversely, many Hitchcock films began as second-rate pulp thrillers but had the seeds to make great cinema, if not great literature.

And we'll have "Close-Up" sections too, where we'll get into the nuts and bolts of the craft, exploring what makes one description better than another. Mark Twain wrote, "The difference between the right word and the almost right word is really a large matter—it's the difference between a lightning bug and the lightning." Hopefully, I'll be able to help you find your own way to catch some of that lightning and trap it in your pages.

And finally, the "Cutaway" sections. My brain takes odd leaps and jumps when I talk about writing.[5] My students learn to bear with me, and

---

[5] Hence the footnotes, like this one.

so will you, but trust me when I tell you that there is a point to everything.

It all begins with your story.

Wide Shot: Decisive Moments

Writing a visually arresting script begins at the structural level. You must make bold choices for your story, choosing situations pregnant with emotion and tension. Answer the basic questions—*Where? Who? What are they doing?*—in clear, simple language. Of every scene, ask yourself, *What do the characters want? What will they do to get it? Who stops them? How do they adjust?*

If you're rolling your eyes because you already read words to this effect at various points in chapters 1 through 11, deal with it. You're reading it again, and not for the last time, *because all the visual style in the world won't make a scene without drama interesting.* Without conflict, without obstacles, your characters are just wandering around. The traditional term for this is "shoe-leather." The untraditional term is "jerking it." You have, at best, 120 pages to tell your story, so don't waste them on characters simply traveling from point A to point B, or scenes where characters get what they want without a struggle, or scenes where two characters talk about a third just to give the audience backstory. In short, avoid scenes devoid of conflict.

Cull the boring moments from your story, and focus on building scenes of decisive moments. That way, you don't burden yourself with trying to inject drama into a scene where none exists. Two people talking in a trailer[6] is not, and will never be, as visually interesting as trying to land a space shuttle on a disintegrating asteroid.[7] But if those two people

---

[6] *True Romance*, written by Quentin Tarantino.

[7] *Armageddon,* story by Robert Roy Pool and Jonathan Hensleigh, adapted by Tony Gilroy and Shane Salerno, and screenplay by Jonathan Hensleigh and J. J. Abrams.

in the trailer are, for example, a Mafia consigliere intent on finding a kid who stole his narcotics, and the kid's father, who's desperate to save his kid's life, the scene doesn't have to be visually arresting. The drama of the situation will suffice. Even the most vivid imagination cannot conjure up images so profound as to distract the audience from the fact that nothing of importance is happening on the screen.

Close-Up: The Emotional Image

Assuming that you've purged all the boring stuff from your story, fill your remaining scenes with moments and images that come loaded with context and emotion. There's an exercise from *The Art of Fiction*[8] by John Gardner that I like to assign to my screenwriting students. They write a brief character sketch, using objects, landscape, weather, etc. to intensify the reader's sense of the character. There's a catch, of course: no parenthetical comments, no internal monologues, no similes ("she's like . . ."). The students must limit their descriptions to external, objective reality— the kinds of things a camera can film. Let me repeat that, in all caps, as if I were shouting at you: THE KINDS OF THINGS A CAMERA CAN FILM.

Most students write a short paragraph. One student did it with a sentence:

She rides in the passenger seat of a dark sedan, her hands tightly clutching the perfectly folded American flag.

It's an ideal sentence for a screenplay. Why? *The specificity of that moment.* When an American soldier receives a military funeral, the flag that draped the coffin is presented to either the spouse or the mother. Either way, that woman has suffered a devastating loss. So much content, from a detail as simple as a folded American flag, *without having to say what the*

---

[8] *The Art of Fiction* may be the single best textbook on creative writing. Gardner also wrote *Grendel,* the story of Beowulf from the monster's point of view.

woman feels. Powerful moments like this need very little description to come alive for the reader. The writer can limit herself to simple physical details and let the reader's emotions fill in the story.

This is why screenwriting instructors always say, "Less is more." "Less" isn't "more," obviously; what we're trying to do is to get our students to find the one image that engages the reader, sometimes doing the equivalent work of a paragraph or an entire scene.[9] Once you've found such a detail, you want to get rid of all the clutter around it, so that the reader can't miss it. The fewer words on your page, the more the ones you have stand out.

Back to that sentence. It's effective, not only because it conveys an image bursting with context and emotion, but because of everything left unsaid. The reader instinctively wants to know more: *Mother or wife? How did the soldier die? How old were the characters? How did they feel?* Don't be afraid of leaving your readers with unanswered questions. You *want* your readers asking questions. The art of fiction lies not in telling the audience what they want to know—*they want to know everything*—but in controlling *which* questions they ask. A reader without questions is a bored reader, who has no reason to turn the page. A reader overwhelmed by questions is a confused reader, who may want to burn the page. By leading off with

---

[9] In my own process, instead of spending hours searching for that perfect image and the words that capture it, I just overwrite the hell out of the scene. I call it "word vomit." Lord knows, it's not good writing, but no one will ever read it but me. Once I finish, I'll go back through the pile of words I just heaved onto the paper, wash away the verbal puke to reveal any rough gems, and edit them until they're shiny. Then I'll move on.

What does this have to do with visual writing? Why am I telling you this? Because it's quite easy to spend hours staring at the blank page, searching for "the right word." "Staring at the page" and "writing" are two different and mutually exclusive actions. It's easier to create the habit of writer's block than it is to create the habit of writing. *Do not create the habit of writer's block.* Write, plenty and often. Don't be precious with your words: Write the crappy, hacked, purple, clichéd version of your moment, your scene, your story.

Then go back and fix it.

a nice, juicy detail—the folded flag, tightly clutched—you direct the reader's questions to follow your upcoming plot instead of wandering off into white, unwritten spaces.

Where will you find the inspiration for moments like this? Photography books. Art museums. Study the great painters. And when you do, study your own reactions. Odds are, if an image moves you, it will move others as well. Now you have to go deeper and ask yourself, *Why does this image move me? Is it the emotional content of the picture itself? Or is there an abstract play between light and shadow and color at work? How would I describe this picture using words?* Nor should you shy away from uncomfortable material.

A personal example: I have many photography books by Joel-Peter Witkin. His subject matter tends toward the deeply disturbing. One particularly strong photograph is of a headless corpse, naked on a stool. Seeing it for the first time, my first reaction was revulsion. But instead of turning away, I forced myself to keep looking. I discovered the dead man was not completely naked: He still had his socks on. The image transformed for me. No less horrific, but now also tragic. This had been a man, like me, who, upon waking, had put on his socks and before the end of the day was dead. My revulsion was replaced by an overwhelming sense of loneliness, and compassion, for that headless man, propped up on a stool, in a morgue somewhere in Mexico.

How can I apply my experience with Witkin's photograph? Well, when I'm describing the scene of a murder, and I want to create more empathy for the victim, I'll add a very mundane detail. Like socks.

Perhaps museums bore you, and my example above has guaranteed that you will never, ever pick up a book of photography. Have no fear. You can find plenty of inspiration in comic books.

Comic books share several similarities with movies. They tell a story with pictures. The images have been laid out upon the page, in sequence, one flowing to the next, not unlike the way motion pictures are edited together. They use the same language, of close-ups and wide shots and cutaways (though comics refer to them as "panels" and not "shots"). It is not exaggeration to say that when you read a well-done comic book,[10] you see one version of a movie in your head, often one better than filmmakers can ultimately capture. I have left the movie theater on more than one occasion, and turned to one of my fellow fanboys, and asked in exasperation, "Why didn't they just use the comic book to storyboard the film? Why did they have to mess with it?"[11]

Which brings us to our greatest source of inspiration: *movies*. Think of powerful images from films and what makes them effective. *The withered plant turns green and unfurls its leaves,* from *E.T.* (Melissa Mathison); *Jeff wipes chocolate icing from Hayley's lips with his fingers,* from *Hard Candy* (Brian Nelson); *Only a single egg remains in the nest,* from *Finding Nemo* (Andrew Stanton, Bob Peterson, & David Reynolds); *The cattle gun rests on the passenger seat of the police cruiser,* from *No Country for Old Men* (Joel Coen & Ethan Coen, from Cormac McCarthy's novel). Each visual detail pops of its own accord, for different reasons, whether it's the symbolic association between plants and life, or the loneliness and vulnerability of the last surviving egg, or the eroticism of a finger brushing soft, feminine lips, or in the case of the cattle gun, the curiosity the unfamiliar device evokes in the audience. These images stand on their own, but put into the larger context of their respective stories, they have great power to incite emotion and move these stories forward.

Returning to my example from *Hard Candy:* In the wider context of the scene, the finger wiping the chocolate belongs to a man in his thirties, and the mouth he wipes it from belongs to a thirteen-year-old girl. The image, in and of itself, remains erotic, but the context—a predatory

---

[10] I recommend anything by Frank Miller, Alan Moore, Brian Michael Bendis, Gregg Hurwitz, Grant Morrison, Joss Whedon, Bill Willingham, Neil Gaiman, and Will "No Relation" Eisner.

[11] Answering this particular question is beyond the purview of this chapter, and indeed my experience, and so I can only refer you to Goldman's admonition: "Nobody knows anything."

pedophile, seducing his next victim—completely subverts it. The conflict between the sensual image and its perverse and antisocial context gives the moment an ugly power that leaves us squirming uncomfortably in our seats. Juxtapositions like this are gold. They trap the audience in a state of anxiety, which must be resolved. And the only way to resolve it is to find out: *What happens next?*

The real magic of cinema takes place offscreen, in the spaces between image and context, between one shot and the next, where the observer's mind puts them together.

As T. S. Eliot wrote, *Between the idea / And the reality / Between the motion / And the act / Falls the Shadow.*

Cutaway: Eisenstein Spins in His Grave

We can't talk about the juxtaposition of images without talking about Sergei Eisenstein.[12] Some of you may have read David Mamet's *On Directing Film*[13] and/or have taken film classes. If so, then you will no doubt be familiar with Eisenstein's montage theory. And if you are, then you know that, upon seeing the previous section, titled "Close-Up: The Emotional Image," Eisenstein rose from his grave, pointed a skeletal digit my way, and cried out (in Russian), "Bourgeois pig! No image comes with context! By their very nature, all shots are uninflected images, devoid of emotion and context!"

Zombie Eisenstein is correct, of course. Images have no emotion, no

---

[12] Sergei Eisenstein (1898–1948), Russian film director and montage theorist, whose films include *Battleship Potemkin, October,* and *Alexander Nevsky.* Arguably one of the two fathers of modern cinema, the other being D. W. Griffith.

[13] Curiously titled, since he talks more about writing films than directing them. Mamet wrote *The Verdict, The Untouchables, Glengarry Glen Ross, American Buffalo,* and a bunch of other great movies; he's won the Pulitzer Prize and been nominated for Academy Awards, and if he wants to tell you a little something about writing drama, you should listen.

context. The images do not move on the screen; they are still images, flashed one after the other. It is the human mind that makes them move. In the same way, the stories we write take place not on the page, but in the minds of those who read them.

Eisenstein's theory of montage—by which we mean *editing*, and not the cliché of compressing time by setting a sequence of images to music—grew from his education in Marxist dialectic, where two opposing forces create a third. He built upon experiments by Lev Kuleshov[14] on how the human brain puts images together to tell itself a story. Kuleshov showed an audience the image of a man and the image of a plate of food, and asked the audience what was going on. *The man is hungry*, was the inevitable reply. He would then show the *exact same picture* of the man and then the image of a knife, and ask the same question. *The man is angry*, came the response. The man wasn't doing anything different—it was the same film clip, a relatively close shot, devoid of content other than the man—but by juxtaposing a different image, the meaning changed completely for the audience.

Thanks in part to Kuleshov, Eisenstein, and the other pathfinders of cinema, filmmakers can exploit this curious ability of the human brain to create stories where none exist, to film thoughts and fantasies and emotions, things that no camera can ever truly capture. We still use the same techniques, all these years later. But before I get into the nitty-gritty, there are a few more "wide shot" principles to share.

Wide Shot: Externalizing the Internal

In a novel, the author can reveal a character's thoughts directly to the reader. Every doubt and longing can be described, in great detail, without the character's actually doing anything at all, other than thinking. Fyodor Dostoyevsky's classic novel *Crime and Punishment* takes place almost

---

[14] Lev Kuleshov (1899–1970), one of the founders of the Moscow Film School, the world's first such institution.

exclusively in the narrator's head. The actual story, from observable events, would be fairly short and direct: poverty-stricken student Raskolnikov takes long moody walks, messily murders an old lady with an axe, and ultimately confesses to the crime.[15] But the reason Dostoyevsky's novel remains relevant after all these years is the internal narration of the main character: His mind has become a battleground where ideas war for supremacy. In this, Raskolnikov embodies the nineteenth century.

In contrast, a screenplay limits the writer to describing observable events a camera can film. As the character Murnau says in *Shadow of the Vampire* (Steve Katz), "If it's not in the frame, it doesn't exist." Since we can't film thoughts and emotions, *we must externalize them.* The most obvious example is having the environment reflect a character's emotional state. We've all seen a leaden sky unleash torrents of rain upon unhappy characters, or lightning flash when a character rages. In fact, we've seen shots like this so often, they've become clichés, used mostly for comic effect.

Fantasy sequences and flashbacks serve the same purpose: externalizing a character's internal reality. Large parts of *Brazil* (Terry Gilliam, Tom Stoppard, Charles McKeown) take place only in Sam's mind; the bulk of *The Adventures of Baron Munchausen* (Charles McKeown & Terry Gilliam) turns out to be a story told by the grandiloquent baron. *Fight Club* (screenplay by Jim Uhls, from the novel by Chuck Palahniuk) takes place entirely inside the narrator's head, from the opening pull-out along his optic nerve to the point when his reality is handed off to the theater audience in the final frame.

Of course, Terry Gilliam and Jim Uhls are not the only writers to jump into a character's subjective reality.

SPOILER ALERT: Verbal Kint tells us the story of *The Usual Suspects* (Christopher McQuarrie), and only at the end do we realize that almost the entirety of the film—indeed, every scene that Kint narrated to

---

[15] Edgar Allan Poe does largely the same thing with one-hundredth of the words in his short story "The Tell-Tale Heart."

us—is a fantasy sequence, a lie, forged by "the devil himself." The only "true" scenes are those set in the aftermath of the massacre, in the hospital with the sole surviving witness, and Kint's interrogation in Agent Kujan's office. The filmmakers could have cut the budget substantially by just filming those scenes, but then the film would have been 120 minutes of Kevin Spacey in a room with Chazz Palminteri. Two great actors, so they might have pulled it off, but it would hardly have been visually compelling cinema.

Not only are these great examples of externalizing the internal, but they also reveal a powerful tool for discovering what visuals you need to tell your story: your point of view.

Wide Shot: Point of View

As I mentioned in "Wide Shot: Decisive Moments," visual writing begins with structure. You have to make story choices that illuminate the protagonist's inner struggles. That's why knowing your characters, and what drives them, is so vital. That knowledge tells you which details are important, which are not, and how to craft your descriptions appropriately. Taken together, these choices create your *point of view* (POV).

Specifically, when I say *POV,* I am referring to the way into your story and how you reveal it to your readers. *Star Wars* (George Lucas) uses a universal, objective point of view. It may be Luke's story, but we don't get to him for some time. Instead, we meet our "stakes" character (Princess Leia), and the villain (Vader), and the chorus (the droids) first. As a result, by the time we get to Luke, we have some familiarity with the setting, and we have an idea of the greater scope of the conflict, even if he doesn't.

Other films choose the subjective route, not letting the audience know anything before the protagonist does. In this approach, the audience identifies with the character. *Saving Private Ryan* (Robert Rodat) doesn't open with a sweeping panorama of the beaches of Normandy. It begins in the claustrophobic landing craft thudding through the waves.

We don't see anything that Captain Miller doesn't. It's not until the battle is over that the camera goes wide to show us the horrific loss of life and we get a sense of the enormous scale of the D-day invasion. In fact, with the exception of the "bookend scenes" at the graveyard[16] and the "stakes" sequence that culminates in the decision to find Private Ryan and "get him the hell out of there,"[17] the entire story plays out with Miller and his squad. If they don't see it, we don't see it. If they don't know it, we don't know it.

The subjective point of view offers a huge advantage to the writer. It's easy for us, as we write, to get lost in our own stories, whether it's two characters in a house, as in *Paranormal Activity* (Oren Peli), or set in the chaos of the Normandy invasion. A character-specific point of view lets the writer ignore all of those details that aren't apparent to that character. The big reveal in *The Sixth Sense* (M. Night Shyamalan)—don't worry, no spoilers this time—works because the story has unfolded from Dr. Crowe's point of view. Only at the end does Crowe's perspective open up to the larger reality. We're right there with him when the truth hits and share his shock and wonder.

Memento (screenplay by Christopher Nolan, from a short story by Jonathan Nolan) takes this even farther. Its story—reflecting the short-term memory loss of its protagonist, Leonard Shelby—unfolds in reverse chronology, small segments of causality working backward toward a revelation not of *what will happen* but *why it happened*. The audience has no choice but to empathize with the character—they're forced to share in his confusion, his reversal of cause and effect. Shelby fulfills Murnau's admonition: *If Shelby doesn't see it, it doesn't exist.*

So: How do you select visuals that reflect the internal reality of your characters without having it rain when they're sad or having the sun come out when they're happy? Here's another great exercise from *The Art of Fiction* that really applies to screenwriting. Gardner wants you to describe an

---

[16] Hated them.

[17] Loved it.

abandoned barn from the point of view of an old man whose only son has died—*without the old man mentioning himself or his dead son.* Then Gardner wants you to describe the same barn, but from the point of view of a young man in love—*again, without the young man mentioning himself or the object of his desire.*

Think of what details one would notice that the other would not. The grief-stricken old man might focus on the rusted old knife used to slaughter hogs, still hanging on the wall. The young lover, on the other hand, might look to the flowering vine that's pushed its way through the broken window and to the green fields beyond.

Another example: Imagine describing a pneumatic pinup in a magazine from the point of view of a heterosexual seventeen-year-old boy. Now describe the same hypersexual pinup from the point of view of the boy's exhausted, overworked, fifty-two-year-old mother, who finds the magazine under her son's bed.

Those two characters will see very different things indeed, one transported by lust into an imagined realm of pleasure, the other wondering, *How much do those things weigh? They must kill her back, poor thing.* In this way, you tailor the environment to reveal character, the same way you make story choices to create drama.

Close-Up: The Director's Job Versus the Writer's Job

You've got your point of view. You've nailed your structure, cut out all the boring parts, and figured out how to turn those internal moments into events a camera can film. It's time to break those events down into shots.

But I read/heard/thought the screenwriter's not supposed to tell the director where to put the camera, you say. You are correct, madam. The screenwriter must make every effort to tell the story without actually suggesting what any given shot should be. First, it's the director's job, and you don't want to be rude to your director. Second, descriptions like CLOSE UP and ZOOM IN and PULL BACK and WIDE don't make for a fun read for anyone who's not well versed in film, and many of the decision makers in the Hollywood food chain aren't. They're successful executives with extensive backgrounds in marketing, law, and business, but not necessarily in filmmaking. While simple shot descriptions work well as shorthand, they can get in the way of readers' immersing themselves in your story.

The problem is, screenwriting requires you to describe a film that exists inside your mind. It's not your job to direct the movie, but it is your job to direct the script. How do you do that without describing a shot?

You imply it.

Here's how it works. Certain actions can't be seen in wide shots. For example, the action *His eyes narrow* won't play unless the audience can clearly see a character's face. The detail would be lost. It's a close-up by default. So are details like *Her fingers tremble* or *His smile doesn't touch his eyes.* Since such actions can only be seen in a close-up, you don't need to tell anyone, CLOSE-UP.

Conversely, other actions need plenty of space to work. These include shots that establish locations, like *Atlanta burns,*[18] from *Gone with the Wind* (Sidney Howard, based on Margaret Mitchell's novel), and other implicitly wide shots, like *Apollo 13 blasts into the sky;* the old cliché *The cavalry crests the hill;* or from *The Avengers,*[19] *Iron Man blasts past an office tower, the Chitauri dragon ship right behind him, tearing chunks out of the building as it slithers through the air.* That sounds like a wide shot to me.

Reveals are trickier and lie at the heart of filmmaking. They create a relationship between two images. The first creates a question in the audience's minds—*What will happen?*—and the second answers it—*This will happen.* The first shot may be a *cause*—*Jack slaps Diane on the ass*—and the second, the *effect*—*Diane straightens, her eyes wide.* Or you can flip the two and start with the effect (*What made Diane slap Jack's face?*) and pay it off with the cause (*his hand on her ass*). Individual screenwriters

---

[18] The two most expensive words in film history.

[19] Written by Joss Whedon, though he didn't write that sentence; I'm just describing a shot I remember from the film.

have their own methods of doing reveals. Some just write prose and trust the director to figure it out. Some actually break out the shot description: CLOSE-UP and WIDE and MOVE TO REVEAL. I like using white space—breaking up blocks of description with the help of the return key—and ellipses. Here's an example from a piece of my own,[20] a sci-fi work in progress:

> *The One Eyed Rider SNARLS and turns to see . . .*
>
> *. . . Deacon's battleshell rising from the black water at the shore. Steam curls from its coilgun and heat sinks. Bloody water runs from an ugly breach in the armor.*
>
> *The One Eyed Rider charges Deacon. Uses the Strider's remaining massive claw to protect his body.*
>
> *Deacon changes targets: marches fire across the Strider's knees, severs its legs, sends it crashing to the ground.*
>
> *One Eye tumbles from his perch, lands at Deacon's feet. Looks up as . . .*
>
> *. . . Deacon's fist comes down. The impact makes a terrible, WET sound.*

You can see how the ellipses work in directing the reader's attention from *this* to *that*. The director could CUT from one ANGLE to another; he could PAN the camera or MOVE it, or play the whole thing in a single master.

But the shots I would use to film that sequence are all there, implicit in the actions I described. A MEDIUM CLOSE-UP of One Eye as he turns; the WIDE on our hero in his power armor, rising from the water. A WIDE of One Eye charging; CLOSER on Deacon when he shifts his aim; WIDE again as the Strider collapses, then a CLOSE-UP of One Eye at Deacon's feet, followed by a CLOSE-UP of the fist. I satisfied my own

---

[20] *The Seven Centurions.*

need to see the story, without imposing that vision on the director. It's there if he wants it, but he's free to imagine it his own way, hopefully making it better in the process.

Close-Up: The Pure, Unemotional Shot

If thinking in shots doesn't come naturally to you, let's return to Zombie Eisenstein for inspiration. Though I don't hew to the emotionally neutral shots that Eisenstein would approve of, understanding how putting one image beside a second to create meaning that transcends either one is

vital to our process. I'll posit an emotion and then two images that might convey the same to the audience when juxtaposed:

THINGS YOU CANNOT FILM	THINGS YOU CAN FILM: THIS . . .	THINGS YOU CAN FILM: . . . AND THAT
Happiness	CLOSE-UP of a woman	Flowers
Love	CLOSE-UP of a man	A woman
Deceit	CLOSE-UP of a woman	Lips moving
Rage	CLOSE-UP of a man	Dogs fighting
Hate	CLOSE-UP of a woman	A man

THINGS YOU CANNOT FILM	THINGS YOU CAN FILM: THIS . . .	THINGS YOU CAN FILM: . . . AND THAT
Murderous intent	A man	A knife
Sorrow	A woman	A tombstone

Wow. I just did an entire relationship in fourteen shots.

Could you write a script that way? Nothing but simple, unemotional, uninflected shots? *The man walks into the room. He looks at the woman. She smiles. Out in the yard, two dogs copulate.*

You certainly could. The ideal film script never just *tells* the reader what's going on in a character's mind. Everything can be inferred from the actions of the characters. Mamet writes this way. Of course, Mamet *can* write this way. First, he makes strong story choices, so that in any given scene, the stakes couldn't be clearer.[21] Second, he is an established, award-winning writer whose scripts attract top-notch actors and directors. An executive doesn't *have* to understand one of Mamet's scripts, because no executive ever got fired for hiring Mamet to write something. His very name protects them should the film not do well.

But perhaps, like me, you are not David Mamet and sometimes have to descend into the less-than-ideal realm. Perhaps you're faced with a key moment, and no matter how you manifest a character's internal struggle, your readers respond, "I don't get it." The truth is, sometimes you just have to tell the reader what's going on in a character's mind. You want to do this as little as possible, but when necessary, *do it.* Maybe you'll write a line of obvious, on-the-nose dialogue for a character to say, with the hope that it won't make it into the final cut.

Confident actors can be your best friend in this instance. Morgan Freeman is known for going through his scripts and crossing out lines, with the explanation, "I can do that with a look." In *Event Horizon,* the studio didn't think the religious aspect of the film was obvious enough and insisted I insert an admonishment from Captain Miller, played by Laurence Fishburne, to the scientist: "You are playing with matches in God's backyard." I hated the line, and so did Fish, who refused to say it.

There's another great reason for writing the bad, on-the-nose version, and it is this: *You might not yet know the answer.* In every single script I

---

[21] If you haven't figured this out by now, I love David Mamet.

ever write, I hit a point where I have to write an on-the-nose, expositional scene—the exact kind of scene that I'm defaming—because I don't know why my character is taking the action she is. Oh, I know from a plot level—she has to do X so that Y will do Z—but not from the character's point of view. My character has become separated from her story. (In screenwriting parlance, this is called *sucking*. So I have to write a scene where the character tells me, in no uncertain terms, in simple, direct language, *what the hell is going on with her*. Then, armed with this knowledge, I go back through the script and insert external details that set up and reinforce this internal conflict. If I do my job well enough, I won't need that expositional scene at all, even a well-written version of it.)

Always search for external actions that reflect the internal world of the character, but don't be ashamed to take that extra step and just spill it. For example, in one of my scripts, I have a drug addict staring down at a crying child: "Jones gazes down at the CRYING child. Emotions ghost his face beneath the skin, rage and guilt."

Any actor can perform the first sentence. The second sentence . . . not so much. But I didn't write it for the actor. I wrote it so that the producers and investors would get the tone of the scene. There are moments in film—a slow push into a character during a moment of decision,[22] for example—that work great on the screen but fail to pop on the page. Hints like the one above help readers who don't think visually to make the leap.

As I mentioned above, experienced actors don't need these asides. In fact, they don't want to know everything, since part of the joy of acting lies in discovering a text. But before your script gets to those actors, it must pass through a phalanx of executives, and even the smartest executive wants to know that they're interpreting the text correctly. For them, the screenplay isn't just a story; it's a business document, one they might

---

[22] Like in Martin Scorsese's *Goodfellas,* when Jimmie decides to whack Morrie. Or in Paul Thomas Anderson's *Boogie Nights*, when Eddie sits on the drug dealer's couch, realizing that his life has absolutely and completely turned to shit and that he is about to die.

be risking vast sums of money upon. *They need to know what's going on, and they don't want to infer a damn thing.*

Of course, there's a middle way between the Eisenstein-Mamet axis of purity and subtext-free, expositional tripe, and that is to describe actions that come laden with context. Let's return to my list of emotions:

THINGS YOU CANNOT FILM	THINGS YOU CAN FILM
Happiness	"They laugh."
Love	"His finger caresses the inside of her wrist."
Deceit	"He can't meet her eyes."
Rage	"He shouts, red-faced." *or* "His lips go white as he bites off his words."

THINGS YOU CANNOT FILM	THINGS YOU CAN FILM
Hate	"She stares unblinking at the back of his head, and cuts herself."
Murderous intent	"He glances at fat bubbling away in the deep fryer and smiles."
Sorrow	"She cries."

Many external actions come already loaded with context, and some are so universal that they're clichés: having someone cry when they're sad, for example. Yes, it shows their emotional state, but it's *boring*, and that is the one unforgivable sin for a storyteller. If you laugh at my incompetent writing, at least you've been entertained. But if I've bored you, I've wasted time you can never recoup.

So take the obvious, boring choice, "She cries," and spin it, to "She refuses to cry." The sorrow becomes implicit, there's more meat for the actor, and any reader will understand what's going on, and not just Sergei Eisenstein. It's also cheating, because you can't film someone "refusing to cry"—they're either crying, or they're not—but it *reads* as if it's visual information.[23] My personal favorite line like this is "He lies." It implies the exact same action as "He says," except now the reader knows the character's thoughts do not match his words. Often, the most interesting scenes come about when characters act against their thoughts—when a couple break up by making love, for example, or fall in love during an argument. Never have a character tell us anything we can see for ourselves. Your dialogue should float above the story—*froth on a cappuccino*—and never have to do the heavy lifting.

In Sum

So how do you tell your story with pictures?

You imagine the complete film, as if you were watching it in the theater. You describe what you see, in simple, clear sentences.

You make strong structural choices that externalize your protagonist's struggle.

You select a point of view for your story that eliminates anything that would distract the reader from your story.

You reveal what's going on inside a character's head—through fan-

---

[23] In fact, an early reviewer of this chapter argued that she could "totally picture someone refusing to cry." Which is exactly what's so great about the description: The reader can picture it. But that doesn't mean an actor can play the action "refusing to cry." A small distinction, but important, because you are writing for actors and need to be aware of the challenges of their craft.

tasy scenes, or flashbacks, or by breaking emotional moments into juxta-posed shots.

You choose character actions that move your story forward and into conflict. No "shoe-leather scenes." No wasting time.

You never have a character speak a word of dialogue that tells the audience something they can see or something they already know.

The Ultimate Cutaway and Brief Coda: Read It Out Loud

How can you tell when your script is a waste of perfectly good blank pa-per and when it is worthy of investing millions of dollars, and years of other people's lives, to film it?

You *read it out loud*.[24]

If it sounds bad, it *is* bad. Go back and fix the bad parts.

Read it aloud again. Some parts that were good will now sound bad. Fix those, too. Keep repeating this process until, when you hear the work read aloud, you nod your head and say to yourself, "That's what I intended."

It's quite simple. It's also a staggering amount of work. Don't ever think—as many new writers do—that typing "The End" on the last page of your rough draft means you're finished. You're not. You're just starting. The end comes many, many drafts later, when you're sitting in a big, dark room with a bunch of strangers, watching your movie.

Reading aloud uses the part of your brain that processes auditory language. This is not the same part of the brain that you write with. When you hear your work aloud, you bring fresh neurons to the table, almost as if another person were in the room with you, bringing a new and unbiased viewpoint to your story.

Reading aloud helps you identify clunky dialogue. You want to write

---

[24] This has nothing to do with visual writing, but it's something I tell all my students, and I would be remiss not to do so here.

dialogue that actors want to say, not that makes them feel that they are, in fact, working. If you can't say it, Anthony Hopkins can't say it, either.[25]

When I was younger, I used to think that the studio would pay Tom Cruise[26] the GDP of a small country to sell my shitty dialogue. The truth is, Tom Cruise gets paid the GDP of a small country to say lines that he would have said for free. No studio has enough money to pay Tom Cruise to say words he doesn't want to say. Money doesn't motivate movie stars to make films—not the movie stars that help you get financing, anyway—which, curiously, makes them that much more expensive.

What motivates movie stars to take a role?

Stories they want to tell.

Characters they want to be.

Words they want to say.

Reading aloud identifies bad lines, and accidental repetitions, and awkward descriptions. You should be able to read your own work without stumbling over any combination of words. When you can hand your work off to another person and they can, without preparation, read it aloud cleanly, your script is ready to share with the world.

If the only advice you take from all this is *read it out loud*, you're ahead of the game.

---

[25] Actually, he can, but you don't want to make Anthony Hopkins suffer, do you?

[26] A star whose involvement effectively green-lights a movie. When I came up in the industry, it was Tom Cruise and Arnold Schwarzenegger. Now it's Tom Cruise and Will Smith; next year, it may be Tom Cruise and Joseph Gordon-Levitt.

CHAPTER 13

Polish Workshop: Making Your Best Even Better
by Michael Weiss

Now Comes the Fun Part

Greetings and welcome to the Polish Workshop. It's been a long road getting here, so grab a drink, have a seat, and let out a long exhale. You have in your hands a screenplay that you've put months of work into, subjected to painful feedback, torn apart, rewritten, and yes, finally, the day has come: You're actually starting to like it. It's okay, you're among friends. You're allowed to admit it here. Quietly.

Because the truth is that pretty soon, you will send your prized little goldfish out to swim in the shark-infested waters of Hollywood. You will enter your script into contests; submit it to managers, agents, and producers; and generally brag about it, pitch it, and send it to every contact you have who's willing to take a look.

But first, you must complete the final step in the feature film writing process: the polish. Now comes the fun part as you put the finishing touches on your script, making sure that it will entertain and impress all future readers. When I was polishing *Journey to the Center of the Earth* (Michael Weiss, Jennifer Flackett, Mark Levin), I knew that the studio executives would be reading the script for the first time, and I had to make a good impression. While that seems like a lot of pressure, I welcomed the chance to go through my script page by page, line by line, and do all the fine-tuning I never quite had the chance to accomplish in my prior drafts.

Throughout my professional writing career (*I'll Always Know What You Did Last Summer;* original material for studios like New Line, Sony, Universal, and Warner Bros.), I have valued the polish stage, because it has allowed me the time to reflect on each scene and do my best work. When you think about the polish process that way, you can almost look forward to it, right?

So let's embark on finalizing your professional calling card and polishing it until it shines. In this chapter, you'll learn how to take a final pass at some broader issues, like tone and theme, making sure that your script as a whole stays true to your vision in those areas. You'll take a look at your scene work, your dialogue, and your writing style. You'll tighten up your page length with an eye toward cutting (lots of cutting), do any final proofreading, and make sure that the tools and guidelines you've used to write your script are still holding true.

How Will I Know When My Script Is Ready to Polish?

With so many moving parts that you want to get right, your script can often feel like a never-ending work in progress. So how do you know when you're close to the finish line? How do you know when you're ready to move from a broad rewriting phase into a shorter, more focused polish step?

The first way to assess your script's "polish readiness" is to look at the nature of the feedback you've gotten on it. Are there still a lot of questions, with bigger issues to clear up? Do the readers think your first act break is still coming way too late? Or do they not buy your ending? If so, your script is not at the polish stage yet.

On the other hand, if the readers' notes are more detail oriented and focus on character nuances, lines of dialogue, and/or action beats, you know that you've made some good progress. At this point, make a checklist of all the comments you've received, and see if you've covered enough of the questions and suggestions in ways that make you feel satisfied. If so, your script has passed the first important test for being in the polish zone.

The second way of knowing when the work is ready is more intuitive: You'll know when you know. This isn't some kind of dodge. It means that, as the screenwriter, your gut will tell you when more pieces of your script are working than in need of fixing. Your instincts and vision will register that there are no major character flaws and no big story problems, your plot lays out properly along a three-act structure, and the script is about the right length—or just a little bit over. When at least 80 percent of your script feels like it's in good shape, then you're in the polish zone.

Ultimately, you need to believe that after this final step, other people are going to read your script and love it. When your checklist and gut are saying yes, you'll know you're ready.

Have Faith in Your Draft

Once you've determined that your script is ready to polish, I want you to embrace the notion that your script does not need any major changes. You aren't rewriting or reinventing. It's time to make everything better. You need to have faith in all the work you've done to get to this point. Don't torture yourself, second-guess every scene, introduce any new characters, add any major plot twists, or do any radical scene shuffling. In fact, I'm commanding you now: Thou shalt not pull any threads on this sweater that might tear it apart!

This phase entails a relatively short time commitment. A typical studio polish is a two-to-three-week job, writing full-time. If you're juggling writing with other commitments, set a goal of around forty to fifty hours of total work, however you divide it up. If you can crank out the pages in a shorter time frame, good for you, but make sure you're being thorough.

If it's taking longer, then you need to find a way to nail things down and finish up, because you do not want the polish to drag on in ways that allow your mind to start wandering.

It's worth noting that you might be taking several passes through your script in this phase as you continue to refine, trim, and proofread it. A weeklong pass might be followed by a series of smaller, two-day sessions. Pace yourself in a way that allows you a few fresh looks—from beginning to end—as you approach a finished draft.

Fine-Tuning Your Tone

There are two big-picture items to think about before diving into the details of the polish. The first one is tone, which you will want to check continuously as you move through your script to make sure it's consistent and true to the genre of the film you are writing. Tone is a somewhat subjective concept, but noticeable shifts can throw off your story and confuse your readers. For example, if you're writing a sophisticated comedy, do you have some silly or raunchy moments that don't quite fit in? Now is the time to tweak them, finding more subtle ways to deliver the same jokes. If you're writing a love story, is it so serious that it's bordering on somber? Maybe you need to add a bit of humor in spots that can spice up the romance and keep the readers engaged. Remember, we're not talking about drastic changes, just small touches to give your script an overall sense of harmony.

How's Your Theme Song?

The other big-picture item to track throughout the script is the theme of your story. In general, script readers want to feel like there's an emotional payoff at the end of the journey they've just been through. The polish phase gives you a chance to take a nice, long look at your work and see if you've delivered the thematic message or resolution that you were shooting for when you started.

Start by taking a "refresher look" at your lead characters. Did they grow, change, or learn? Are they capable of doing or saying something that wasn't possible when the story began? If you are at the end of your script and find that your story isn't quite reaching those dramatic heights, seek out some moments in your current draft—don't start thinking of new ones—that could be polished in a way that allows them to deliver your theme. For instance, can you find a line of dialogue or a small action that might drive home your point?

At the end of *The Descendants* (Alexander Payne, Nat Faxon, Jim Rash), there is a wonderful affirmation of the movie's theme of the power of love and acceptance as Matt King (George Clooney) watches TV with his two daughters. It's a quiet moment that shows the family is going to be all right, despite their mother's death, and that they have grown to love and respect each other. Matt even knows what kind of ice cream his daughter likes now, something he had no clue about at the start of the movie. It says a lot about the characters and lets the viewer know that this journey was worth taking.

In particular, scrutinize the final images of your script for its thematic content, because this is one part of the script your readers will not skip. In fact, if anything, they will skip *to* the end, to see if you have paid them off properly for their time.

Setting the Hook: Polishing the First Ten Pages

Keeping in mind the big-picture items of tone and theme, it's time to dive in and start polishing. Let's start at the beginning. When teaching my UCLA Extension Writers' Program classes, I constantly emphasize the importance of the first ten pages of a screenplay, especially the "page 10 moment," or what some instructors call the "inciting incident." It's that point, very early on in your story, where the reader is totally hooked, so that he or she *has* to know what comes next. In the polish phase, you want to hone in on that moment to make sure it's really sharp, on both a character and a story level.

A great example of setting the hook is in *The Fugitive* (Jeb Stuart, David Twohy). Thirteen minutes into the movie, its hero, Dr. Richard Kimble (Harrison Ford), stands before a judge, accused of murdering his own wife. The judge declares, "It is the judgment of this court that you be remanded to Illinois state penitentiary at Menard, where you will await execution by lethal injection, at a date to be set forth by the attorney general of the state. May God have mercy on your soul." He slams down his gavel, and the hook is set! Does it work on a character level? You bet, as an innocent man is now convicted of killing his own wife. On a plot level? It's a shocking situation, as we have no idea how Kimble will escape execution, let alone figure out who the real murderer is.

You've got about ten pages to really grab your reader. Ask yourself one more time: Have you clearly set the stakes for your hero? Is the moment emotionally strong enough? Is it as visual as it can be? These ten pages demand your utmost attention, because if they're not strong enough, you run the risk of losing your reader altogether. Remember that agents, managers, and producers have piles of scripts to read. They will be quick to judge you and your material, so you better get this hook right.

Scene Therapy

The polish phase provides the opportunity to take a hard look at the specifics of every scene in your script—without, of course, changing too much. Your goal is to trim, shape, and elevate each scene to make sure it pops and sizzles on the page.

Advance Plot, Reveal Character

Your first test is to look at each scene and ask, "Does this scene advance plot *and* reveal character?" Without a doubt, the best scenes do both. If you find a scene coming up short in one department, see if there's a way to make a quick but effective tweak.

The memorable "rooftop toast" scene from *The Hangover* (Jon Lucas,

Scott Moore) is essential to the plot because the drinks turn out to be laced with drugs, sending the whole movie spiraling forward. But the scene is elevated by the character reveal, through the rambling "wolf pack" speech delivered by Alan (Zach Galifianakis), which shows that he's weird, strangely bonded to the other guys, and when he cuts his hand, just a bit dangerous. The writers took what could have been a simple, plot-driven event—a toast—and turned it into a character's defining moment. As you look at your scenes, spot the ones that simply move the plot, and find a way to add some character flavor to them.

By the same token, figure out whether the more character-driven scenes can be adjusted a bit through dialogue or a touch of action to affect the plot as well. In *Twilight* (Melissa Rosenberg, from the novel by Stephenie Meyer), there is a magical, daring, and romantic sequence in which Edward (Robert Pattinson) takes Bella (Kristen Stewart) flying through the trees. In addition to revealing character effectively, this sequence also advances the plot when Edward's father, Dr. Carlisle Cullen (Peter Facinelli), observes, "He's been alone too long . . . But how can it end well?" It's a quick, simple reminder that the deeper Edward and Bella fall for each other, the more dangerous it is for everyone involved.

Scene Stacking

A common mistake is to stack together scenes that repeat the same emotional trait or plot point without taking the reader deeper into the character or story. On the other hand, scene stacking can be done well, as seen in the second half of *Knocked Up* (Judd Apatow), when Ben Stone (Seth Rogen) is putting his life together in a series of quick beats— getting a new job and a new apartment, creating a nursery, and reading a baby book. The scenes are short, and each one presents a unique aspect of Ben's new maturity. And they add up to a big plot moment— where Ben proves that he's capable of being a good father. As you go through your script, look for these sequences and ask yourself if each moment is necessary. If you find a scene that's superfluous, now is the time to cut it.

What's This Scene All About?

The next question to ask is "What's the purpose of this scene?" Oftentimes, it's not until the polish step that you can reliably answer that question in relation to the rest of the script. In *The Bourne Identity* (Tony Gilroy and W. Blake Herron), there's a memorable scene early on in which Jason Bourne is sleeping on a park bench in Switzerland, still unsure of who he is and what has happened to him. A couple of police officers start to hassle him, and in a jarring display of martial arts, he disarms and knocks them out. Bourne realizes, in that moment, that he's got the deadly skills of an assassin—even if he doesn't know why. The scene is lean, tight, and focused on the one concept that drives the whole movie forward: "I have deadly skills, but I don't remember who I am."

When you can identify your scene's true purpose, you can trim it down to its barest, most dramatic essentials. For the most part, all the action and dialogue of the scene should convey that single idea. Cut out any characters or plotlines that aren't important, add a line or two of dialogue to make your scene's core idea very clear, and use the techniques covered in the following sections to highlight what you want to get across. Polish tip: If you have a character in a scene with nothing to say, it's a sign that he or she probably shouldn't be there.

Fire Up the Trailer Moments

Whether you're writing action, comedy, suspense, or drama, your script should contain a certain number of "trailer moments." These are big, original scenes that define your story and create lasting memories—basically, all the great stuff that an audience sees in the movie's trailer. These moments should be in place by now. In the polish step, you have the chance to take them to the highest level possible.

Keep It Simple

There's an engineering acronym that is quoted frequently in Hollywood: "KISS," which means "Keep it simple, stupid." The trap in writing a trailer-moment sequence is that if it gets too complicated, it reads like the operating instructions to a garbage disposal: *Tighten bolt A, attach hose B, toggle switch C, run water, and shred food.* Here's your chance to open your writer's toolbox and freshen up your scenes so they are not too dense, boring, or confusing.

Start off by identifying the funniest, coolest, scariest, or most dramatic moment in the scene—the one that's so unique, people will be talking about it after they read the script or see the movie. A classic example of such a moment is the dirt-bike chase in *E.T.: The Extra-Terrestrial* (Melissa Mathison), which builds to the iconic image of E.T. and Elliott (Henry Thomas) soaring past the moon. Find those moments in your scenes and make sure everything is working to serve them.

Next, thin out any nonessential bits or pieces so that the trailer moments flow fast and are easy to understand. Cut any moments that are repetitive or feel like overkill in describing an event. Finally, use some of the tips found in the upcoming "Style Points" section to highlight the pieces of the trailer moments that you want to stand out.

Make It Better

When I was writing *Journey to the Center of the Earth,* I knew from the start there was going to be a roller-coaster-style cart ride through an old mine, to be shot in screen-bursting 3-D. In my polish, I made sure to include some key elements that would make the scene pop: a spooky reveal of some skeletons, a big mine-cart jump over a missing section of bridge, and finally, a tunnel section made of diamonds, which would become a plot point later on.

This step takes time, sitting with your "trailer" scenes, looking for small ways to make them more exciting, funny, or dramatic. If it's a comedy, can you take the humor one step further? If it's a horror film, can you add a visual cue that's scarier or more shocking? Can you add a twist that is distinctive and genuinely surprising or a great line of dialogue that punctuates an emotion? Remember, these trailer moments should be original and memorable. You have the time now to polish the details, so when the reader puts the script down, he or she cannot stop thinking about these indelible scenes.

Scene Transitions

Screenplays are like puzzles, with a series of scenes laid out in interlocking order, building toward one large picture. In the polish stage, your goal is to make sure that the scenes fit together in the tightest, most dramatic of ways as well as maintain their momentum as they fall into place. This process requires you to take a hard look at your transitions and ask yourself if the end of every scene is as dramatic, funny, thrilling, or clever as it can be.

Cause and Effect

A general guide for your script is that the action and events of your scenes should have a cause-and-effect flow, even if you have a few different story lines running. In the polish phase, you want to make sure this cause-and-effect flow holds true—that your scenes link up smoothly and the way they connect is clear to the reader.

Slumdog Millionaire (Simon Beaufoy) offers an excellent example of cause and effect in a script. The hero, Jamal (Dev Patel), is desperately searching for the love of his life, Latika (Freida Pinto). A sequence of his hunt goes like this: While working at a call center in Mumbai, Jamal uses the center's technology to track down his missing brother, Salim (Madhur Mittal). Jamal confronts Salim for help, but Salim says he doesn't know where Latika is. Jamal doesn't believe him and follows Salim to the home of a local gangster, where Salim is working. Sure enough, he finds

Latika there and asks her to run away with him. Each scene offers information that leads to the next. The entire sequence builds upon one question: "Where is Latika?"

Now look at your own script and analyze each scene and the connections among them. If you're coming up short, find a line of dialogue or a small bit of action that can work as some glue. If you have two scenes together that really don't fit in any way, as a last-resort attempt to keep your pacing right, consider shuffling things around.

Trimming the Connections

Finding words, lines, and moments to cut is one of the keys to the polish phase, and these transitional spots are where you can often find some content worth chopping. There's a screenwriter's creed about scene transitions coined by the legendary screenwriter William Goldman (*Butch Cassidy and the Sundance Kid, The Princess Bride, Marathon Man*) that is commonly paraphrased as "Cut in late, cut out early." "Cut in late" refers to the beginning of a scene, and it means starting as deep into the drama or action as possible. It's a reminder not to waste time, energy, and most importantly, page length on transitional moments—a person getting out of a car, knocking on the door, asking to come inside.

"Cut out early" applies to the end of scenes. When the drama has made its point, cut out and get to the next scene. If you need a reaction shot or one line of dialogue to punctuate the moment, that's cool. But just as with the opening, there's usually no need to see a character leave the room or offer meaningless good-byes once the drama has peaked.

There's a great example of this technique in *The King's Speech* (David Seidler), which won the 2010 Academy Award for Best Original Screenplay. In one scene, the Duke of York, later King George VI (Colin Firth), is at home with his wife, who has suggested he hire a speech therapist. Until now, the duke has resisted. When he finally has a change of heart, the movie directly cuts to the next scene—in the therapist's apartment, with the duke and his wife on the couch and the duke saying, "Strictly business. No personal nonsense." There are no transitions, no wasted words. It's a sharp, deep cut right to the heart of the action.

Dialogue Polish

As you trim your scenes down to their barest essentials, you'll have the opportunity to review your dialogue once again. In some regards, this is the most important element upon which to feast your brain during the polish phase. When crafting your first draft and even your revision, I'd generally advise you not to ruminate too long over your dialogue. In those script phases, so many pieces are moving about, so many things are changing, and you never know what's going to stick. Why kill yourself coming up with the best three lines you've ever written, only to realize you're going to cut that speech or exchange? Or even cut that character?

Those times are over. Now it's time to deliver the funniest, saddest, wittiest, and craziest dialogue you've ever written. Give yourself plenty of time. Read your words out loud to hear how it sounds. Don't move on until you're satisfied.

Be Consistent

Aside from making your characters great, the most important thing you can do is to make their voices consistent. The executives reading your polished draft haven't spent the past few months getting to know your characters. They haven't workshopped the script with you to understand the relationships. This will be the first time they encounter your script, and you must keep them on track by ensuring that all the dialogue fits your characters and that each character's voice remains consistent throughout the script.

In *The King's Speech*, the first time the Duke of York meets his speech therapist, Lionel Logue (Geoffrey Rush), the duke—"Bertie"—remains stoic and formal at all times, while Lionel is provocative and unconventional.

CUT TO THE CHASE

                    BERTIE
Aren't you going to start treating
me, Doctor Logue?

                    LIONEL
Only if you're interested in being
treated. Please, call me Lionel.

                    BERTIE
I prefer Doctor.

                    LIONEL
I prefer Lionel. What'll I call you?

                    BERTIE
Your Royal Highness, then Sir after that.

                    LIONEL
A bit formal for here. What about your name?

                    BERTIE
Prince Albert Frederick Arthur George?

                    LIONEL
How about Bertie?

                    BERTIE
        (flushes)
Only my family uses that.

                    LIONEL
Perfect. In here, it's better if we're equals.

> BERTIE
> If we were equal, I wouldn't be here. I'd be at
> home with my wife and no-one would give a damn.

Notice how each man—and each bit of dialogue—stays true to character.

One tip for keeping your dialogue consistent is to create a chart of your characters and assign them each a simple point of view, something that sums up their attitude about life. As you look over your dialogue, check it against this chart. Is an "eternal optimist" saying a few negative things that would be out of character? Is a serious character suddenly making jokes? At this point, you should have a clear grasp on your characters and be able to fine-tune every line to fit their personalities.

The "Dialogue Read"

There's a dirty little secret in Hollywood that I picked up on during my time as a development executive at Miramax Films and as a professional script reader. It's called a "dialogue read," and it literally means that someone skims through your script, picking up most of his information through chunks of dialogue. Remember, the agents, managers, and producers have piles of scripts to read, so they need to move quickly. It's easier to read snappy passages of dialogue than it is to read long passages of detailed description.

Am I suggesting you jam every plot point into on-the-nose, expository dialogue? Not at all. But in the polish phase, you want to see if there are any bits of dialogue that would help to emphasize or add clarity to your story.

For example, around twenty-seven minutes into *Black Swan* (Mark Heyman, Andres Heinz, John McLaughlin), ballet director Thomas Leroy (Vincent Cassel) lays out his goals for Nina (Natalie Portman) when he states, "I knew the White Swan wouldn't be your problem. The real work will be your metamorphosis into her evil twin." You might think that's an obvious line for this film. But it stands out on the page and goes a long way toward telling the reader what's happening with the plot and where the heroine stands on her journey. Essentially, it's *telling* us what the second act is going to be about: Nina's metamorphosis.

It wouldn't hurt to go through the different sections of your script and find a spot or two where you can add this kind of helpful dialogue that acts as a mile marker for the reader.

Let It Zing!

Another "polish phase" technique is to look for spots of dialogue at the end of scenes that you can strengthen by adding "zingers." These are bits of dialogue that can act as punch lines to button up a scene or well-crafted setups to the moment coming up next.

When *The Hangover*'s rooftop scene ends with Phil (Bradley Cooper) toasting, "To a night we'll never forget," it's a comically prophetic line that sets up the ensuing situation, in which the guys wake up with memory-erasing hangovers. In *The Town* (Peter Craig, Ben Affleck, Aaron Stockard), there's a fun zinger at the end of a quick scene between tough guys Doug (Ben Affleck) and Jem (Jeremy Renner):

```
INT. JEM'S APARTMENT — FIFTEEN MINUTES LATER
Doug walks in. Jem is watching television.


                    DOUG
        I'm asking for your help. I can't tell
        you why, you can never ask me about it after
        and it involves hurting people.


Jem stares at him, eyes thoughtful.


                    JEM
        Whose car we gonna take?
```

Zing! The scene cuts right from there to the guys driving off to commit a crime, and that singular line reveals the bond between these friends and Jem's darkly comic zest for danger.

Of course, one of the greatest zingers of all time is in *When Harry Met Sally . . .* (Nora Ephron) in the scene in which Sally (Meg Ryan) fakes an orgasm in a diner booth. There's a pause after she finishes, and then an older woman in the background delivers a killer line: "I'll have what she's having."

Style Points

One of the ways you're going to be judged as a writer is on your style, which comes not only from your dialogue but also from the way you write your action and scene descriptions. The irony is that in the best screenplays, style is simply an economy of words, done right. The sign of a true amateur is when a scene description contains unnecessary detail and emotional content.

So your first step in a style polish is to put your script under a microscope, looking for extraneous sentences and words. Be alert to places where you've gone into excessive detail about what someone's apartment looks like, or how dinner is being served, or what someone is wearing. The shorter these descriptions, the better.

Put It on the Screen

In my Writers' Program classes, we conduct "table reads," in which scripts are read out loud, with students taking on the different roles. Oftentimes, we learn the most from the narrator, who reads out the scene description and action. Students have noticed how often the narrator tells us things that the movie's audience wouldn't see on-screen.

For example, in the description "Sarah enters the room with Courtney, who was her best friend in college until she dropped out to pursue acting," we're being given background information that would not be apparent to a movie audience. In "Joe looks around the party, realizing these people would never have taken him seriously before his big inheritance," we're getting the character's inner thoughts, which can't be filmed.

This problem is not just logistical but also stylistic—in a way, you're cheating by telling us what to think, rather than letting the characters and situations reveal this information. Professional readers will spot this weakness in an instant and very likely be turned off by your style of storytelling. Use the polish phase to tweak or weed out such elements, and your style will be that much crisper and smarter.

A Touch of Spice

I'm going to contradict myself slightly here and say that, occasionally, good writers can bend the "put it on the screen" rule by supplying some information that isn't on the screen to spice up their style. In *Good Will Hunting,* screenwriters Ben Affleck and Matt Damon paint a picture of the movie's core group of buddies in a quick and clever way: "All four boys speak with thick Boston accents. This is a rough, working-class Irish neighborhood and these boys are its product."

When you can use a lean style and effective word choice to convey a concept without wasting time on details, consider it. For instance, instead of describing the physical dents and rust on a boat, you might say, "She's been through enough storms that the next one could be her last." While it's true that you are "telling" and not "showing" us something about the boat, you are imparting a feeling and conjuring up imagery that will stick with the reader. Keep in mind, however, that this rule bending should be used only when it will *save* you from lengthy descriptions while adding a little bit of pizzazz to your style.

Typing with Style

There are also ways to ADD STYLE that can make your action POP on the page, simply by the way you type it. You see how I did that there—putting the significant words in ALL CAPS? If we were texting each other, you'd think I was angry. But in a script, using ALL CAPS is a way to draw your reader's attention to just the right words at just the right times. If you have an action scene and want the readers to remember an EXPLOSION, go ahead and use this technique. You could even underline an important series of words, if they were <u>something you didn't want the reader to miss</u>.

You can also pull out a single line to draw the reader's attention to a moment.

The white space around it will help highlight the drama of the moment.

These aren't tricks; they are style tools that professional writers use throughout their scripts. Remember that as you're putting the finishing touches on your characters, story, structure, and dialogue, you should be polishing your script's style as well.

The Lean Cut

The best read is a fast read! You want to make sure that your scene descriptions, action, and dialogue are as lean as possible, without losing any of your dramatic impact. In general, the more trimming you can do, the better the read and the more your readers will be impressed with your work.

I'll give you another little secret from my former life as a development executive, and that's about the value of "keeping it lean." Back when people used to print scripts, the first thing we execs did was flip to the back page to see the page count. Today, readers check the page length of the PDF file, and in an instant, a judgment gets made. It's like Goldilocks and her three bowls of porridge. An 84-page script? Too short. A 138-page script? Way too long. Somewhere around 105 to 110? Just right. There's a reaction that script length gets, and I've been in the trenches long enough to know that you want to be in that sweet spot.

For the most part, screenplays come in a little too long, so the polish phase becomes a very serious game of "What else can I cut?" Even when you think you've hit the wall and the next cut will ruin your script, there are still plenty of ways to keep trimming, because you have to get your script to the right length, *no matter what it takes*. This polished draft is your calling card, and it has to be tight. Here are a few style tips to help you take your cuts deeper.

Punch Out Your Slug Lines

Slug lines (those capitalized headings that signal a change of scene, location, and time) take up a lot of page space, so look around for scene headings that aren't needed. You might spot a handful of slug lines in an action scene that can be condensed, or find slug lines in transitions or establishing shots that can be cut or moved into the body of another scene. For example, let's say a thief is running through a shopping mall. You might have started out writing it like this:

```
INT. SHOPPING MALL — DAY
The thief runs through the mall, looking over
his shoulder at the cops.


INT. SHOPPING MALL — FOOD COURT — DAY
The thief gets to the food court and ducks
behind a garbage can.
```

To save space—and keep the scene more fluid—you could change it to this:

```
INT. SHOPPING MALL — DAY
The thief runs through the mall, looking over
his shoulder at the cops. He gets to the FOOD
COURT and ducks behind a garbage can.
```

You'd be surprised how removing just a few of these slug lines can cut your page length quickly and make for a smoother read.

Cut Down Your CUT TO Habit

You don't always have to use CUT TO at the end of every scene. In fact, you almost never have to use it, especially in a spec script, in which you should consciously avoid directing or editing on the page. We know you're cutting from scene to scene; you don't have to remind us. Like slug lines, these little monsters eat up tons of page space. Occasionally, a CUT TO helps a specific gag. For example, a guy shows up for a job at the circus but is told the only job available is as a clown. The guy says no way, I'll never be a clown. CUT TO: the guy standing in a clown suit. There are some select moments where you might want that kind of hard transition. But for the most part, save yourself the page space.

Omit Danglers

A *dangler,* also known as an *orphan,* is a word or two that comes at the end of a sentence but takes up a whole line of space. You must hunt down these pesky varmints, as they may be adding pages to your script. For example, the word *inside* is the dangler on these four lines:

```
A horse-drawn carriage pulls up to a magnificent
hillside castle. Guards open its doors. Scarlett
and Jonathan step out of the carriage and walk
inside.
```

What a waste! Watch as I magically turn four lines into three, without losing any content:

```
A horse-drawn carriage pulls up to a magnificent
hillside castle. Guards open its doors. The
couple exits the carriage and walks inside.
```

The same trick can be done with dialogue, where one or two words dangle at the bottom of a block. It seems simple. Almost unnecessary. But I guarantee that if you find and fix ten or twenty danglers, you will lose a page or two without sacrificing anything important. In fact, your script will suddenly seem tighter and faster-paced.

The Proof Is in the Polish

There is one part of the polish that's going to be a bit tedious: proofreading. You want to save that until the very, very end, when you've executed every single other step. And when I say *proofreading,* I mean going page by page, line by line through the sucker. Read the script out loud, listen for any and all errors, look for punctuation gaffes or flat-out broken sentences. Look for lines that accidentally get repeated or lines that were left out. Take your time. Get a friend or two to double-check it for you. Do everything you can to get it right.

You'd be surprised how many "polished" drafts come in loaded with mistakes—right on the first page—because the writer thought that *polish* really meant "skim." You have to be your own editor here. Pretend that the script has been submitted to you, and now you're looking for mistakes. If you're not sure about a grammatical phrase, look it up. Run your computer spell check. Slowly. Carefully. Make sure when you hit the "replace" button on your spell checker, you haven't just corrected *anotated* to *anointed* when you really meant *annotated.* Trust me. It happens. You've come this far. You don't want sloppy errors on your calling card, right?

How Do You Know You Are Done?

At the start of this chapter, I gave you some guidance on how to know when your script is ready for the polish phase. At this point, you're probably wondering, *How do I know when I'm actually done with the polish?* Here's a checklist that you can use when you get to the end of it, to see if you've done all the work.

- Have you covered all the questions and feedback given to you in your previous draft?

- Did you follow your game plan, not making any major character or plot changes?

- Is your tone consistent throughout?

- Is your theme clearly stated and fulfilled in a satisfying way by the end of the script?

- Are your first ten pages as engaging and sharp as possible?

- Do your scenes advance plot and reveal character?

- Have you taken your trailer moments to their highest, most memorable heights?

- Are your scene transitions fluid? Do you have any repetitive scenes left?

- Is your dialogue consistent throughout your script?

- Have you added some zingers at the end of scenes?

- Is your style lean and effective? An economy of words, done right?

- Have you cut out any descriptions that seem like cheats and cannot be filmed?

- Have you used your style tips to highlight important moments?

- Have you gone through and trimmed as much as possible, using every technique?

- Is your script at the right page length?

- Have you proofread the script until it is absolutely perfect?

Are You Having Fun Yet?

Okay, let's do it again. Take a deep breath, and then let out a big exhale. Really, try it.

In addition to being relieved and satisfied by completing this final step in the feature film script process, I hope you are also soaking in your enormous accomplishment.

On the specific level, I am referring to the achievement of completing the polish process: every scene you refined, every trailer moment you nailed, every transition you perfected, every stylistic device you used to the best of your ability, and every item you checked off your list with confidence. Your gut tells you that you've polished your script until it gleams, and you have faith in the final product.

But even more importantly, you have *finished your screenplay*! While many people dream of writing a movie, relatively few have the discipline and dedication to tackle the process from the ground up. Think of the enormity of your achievement. As you worked your way through *Cut to the Chase,* you created a compelling story and characters and constructed a well-crafted plot and tight outline. You worked through the grueling process of writing the first draft and subsequent revisions, and zeroed in on the art of scene construction and movement. You tackled the nuances of dialogue and visual storytelling, and last but not least, you polished your creation. You survived self-doubt, trusted the process, and managed your time to give priority to your writing.

Therefore, by the powers granted to me as the author of this chapter, I salute and congratulate you on becoming a feature film writer! No matter what the future may hold, you have done everything you can to make your script as great as it can possibly be and to make your dream a reality.

SECTION IV

Being a Professional
in the Movie Business

CHAPTER 14

Demystifying the Business of Feature Film Writing

by Laurence Rosenthal

When it comes to the film business, there is no one formula for success. What works today may change tomorrow. *Who* works today may change tomorrow as well.

What doesn't change is the fact that movies are a fascinating fusion of art and commerce, and the two cannot be separated. The most successful writers, producers, directors, agents, and studio executives understand this fact and don't confuse it with the magic, glamour, and fantasy the movie industry promotes.

Companies and corporations conduct an exhaustive amount of research to determine the future potential of a film story, because the stakes are huge and jobs are on the line. They invest millions of dollars (sometimes hundreds of millions) in order to produce, distribute, market, and promote a product whose worth is generally determined in one weekend—especially now, with audience members posting their reviews during the first screenings.

As a preprofessional, your first job is to explore the creative decisions you make in your evolution as a writer and to learn to write the best scripts you can. When I teach the "Writing the First Screenplay" sequence for the UCLA Extension Writers' Program, I tell my students that while they write (and rewrite) their scripts, the greater their understanding of the system and how to navigate through it, the better their chances are for success. Understanding the business of feature film writing is power.

When I was director of development at Woods Entertainment, where we made *Things to Do in Denver When You're Dead, Beautiful Girls, Citizen Ruth, Wide Awake, Kate and Leopold, Kids, Cop Land,* and *Scream,* I remember how enthused writer/director Alexander Payne (*Sideways, Election*) was about a wonderful actress who auditioned for the role of Ruth in *Citizen Ruth.* This actress was a revelation on her audition tape, but she didn't get the part. The title role went to Laura Dern, because she was a "known entity" that Miramax could sell to foreign distributors— remember: Art plus commerce equals movies. And the fact is, Laura Dern won a best actress award at the Montreal World Film Festival for her portrayal of Ruth, and the movie earned several nominations, awards, and increased visibility for the film's cowriters, Alexander Payne and Jim Taylor.

This chapter aims to give you knowledge and tools an aspiring screenwriter needs to combine the heart of an artist with the head of an entrepreneur. You'll understand the critical role that branding plays, both in today's film industry in general and for you as a new writer. You'll learn the various routes a script can take to be seen, represented, and sold, and what roles readers, agents, managers, attorneys, producers, and other buyers play in this process. You'll get a grasp on how studios, with their hierarchy of junior execs through chairmen/women, function, and how they factor into your script's journey from your hands to the screen. Finally, throughout this chapter, you'll learn the importance of cultivating relationships at every level.

Screenwriting is a *career;* it's not a one-shot affair ("I'll sell my first script and make a million dollars"), as many people believe. So what does the reality of this roller coaster of an industry look like, and how do you proactively engage in it?

Understanding the Power of the Brand

Movies as Brands

When I started in this business, the split between foreign and domestic box office was 70 percent North American market and 30 percent international. Today, the lion's share of a commercial film's revenue comes from foreign distribution, which makes branding—those elements that make an entity recognizable—especially key to a movie's chances of economic success. Financiers and studios feel much safer pushing a brand that the national, and especially the international, public already has an established interest in; these properties are, in a way, presold. That's why there are so many sequels, prequels, remakes, reinterpretations, and adaptations of popular novels and comic books.

For example, the ten top-grossing movies from July 8 to 10, 2011, the heart of summer blockbuster season, consisted of six sequels (*Transformers: Dark of the Moon, The Hangover Part II, Pirates of the Caribbean: On Stranger Tides, Fast Five, Kung Fu Panda 2, Cars 2*), one prequel (*X-Men: First Class*), and two originals—though one was adapted from a comic book: *Thor* and *Bridesmaids*.

Granted, it's highly unlikely the producer of the next *Pirates of the Caribbean* will tap you, early in your career, to write the script, but consider this: *Pirates of the Caribbean* franchise creator Stuart Beattie was a new screenwriter with only one small, independently produced Australian feature under his belt when he sold his script based on a ride at Disneyland. And by the way, he developed the screen story of *Pirates of the Caribbean: The Curse of the Black Pearl* as a student in Writers' Program screenwriting classes. The point is that *someone* has to write the first script in what might become a highly successful franchise. And even if your goal is to write an intimate, character-driven, quirky love story and seek independent financing, it's important to have a strong handle on what sells, what's getting made, and what tends to have the biggest box office.

Movie Stars as Brands

Movie stars are also brands; they are the power center of the business. They're not getting paid $10 to 20 million for eight weeks of work on the set; they're getting paid for the value their names bring to movies. Stars like Johnny Depp "open" a movie, meaning that their fans turn out on the opening weekend and set the stage for financial success. These movie stars know it too, which is why they associate themselves with similar product, time after time. As an audience member, you know what to expect from a Tom Cruise movie or a Will Smith movie, and that's what makes these actors bankable.

However, many movie stars want to appear in films that not only highlight their brand but also enhance it. George Clooney is a perfect example of a movie star who has built his career by finding the balance between commercial work in movies like the *Ocean's Eleven* franchise and more evocative roles in films like *Syriana*. That movie did well enough, but it wouldn't have been made without its star. The people at Warner Bros., who distribute *Ocean's Eleven*, wanted to work with George Clooney again, and that's why they made *Syriana*, which won the actor his Academy Award.

In my personal and professional experience, I've never met an actor who didn't dream of giving an acceptance speech at the Oscars, and you can pretty much count on the fact that he would be so honored for an original *Syriana*-style turn rather than an *Ocean's Eleven*—or *Twelve* or *Thirteen*. This is where you come in. If your unique voice and vision have the power to capture a star's attention, you are increasing your chances of winning this high-stakes game. Getting a major movie star attached to your screenplay is the ultimate objective for the studio, and therefore for you, because it helps to get your movie made.

The Director as a Brand

In addition, there is a group of directors who, like actors, have brand appeal. Spielberg. Scorsese. Cameron. Burton. When you know them by one name, they're a star. Okay, sometimes it takes two names, but only to differentiate, as in the case of Spike and Ang Lee. The point is that there are directors who are stars in their own right, because their singular creative vision brings people to the theater. Along with studio executives, agents, actors, and producers, directors want to discover an original, refreshing voice and an idea that's bold and daring, but at the same time they need to maintain their positions in the hierarchy of Hollywood. In this business, everyone has a personal interest.

Moreover, there is a "subset" of brand-name writer-directors. Some of those, like Quentin Tarantino and Woody Allen, only direct material they write, so the chances of getting them attached would be nonexistent. Others, like Guillermo del Toro, direct both other writers' and their own work.

Branding Yourself as a Writer

Do you notice a consistent theme here? The most successful movies, stars, and directors are identifiable by the style, genre, vision, and point of view with which they are most closely associated. The same is true for writers, and so when you are writing and polishing your first batch of scripts, you should be keeping this central question in mind: "What kind of a career do I want?"

I know that we all like to think of ourselves as writers with great range. By nature, we want to exercise our talents and pursue a variety of genres, and you will be able to do that, but not now—not until you have established yourself as a unique, qualified voice. Studios are towering bureaucracies with a hierarchical structure; once anyone at a studio meets you and is enthused about your work, be prepared to offer them more of the same, only different. Remember, this is what they want, and this is your *career,* so be prepared with at least several scripts and plenty of concepts that create a niche that allows you—and eventually, your agent—to "sell" you for specific, recognizable, and consistent material.

In fact, ironically, most first-time produced writers get branded coming out of the gate—that is, whatever you sell first is assumed to be your genre, and many writers complain that breaking out of that box can be hard. So be prepared to brand yourself carefully.

Choosing Your Subject Matter

The Content

My friend Alessandro Camon, a truly successful producer (*Thank You for Smoking, The Cooler, Wall Street: Money Never Sleeps*) and Academy Award–nominated screenwriter (*The Messenger*), tells me that studio executives are essentially "managers of intellectual properties who are always looking for material that will get the best actors and directors excited." It's up to you to provide them with that material. What are the kinds of movies a new writer can write that give them the best chance of catching the eye of someone in a position to "make the magic happen"?

Original Work

There is always a market for fresh work; think about Diablo Cody's *Juno*, a quirky, original script that catapulted her into a brand of her own. The good news here is that you don't have to write a big action movie with huge franchise potential. However, you *do* need to approach your feature concepts with a clear view of the brand you want to establish and the possible financial rewards for the investors; there is way too much money at stake to ignore this reality, particularly these days with the narrowing of distribution channels for small, independent films. *The Hangover* was a wild, funny movie that made everyone who read the script laugh out loud. In addition, it was the perfect piece for the biggest segment of today's film audience, adolescent and postadolescent boys, and its success led, of course, to its sequel: *The Hangover II*.

Adaptations and the Public Domain

Another route for new screenwriters with a savvy eye on their content is to write stories that are adapted from classic works whose titles evoke recognition and are available in the public domain—meaning they are no longer protected by copyright law. Typically, if a work of fiction was copyrighted in excess of seventy-five years ago, it is available in the public domain. If the authors have been dead more than one hundred years, it's safe to say that their works are available in the public domain.

However, a court of law is not going to uphold advice you were given from a screenwriting book. Public domain is a legal issue, and it's not absolute across the board. It can differ from country to country, which means that you should check the status of whatever work you plan on contemporizing. This due diligence includes consulting an intellectual property attorney and/or investigating the chain of rights through the Library of Congress (if the property was originally literary). There are also a number of websites that will aid your research in determining the status of a work of art and its availability in the public domain.

If you do have the ability, through finances or in some cases relationships, to adapt a property that is still protected by copyright law, make certain that you have the exclusive rights to it. I once had the idea to do a remake of a Billy Wilder movie called *The Fortune Cookie*. I was so all-fired set on my new take on the material that I just wrote it and pitched it to Bette Midler's company. They liked the idea—so much so that they optioned the rights on their own and left me out of the equation. Boo-hoo for me. The lesson here: Don't write anything unless you know you have the right to do it.

Understanding How Twenty-First-Century Representation Works

While getting an agent to represent your work is still the gold standard, the new business model is that an agent is part of a team that includes a manager and an attorney. It's important that, as a new writer, you know exactly what roles each of these team members plays, what kind of agent most likely will represent you, and what you can—and can't—expect from them in helping you forge and manage your career.

The Agent

According to a very dear friend of mine who is a top-flight agent, "an agent is a guide, a wise man [or woman], and a strategist for content and ideas. In a sense, they are your first producer." All of this is true. Agents are the people whose experience and relationships make them an invaluable resource to you. Furthermore, their perspective on the ins and outs of the way business is conducted, who's who, and what content is being sought after in Hollywood can be a pivotal factor in determining your success as a screenwriter. They also have a deep-rooted economic interest in your success, which usually makes their advice more reliable than that of family and friends, who are emotionally invested in your immediate happiness.

Established Agents and the Bottom Line

However, what you need to understand up front is that the role of agents has changed from the "old days" (i.e., not now), when any good agent would read every draft of your work and offer constructive feedback. You could count on your agent to be your best critic when the script didn't work, and your biggest cheerleader and supporter when it did. Though the agents I interviewed for this chapter all insist they are hand-holding coddlers, experience dictates otherwise.

Regrettably, in today's market, there aren't many agents who will read more than a first draft of assignment work. For the most part, if you're not paying the phone bill for a busy agent, he or she won't spend the bulk of his or her time soliciting on your behalf. It's true the big agencies have clout, but they are going to use that clout with their established clients who garner greater fees. It's only natural that they are going to focus their time and resources on clients who bring in the big bucks.

Agents may give a new writer a brief honeymoon of activity (submissions and meetings) of perhaps three months or so, and then they will expect the phone to ring—or for you, the writer, to bring in your own networking/buyer interest based on the meetings the agent initially arranged. Basically, if you sign with a big agency as a new writer, you should view your agent as a salesperson and rely on a manager to help you develop your work—more on that member of your team shortly.

Agents and New Writers: The Good News

Does this mean you should despair? Not at all, but it suggests that finding an agent whose career path is more aligned with yours may work to your greater advantage, keeping in mind that this may prove to be your most important relationship in your career. Most established agents don't accept unsolicited material; my friend the top-flight agent only looks at writers who are referred to her. However, she notes that assistants and baby agents are often open to new writers, because they are at the beginning of their careers and want to make their mark. This underlines a fundamental aspect of the movie business: It is a business based on relationships, including how you get an agent and if you get the right one for you at this point in your career. So choose your agent well. The Writers Guild of America offers a list of reputable agents that can be accessed for free on their website at WGA.org.

How the Writer-Agent Relationship Works Best

Let's assume you have done just that: made the perfect new writer-agent match. For his or her 10 percent, your agent will invest time, passion, and capital in your screenwriting career. It's been my experience that agents define themselves as career builders, and the best of them are. Their goal is to push product, so they are forever looking for promising screenwriters whom they can propel into lucrative careers. Agents who are fully on board with you and your projects will help you get your foot in the door and will ultimately negotiate your deals and (hopefully) field offers, so it is in their best interest to consider long-term goals as well as the most immediate future. Still, it's your job, to paraphrase sports agent Jerry Maguire (Tom Cruise) in the movie of the same name, to help them help you.

Respect your agent and take his or her advice. Understand that he or she is looking out for the best advantage for you, because what serves you serves him or her. Good agents have good reputations. When I worked as a development executive, I would get submissions from dozens of different agents. After a time, I'd come to recognize who had good taste and who was just hawking whatever wares they could sell, and I would approach that screenplay with greater consideration based on the value of the agent's imprimatur. When you seek out an agent, check out who else he or she represents.

Agents, Writers, and Relationships: Social Skills, Research, and Manners Matter

Never assume that creating great scripts is enough to launch your career and that an agent will take you on based solely on your writing ability. While there may be some occasional blogger who gets a one-shot deal based on the content of his Internet musings, it's vital that the contemporary screenwriter can enter a meeting and engage the executives and creatives in a conversation that builds rapport.

Writers who are adept at building relationships are, unequivocally, the writers who work most frequently. Focus on building these relationships even *before* your first meeting. Research the people you are meeting with, learn everything you can about their company and what films they've produced, and never leave a meeting without establishing a reason for further contact. Google and the Internet Movie Database (IMDb .com) are great, free resources. At some point, if you are in the position to do more, the paid website IMDbPro.com is very useful and detailed. Studio System (StudioSystem.com) is much more expensive but is the way that most higher-end execs at studios check out the writers—and one another—and is accurate and current.

Finally, don't underestimate the power of old-fashioned manners. I'll share several last pieces of advice from my top-flight agent friend: Be kind to assistants. They are the agents and producers of the future. And from her point of view, a follow-up thank-you note makes a positive impression, because it suggests that you appreciate someone's time and consideration.

The Manager

In creating and sustaining twenty-first-century writing careers, managers have come to fulfill a vital position. Managers have taken over much of the creative side of the agent's work, including sending out scripts as samples and setting up meetings for their writer clients. They tend to be more accessible on a day-to-day basis than agents and are more prone to give you feedback on each and every draft. Managers also consider long-term career objectives and help their clients maneuver through the business aspects of the film world by tapping into their relationships.

A lot of managers started off in the business as agents, so they have political savvy and connections. In general, managers have fewer clients. Whereas an agency may represent a slew of different screenwriters competing for the same open assignment, a manager will have one screenwriter who specializes in any specific genre. Therefore, managers are less encumbered by the multiple allegiances that can work to your disadvantage at a large agency. This also allows managers to go to bat for you in concert with your agent, which serves to make a valuable impression on potential buyers. One person touting you is good; two is better.

Managers charge 10 percent as well, so they share in the investment of your career. However, they cannot legally negotiate contracts on your behalf. That is the exclusive domain of an agent or attorney. A lot of writers find managers first and then their managers help them secure agents; other times, it's the opposite and an agent will help you find a manager. Though their spheres of influence can sometimes overlap, more often than not, managers and agents complement each other. They are both important, because, in the minds of the industry, they represent you.

The Attorney

Some screenwriters also have attorneys, who bring their own wisdom and relationships to the team's sales effort. Like agents and managers, attorneys have developed key associations in the business that they can access on your behalf, and like agents, they can negotiate deals. Attorneys generally charge a 5 percent commission, so it's uncommon for neophyte writers who have not yet proven their economic value in the industry to engage an attorney; 5 percent of the Writers Guild minimum or thereabouts is not a lot of money to an attorney.

There are attorneys who charge an hourly fee. However, this can get expensive as hours add up. Still other attorneys may, given their time and inclination, give you some pro bono help if they feel they are investing in a potentially profitable relationship. It's rare, but it happens. It's more typical to hire an attorney after you've sold a couple of projects and your "quote" (how much you make per project, based on what you were paid for the previous project) is established. This addition of an attorney to your team is something you should discuss with your agent and manager, who will help you assess the added value of an entertainment attorney.

Writing to Be Read: Presenting Your Material

You and the Reader

Once you have representation, what usually happens when a new screenwriter's script gets sent to a studio or other entity capable of buying it? Keep in mind that more than fifty thousand scripts are submitted to the Writers Guild of America each year and that it's not unusual for production companies, agencies, studios, and development executives to receive anywhere from ten to fifteen screenplays each *day*. Add to that equation this rather ironic open secret: No one in Hollywood likes to read.

The potential buyers' solution to dealing with this deluge of scripts is to hire a vast pool of freelancers called "readers." Readers are paid on a per-script basis to read, comment upon, and assign your script a "Pass" (thumbs down), "Consider" (maybe), or "Recommend," which means that your script goes forward to the next level. (The more rarefied position of "story analyst" is a union reader who performs this role for the executives at major studios.)

The process goes like this: The reader writes "coverage" of your script, which consists of a logline, or premise that indicates the general nature of the story, followed by a one-or-two-page synopsis of the plotline, and ending with overall comments on the script's relative merits and flaws and the "grade" of "Pass," "Consider," or "Recommend." A "Recommend" is the exception rather than the rule, because the reader's job is to zero in on the very small handful of scripts worthy of a producer or film executive's time and consideration.

Therefore, readers are paradoxically very important characters in the film industry. While on one hand they are in a relatively low-paying position, it is nevertheless a super-significant position, because they are the first in line to decide if your script is worthy of another look.

What does this mean for you? Among other things, it is imperative for you to understand that your screenplay is your sales tool, and its objective is to induce producers, directors, and talent to want to make your movie. In addition to being the absolute best writing you can achieve, the script should be clean, easy to read, and appealing on every level, including a professional presentation using standard industry formatting and correct spelling and grammar. Almost all scripts are sent by e-mail now as PDFs. If a hard copy is requested, the correct binding, down to good-quality brads, is a must. In all cases, the script must be pristine. In a world dominated by no's, you want to give the reader—and everyone else who might see your script—reasons to say yes.

You also want to bear in mind—pretty much constantly—that this is a business of relationships, and that includes you and the reader. It's rare to find a good screenplay, and when a reader does so, he or she often becomes a new writer's first champion. I recall quite vividly reading the coverage report for the screenplay of Charlie Kaufman's *Being John Malkovich,* in which the reader wrote something like, "This script would no doubt be hailed as a masterpiece on the planet on which it was written." While I wasn't in a position at that time to consider the movie, my interest in reading the work of Charlie Kaufman was certainly piqued, and I wasn't alone. The reader's coverage of *Being John Malkovich* generated industry-wide intrigue and called attention to Kaufman's unique and individualistic voice.

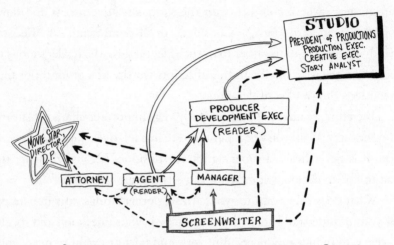

STRAIGHT LINES REPRESENT DIRECT, CONVENTIONAL ROUTES
PERFORATED LINES REPRESENT POSSIBILITIES BASED ON RELATIONSHIPS

The Chain: How a Script Gets Seen and Sold

Again, allow me to reemphasize the importance of readers. Everyone uses them: agents, producers, studios, movie stars, and directors. And, as you can see from the illustration above, different readers may be employed at different stages of your screenplay's trajectory into the market.

It's most likely that your agent will initially pursue a producer, especially if this is your first screenplay to make it to market. The producer will then take it to either the studio or financiers, with attachments or not.

The question "Does your agent and/or manager attend the subsequent meetings?" has been posed in my class. It's been my experience that they usually don't. However, they might want to, depending on your relationship and, frankly, their comfort with the way you present in a room.

Kevin Williamson: From Unknown to A-List Writer—the Power of Relationships

Whenever you have the chance to build relationships, take it. I was the director of development at Woods Entertainment when, on a beautiful spring day, my office received two "hot" specs that needed to be read right away. Everyone dropped everything and began to read the thriller with the fantastically engaging opening sequence of a woman escaping from an asylum. They loved it. I, on the other hand, thought it fell apart after the first act. I then picked up the second screenplay, about a group of teenage kids who planned revenge on their sadistic high school teacher, and found it well written, tongue-in-cheek hilarious, compelling, cinematic, and chock-full of great characters—in short, far superior to the first script. As it turns out, I was a majority of one; everyone else, my producer boss included, dismissed it.

Even though I couldn't get the higher-ups in the company interested in the screenplay, which at the time was called *Killing Mrs. Tingle,* I was in the position to invite the screenwriter, Kevin Williamson, to a meeting to discuss other projects he might be developing. (Little did I know then that Kevin Williamson had written *Killing Mrs. Tingle* while taking classes at the UCLA Extension Writers' Program. No wonder it was so good.)

Williamson came to our office. He was neat and relaxed, articulate and thoughtful. In short, he presented himself in a professional light. I told him what a fan I was of his script and assured him that I would love to read whatever else he might be working on. He accepted the compliment with grace and equanimity. He didn't say anything along the lines of "If you liked it so much, how come you didn't option it?" even though the thought raced through my mind, if not his. My boss, who never read the original screenplay, smiled and agreed. Williamson then spoke in vague terms of the two projects he was working on at the time and mentioned that one of them would be ready in a couple of months. He left after planting that seed. My boss immediately called Williamson's agent after the meeting and said, "We want to see everything he writes."

Months passed, but long story short, because I had evinced interest in Kevin Williamson and took the time to meet him, I was one of the first people who got the chance to read his next screenplay, which eventually was entitled *Scream*.

Scream and its sequels have so far made over $400 million worldwide and launched the spectacular career of Kevin Williamson, who shortly after was able to set up *Killing Mrs. Tingle* (it became *Teaching Mrs. Tingle*) and his seminal television series *Dawson's Creek*. The point is, sometimes a good spec script is enough to launch a career (he subsequently developed *The Vampire Diaries*), and you never know who in the business might be in the position to do it. Here was a writer whose work I really responded to, and the rest is history.

It helped, of course, that the company I worked for had a deal with Miramax Films and the Weinstein brothers always had a special place in their heart for horror films. We were the right producer working for the right studio for that project—but the first step was making that connection and building the relationship.

What Williamson understood is essential: When you get the chance to meet with a producer or studio executive, know that you have one shot to make an impression. I'm not telling you to limit yourself; I'm telling you to focus, because one screenplay in thousands gets sold. If you, as an unproduced writer, have ten scripts and talk about all of them, the producer and the studio executive will start thinking, *How come this writer's got so much material and never been produced?*

So pick your very best work to talk about and stay consistent with the genre of the screenplay that triggered the meeting. Meetings can lead to building a fan base of producers and studio executives around town. Producers are always looking for the next big project. Studio executives have specific assigned writing slots they will need to fill, and it helps them immeasurably to define writers by their fortes; that way, when a suspense thriller writing assignment opens up, they're going to think of that writer they met with who writes great suspense thrillers.

Understanding the Money Behind the Movies
The Producer

Let's say your script gets a "Recommend" and goes to the next level; that might mean your script gets in the hands of an actor, a director, or even a director of photography. Most often, however, producers are the ones most likely to get the ball rolling on your script, and their first task is to determine how your story suits their sensibilities and how the financing for your story will be acquired. A lot of people labor under the misguided notion that producers put up money for movies to be made. In reality, it's the producer's responsibility to find the money to get the movie made.

Your agent and/or manager will undoubtedly help choose the best possible producer for your particular screenplay, but you cannot leave it to them alone. Agents appreciate clients who are proactive and determined in their approach, which includes your own researching of producers and the kinds of projects they pursue. Producers of note have relationships with studios and financial entities, and depending on their track record, they may also have some clout. Scott Rudin is a great producer. His record for financial and artistic successes is extraordinary, so he wields tremendous influence as a producer. So does Jerry Bruckheimer. Check out their credits and you'll understand why. Obviously, you want to align yourself with the strongest producer possible.

Even though you and your agent have agreed that your screenplay is ready to go into production tomorrow, invariably your producer will want you to tinker with it some more. Producers by and large are very smart people. They love movies and have what it takes to make them, but they also have egos. They're going to ask you to make changes. It's inevitable, so keep an open mind. They didn't get where they are by accident.

Still, there are times you will disagree with the changes they ask you to make. And you will make them anyway, because success in this industry is not contingent on a single produced film; it's contingent upon building relationships that constitute a career.

Keep a big-picture perspective. In the best-case scenario, you will be working with these people again and you want to be in it for the long run. So try to implement their vision without selling out your own. Oftentimes, creative compromise can result in inspiration.

Ultimately, a producer will help to package your film, meaning he or she helps get "elements" attached. *Elements* refers to the previously mentioned actors and directors whose names get studios and financiers on board to make the film. Producers also know exactly what studios are looking for and can use their influence to get financiers to agree to back their films.

The Studios

Studios are financial entities that manufacture, market, and distribute product. In contractual terms they are referred to as "the buyer," because they take the ultimate financial risk in promoting your product.

As with every other phase of your professional journey, it's important to make friends everywhere: from the assistant to the creative executive who first championed your screenplay, to the production executive who fought for your project, to the VP of production who's in charge of your project, to the presidents of production, marketing, public relations, and beyond. Never lose sight of the fact that a film studio is a factory and all of its employees function to promote the sale of your project, which is a stepping-stone for your career.

An Alternate Route

The studio system has changed a lot in the past decade. There are fewer studios to speak of and fewer production companies with exclusive deals at studios. Consequently, less funding is allocated for the development of new projects these days. That results in more screenwriters writing more on speculation ("spec").

The upside of this equation is that screenwriters own their work and can sell it to whomever they please. As I discussed at the outset, movie stars and directors are brands and can hold substantial clout when it comes to finding financing in this industry. The good news is that in this new paradigm a lot of actors and directors have their own production companies (for example, George Clooney and Brad Pitt, among many others), which means that your agents and managers will have avenues to package your screenplay before bringing it to the studio for financing. This adds considerable value to your screenplay, so that when you do take it to the studio (or other available financial entities) with the imprimatur of a star or star director, you have a greater shot at getting it made.

Final Pointers and a Word of Encouragement

If all of this were easy, there would be a lot more movies made, and let's face it, they would be better. Writing the screenplay is only half of the equation. Selling it is the other half, and it's even more challenging. Some of the best stories I've ever worked on have gone unproduced. Some of the best people I've ever worked with have moved on to have extraordinary lives and successes in other arenas. There's a lottery-like quality to the way success works in this industry, but if you want to win, you've got to buy a ticket.

In this chapter, I've endeavored to make sense of how things work, but of course many varying truths exist simultaneously, and it's impossible to make sense of it all. Nevertheless, there are some words of guidance I'd like to share to help you in your approach to a career in screenwriting.

- The unreturned phone call is the new no. If someone is interested in your work, they're going to find you. If they're not, three dozen messages or e-mails are not going to make them more inclined. This is the world we live in.

- Don't be one of those people who claim to be a "volcano of ideas." Right away, people know you're an amateur. Writing is hard work that takes enormous concentration and consideration. Show that you are thoughtful, professional, and polished, and that you are infused with passion about your story.

- Be dialed into what is happening in the world. Stay attuned to trends and local and world events. A great true story has an automatic hook to it. Financiers know this. It helps them sell movies. Think *The Social Network*. Think *Argo*.

- Finally, be realistic and patient. Your screenwriting career is a marathon, not a sprint, and each hurdle will take you further. You will sometimes suffer setbacks, and you can use these to make you stronger.

Ultimately, you must find passion and determination through your work, and that passion will translate to the reader, be it agent, producer, or studio executive—and ultimately to the viewer in the darkened theater. As I stated at the start of this chapter, there is no one formula for success in the entertainment industry. Despite all my emphasis on business and branding, I am drawn to a quotation from the poet Samuel Taylor Coleridge, who said, "What comes from the heart, goes to the heart." In the end, you must let your heart be your guide. Use it to light your path and shine it upon others. The paradigm shifts when someone does something startling and original, and you can be that someone.

CHAPTER 15

Launching and Sustaining
a Feature Film Writing Career

by Deborah Dean Davis

Hello, I am Deborah Dean Davis and . . . I am a writer.

I have been paid to write for Steven Spielberg, Ivan Reitman, and Meg Ryan (twice). I wrote *It Takes Two*, Mary-Kate and Ashley Olsen's highest-grossing film. I wrote a ton of TV at the beginning of my career, including multiple episodes of *Knight Rider; Magnum, P.I.; The Fall Guy; The Incredible Hulk;* and *Star Trek: The Next Generation*. If I had worked a regular job, say, at Trader Joe's . . . day in and day out, I would have ended up making the same amount of money. Yes, on occasion, I have depended on the kindness of strangers. But I've never *had* to sleep on anyone's couch. Although there have been some dry periods, for the most part it's been a terrific ride.

There have been many marriages, as many divorces, trips all over the world, homes purchased and sold, one daughter sent to private schools and UC Berkeley. I own one pair of Gucci shoes and I've hosted more dinner parties than anyone you know, unless you know Martha Stewart. All the above-mentioned "life" was paid for with the money I have made writing. That, I hope, makes me crazy enough to tackle the delicious title seen above and gives you the confidence to be open to what I have to share with you.

Every time I teach my UCLA Extension Writers' Program seminar, "Selling Yourself and Your Work: The Business of Being a Screenwriter," the primary questions my students are desperate to have answered all deal with . . . money. How much did you sell your first screenplay for? Answer: scale. How many screenplays have you sold? Answer: more than twenty. How long before you could stop your day job? Answer: what day job? This need for quantifying might stem from an innate lack of security or from fear, but more likely, students just want some concrete assurance that being a writer makes sense. I tell them that it's how you spend your life that counts, that the way you spend your life should feed your spirit, and if writing does that, the choice to commit to this writing thing becomes clearer.

Hopefully, this chapter will help you with any lingering commitment issues and make becoming a feature film writer seem more doable by giving you lots of practical tips and guidance on how to declare and prepare yourself as a writer, how to open career doors (yes, perseverance and grooming count!), and how to keep those doors open over the long haul by keeping your creativity, health, writing habits, and professional skills sharp and intact. My assumption is that each and every one of you reading this miraculous book is a writer, hallowed be thy name.

Launching Your Feature Film Writing Career

There are too many well-documented and wildly diverse ways successful feature film writers have broken into the business for anyone to claim there is an exact formula. And anyone who tells you otherwise is blowing smoke up your ass. Each and every one of you must find and follow your unique path to achieve your personal and definitive career launch.

You might win a prestigious screenplay contest. You could begin by signing with an agent or selling a spec screenplay. You could be hired for an internship at a high-profile production company (one of my Writers' Program students just started interning for Academy Award–winning producer Dan Jinks [*American Beauty, Milk*]). Maybe signing with an understanding manager is right for you. Or you could move from Nebraska to Hollywood and land the punishing but fruitful job of PA (production assistant) in a writers' room on a hit TV show.

Many roads can lead to launching your life as a screenwriter, and the only proven way to find the right road for you is to get out of the house and start walking. That said, there are a few hundred potholes in each and every road, so here's some advice that I share with my students to make their journey smoother, faster, and more productive.

Come Out of the Closet

Repeat after me: "I am a writer!" Sorry, I can't hear you. Again. "I am a writer!!!" That was better. Not great, but better.

A guy I knew became a PA at Universal Studios. The writing staff loved the way he grasped the nuances of their coffee orders. But he never told them he was a writer, and his big break was squandered. If you ever want anyone to take you seriously, you must begin by taking yourself seriously. Tell *everyone* that you are a writer. If you're shy, start small. Go to any drive-through restaurant and when the machine asks what you want say, "I'm a writer and I want two tacos and a Coke." Declare yourself!

I know, I know, coming out of the writer closet is hard for a lot of writers to embrace. "Why can't I just write, like, late at night, when no one knows what I'm doing, so no one will, like, ask to read what I'm writing?" Isn't screenwriting the perfect career choice for a thinker, an introvert, an intellectual, an agoraphobic? There is nothing wrong with being an introvert, but this is *show* business, and those of you who want to write for the big screen must, yourself, be willing to join the big party. Why? In one word: trust.

There is no way you can launch or sustain a feature film writing career without inspiring trust in other professionals: agents, producers, directors, actors, studio executives. You must be able to say, "I am a writer."

Everything Is Really Important, Even Your Shoes

The best example I have that there is no detail too small or too obvious for you to concern yourself with when undertaking the task of becoming a screenwriter is the following. The late, great UCLA basketball coach John Wooden used to eat at a deli near my home in Encino every Wednesday. One day I asked him, "What is the most important thing you taught every athlete on every one of your teams?" Well into his nineties, Coach Wooden answered without hesitation: "The most important lesson was the first: how to put on your socks and shoes. No creases in the socks or you'll get bad blisters and that'll affect your game." He's right, you know. Take care to avoid blisters that will affect your game.

Blisters, in the case of a professional screenwriter, could be tardiness, bad breath, inappropriate clothing, dirty hair, or an iPhone with "Ass Like That" by Eminem for a ringtone. Is it right to be "green" and conserve paper? Yes. Should you print your sample script on the back of your college paper on venereal disease? No!

You might be thinking, *Shoes?!* Actually, shoes are pretty darn important, too. Most of the time, the offices that writers find themselves in have chairs or sofas with nowhere to hide their feet. Don't get caught wearing the same shoes you wore yesterday to take your puppy to the dog park, because the people you're selling to aren't even listening to your story; they're looking at your nasty-ass shoes. So buy a pair of meeting shoes. I'm sorry. I know you're a starving artist! Google "shoe repair" and learn about eBay, Loehmann's, Nordstrom Rack, and Target. It's better to wear an unscuffed, stylish pair of cheap shoes than a ratty, dirty, scuffed pair of Pradas.

Also, it's safe to assume that everything, from the shoes up, is just as important. *Do not sabotage yourself.* There is no such thing as an unimportant detail here. John Wooden's teams won a ton of NCAA championships. There's a lot to be said for avoiding blisters.

"Don't Ever Let Anyone Stop You from Dreaming" (and If Necessary, Break Up with the Witch/Bastard)

There is a scene in the really ancient film *National Velvet* starring twelve-year-old Elizabeth Taylor that kills me. I don't even have to watch it to get goose bumps. The already-gorgeous Elizabeth plays Velvet Brown, a country girl with a passion for horses who ends up training a horse she wins in a lottery for England's most famous race. Velvet sits at her desk in an old-fashioned rural schoolhouse, daydreaming, staring out the window. She's probably imagining all the iconic horse jumping to come. Anyway, she gets in a lot of trouble for not paying attention to the teacher. When her big-boned mom finds out why Velvet had to stay after school, you expect big-time trouble. Instead, her mother firmly tells her darling daughter that there is nothing more important in life than . . . dreaming. "Don't ever let anyone stop you from dreaming." Tears. Tissue. Thank you.

Why does this little inconsequential scene resonate? Because when you commit to living the life of the artist, when you long to become a screenwriter, you spend a great portion of your time looking out the window. I am very proud of my student Terrence Michael, who stuck with his dream of being a writer by studying his craft at night, after work, eventually entering and winning second place in the 2010 UCLA Extension Screenplay Competition. That led to his getting an agent, a manager, a spot on the prestigious Black List, and a couple of projects set up. I am equally proud of my two students who got . . . divorced.

Listen up! If there is someone in your daily life who gives you crap about staring out the window, get rid of them. To launch your career, you need to be surrounded by people who nurture your creativity. Fact. This doesn't mean you can't get notes on your pages from your mom. It means you need to get a second job and move out if she insists that taking out the garbage is more important than "that nonsense" you keep "wasting your time with" on that expensive laptop you bought.

In *Tropic of Capricorn,* Henry Miller says, "I had to learn, as I soon did, that one must give up everything and not do anything else but write; that one must write and write and write, even if everybody else in the world advises you against it, even if nobody believes in you. Perhaps one does it because nobody believes; perhaps the real secret lies in making people believe."

Screenwriter-turned-psychotherapist Dennis Palumbo, writing about the ability of a screenwriter to keep on keeping on in *Writing from the Inside Out,* says, "Limit contact with non-supportive family and friends. A seemingly obvious suggestion, I'm always stunned at how often writer clients will reveal their creative concerns to the wrong people in their lives, folks whose own agendas—unconsciously or not—contribute to reinforcing the most self-defeating aspects of a writer's personality. Avoid such people like the plague. Turn off your phone's ringer, put a 'condemned' sign outside your apartment building, assume a false identity, and move to Cairo—whatever it takes!"

I divorced one of my husbands after I sold a two-hundred-page bible for a TV series to NBC, and he said, "Terrific! Now I don't have to read it. I'll just watch it." Ummm, no, not so much. The people who make you feel foolish for staring out the window don't belong in your day-to-day life. Or you can move to Cairo. Your choice.

Join a Gym, Eat Healthy, Be Fit

This is my least-favorite thing to talk about. It just doesn't seem fair that a writer should have to worry about this kind of thing. I mean, we just sit and type, right? Wrong. Writing is hard work. Real research (not just firing up Wikipedia) is often physically demanding. When Paramount Studios hired me to write a romantic comedy that took place in the world of heavyweight boxing, I trained/researched for two weeks with the current heavyweight contender at Caesars Palace. I'm talking road work (seven miles) every morning at five A.M. If that doesn't convince you, then there are many annoying articles by brilliant doctors connecting brain health to physical health. Also, consider the actors and actresses you write for. Have you seen Jonah Hill?! Even he lost weight. Eventually, someone is going to want to meet you face-to-face, and every bit of anthropological research supports that the healthier you are, the more others will be drawn to you and listen to your ideas, and they'll even be more apt to give you a job.

Sign Up for an Acting Class

Let's skip over the obvious reason this is a good idea: You want to write for actors, so you might want to find out what it's like to be one. One of the first things I ask my students to do is write down the five things they feel they need to do in order to make their dream of becoming a professional screenwriter a reality. Only one student, ever, listed taking an acting class on her original to-do list. At the end of the seminar, 99 percent of them write "Take an acting class" in the number one slot.

Why? Because to become a good storyteller, you must be able to master the art of sincere and entertaining communication, and most writers need professional training to learn how to do that. Speaking words will not elicit emotions in others if you, the writer, are unable to feel and convey your own. You can learn to let down your inhibitions and go for it, whatever "it" is. Acting class will help you in more ways than I can say. Is that you I can hear screaming, "No way!"? Carl Jung said, "Neurotics are people who refuse to suffer." Yes, that was me daring you to take an acting class.

Find and Sign with an Agent/Manager
(Or, How to Turn *No* into *Yes*)

This is usually first on every wannabe writer's to-do list. Agents are terrific. They are superheroes in the realm of calling back 150 people a day.

They are especially wonderful if you never, ever expect them to *get you a job*. You are the only one who can make that happen. Once you understand how huge your part is in becoming a working writer, having an agent and/or a manager will be extremely helpful to you. Hopefully, you are related to someone in the business who can ask an agent to read your work. If that isn't the case, hopefully you are related to someone who knows someone in the business who can ask an agent to read your work.

No? Then be aware that there is a master list of all the agents in the known world available to you at the Writers Guild of America. If you're in Los Angeles, take a drive over to WGA at 7000 West Third Street, Los Angeles, California. Or just log on to the website WGA.org and print that sucker out. Then what? You need to write query letters to agents you carefully select. This is fun. The wonderful news here is that you are a writer, right? This is your weapon, your key to the Emerald City, your lottery ticket. Use it! Make your query letter short, personable, unique (as in your unique voice), punctuation-and-spelling-error-free, and on point. Don't send a query letter to every agent on the list! Make a concerted effort to learn something about the agency/agent you're targeting: what they've sold, who they represent. Make sure you don't waste your time or theirs— e.g., begging a TV agent to represent your spec feature screenplay.

I'm often asked how I got my first agent, and I'll tell you if you promise *not to try this at home*. I was taking classes at UCLA Extension Writers' Program, and I found out that Charlotte Brown, a producer on a TV sitcom that I had written a spec script for, was giving a talk on campus. I sat in the front row. When she asked if there were any questions, I raised my hand. She called on me. I asked, "Will you read the sample script I've written for your show?" She was horrified, and she told me and everyone else in the room how inappropriate my question/request was. She went on to say that, legally, she would never read a script unless it was submitted by an *agent*. My hand shot up again. Of course, she didn't call on me.

After the lecture ended I had a fifty-fifty chance of picking the correct stairwell to catch her: stage left or stage right. I went left. And Miss Charlotte Brown found me waiting in the stairwell like a serial killer. She seemed frightened. I assured her I wished her no harm. All I wanted was the name of an agent, one that she respected, so that I could submit my spec, which I felt confident would then be submitted to her. There was absolutely no way she would recommend an agent. I was taller than her, a lot taller. Maybe that had some bearing on the situation. I don't know. Anyway, despite her animosity, I begged, "Give me a name. Please!"

Finally, she rattled off a string of names that meant nothing to me; they all sounded like legal firms or gynecologists. And then she told me that if she ever found out I had said she'd recommended me . . . there would be hell to pay. I flattened against the wall and she scurried past. The only names I remembered were Robinson and Weintraub. I called them first thing the next morning and left the following message: "Tell Mr. Robinson that Charlotte Brown made me swear to let him know she *did not* recommend me!"

And Stu Robinson thought this was really funny. He wanted to read my script, which he loved, and he signed me as a client. He was my agent for years. I never saw Charlotte Brown again, but I very much appreciate the part she had in *helping* me to get my first agent.

Find and Hire an Entertainment Attorney

This is another entry that should end up on your to-do list if it's not already there. It's also right up there with things I don't like to talk about. When I sold my first spec original screenplay, I did not have my entertainment attorney look over the contract. Yikes! My agent said everything was in order and I was lucky to receive $10,000 option money against $100,000 total sale price, which wasn't payable until production began or within two years—*if* they decided to re-up the option. Cut-and-dried, right? I signed the contract. They flew me to New York to meet the producer and get notes. Very exciting!

Shortly after I turned in the new draft, the producer sold my script (which was legally now *his* script) for $1,250,000 to Orion Pictures. No, I didn't even receive a thank-you note. The producer bought a prime piece of property in Tahiti with "his" money and told me that if I was ever in Tahiti I could stay in his guesthouse. Before you throw up, know that since then, I have made well over a million dollars from other buyers who liked the script and hired me on other projects. Still, I hope I've made my point. Hire an entertainment attorney and have him look at *every contract* before you sign. Five percent (a typical entertainment attorney's fee) of $100,000 is $5,000. That's all it would have cost me to make $1,250,000.

Take Classes at UCLA Extension Writers' Program/Make Friends with Other Writers

The professional writers who teach at UCLA Extension are over-the-moon exceptional. If you don't live in Los Angeles, no problem. You can take Writers' Program's screenwriting classes online, from anywhere in the world. Trust me on this one . . . take a class or two or fifteen. And it's not just about the teachers; the other writers in the class are super-valuable connections.

Sometimes all it takes is a friendly voice urging you to keep plugging away, that writer's block is nothing but a well-disguised breakthrough, and that you have been sitting at your computer so long that you truly need to take a shower, wash your hair, and change your sweatpants. The buddy system, it turns out, works very well both in war and in launching a career as a screenwriter. Find as many writer buddies as you can and hold on tight. Leave No Writer Behind!

Enter Screenplay Contests

Yes! Investigate and enter contests. I am a huge fan of the UCLA Extension screenplay competition for obvious reasons. Since it is limited to Writers' Program students, the chances of placing and accruing significant possible benefits—getting an agent, a manager, maybe even optioning or selling your script—are very good, especially relative to many contests. In addition, there are others with their own distinct advantages. My student Steven Lamm says,

Screenwriting contests vary greatly in principle and prestige. Some contests offer lucrative rewards, generally in proportion with their size. However, for the burgeoning screenwriter the primary benefits are essentially twofold. First and foremost, contests allow one's work to be read. While this benefit seems more or less obvious, getting one's work read in Hollywood should never be taken for granted, especially for a writer at the beginning of his journey. Consequently, work that enters the public domain can lead to management, representation, and even production.

Secondly, contests provide writers a valuable opportunity to receive feedback from professional readers. Of course, every opinion is subjective, yet contest results give writers a range of data points to gauge their current ability. For an additional fee, most contests offer a coverage service detailing the judge's (or judges') specific critique of a script. As aforementioned, contests come in all shapes and sizes. The undoubted champion is the Nicholl Fellowship, totaling over 7,190 entries in 2012. After Nicholl, the pecking order is highly debatable: Sundance Screenwriters Lab, Scriptapalooza, the PAGE International Screenwriting Awards, BlueCat, StoryPros, and the Austin Film Festival are all highly respected contests that have launched various careers.

The bigger competitions offer greater rewards but at the risk of harder competition. Thus, it makes sense to enter some smaller competitions to improve one's chances of success. After all, it only takes one great connection to start turning daydreams into dollars. In general, contests range from $40 to $75 per entry, with prices staggered upward toward the final deadline. Many contests break up their competitions into a variety of genres (action, comedy, etc.) and less often into separate mediums (feature length, short, pilot). As almost any contest can be accessed on-line, almost any contest can be researched online. There are some scammers lurking on the web, so one would be well served to look up user reviews for lesser-known contests on websites such as MovieBytes.com.

Steven's results: *Finalist:* StoryPros, Blazing Quill, the Indie Gathering, Screenwriter Takes All, ScriptVamp. *Winner:* the Texas International Film Festival.

Steven, I think, is most definitely on his "unique path."

Network Like Your Life Depends on It

Give it some thought: Do you know the name of at least one person in the wide world who might be able to help you get your foot in the door? Call that person. That's all there is to it. Check that nagging "if" off your to-do list. You'll get the help or not. Better you should pull the Band-Aid off fast, find out, and move on. But no matter what happens with your second cousin's ex-boyfriend who knows a guy who did something on the last Cameron Diaz film, be open to the possibility that everyone you bump into might be the person who will help you fulfill your dream. Accept invitations anywhere that you might meet anyone. The most miraculous connections can come from the most unlikely encounters.

If you have the opportunity to go to any industry events, make sure you not only go but that you *do not drink anything* at the reception. It is an absolute truth that when you walk around holding a glass in your hand, said hand promises to be cold, wet, and clammy. That is not the hand you want to use when you shake hands with the president of Sony.

Yes, force your way into the airspace of the most important person at the event. Do whatever it takes, other than using tae kwon do. Make eye contact, extend your room-temperature hand, and offer any old generic congratulations. This isn't the person you are out to impress. It's the rest of the room. All eyes are on you, and if you're lucky, the big shot is bored with people trying to get things from her and she just might spend a moment with a nonthreatening struggling wannabe screenwriter. Once your audience with the pope is over, other people will suddenly want to talk to you. Go for it.

In general, remember that *everyone you meet might be the one who helps you realize your dream*. So, play nice, *be* nice. This is different than being phony. Way different. These are good training wheels for life. If we treat everyone we meet with a degree of respect, a shred of importance, good things will happen whether or not the person we are kind to is the one who ends up giving us a feature film assignment.

Personal Networking Story #1

I was twenty-three years old and the only credit on my résumé was the Halloween show at Six Flags Magic Mountain. I was at a club and a stranger asked if she could sit at my table. I was nice. She ended up being a temp at Universal. I told her I was a writer. A week later she snuck me onto the lot and into a writers' meeting for a TV show. I was the only one out of twenty professional writers that the producer asked to stay after the meeting. I was hired to write my first prime-time teleplay. Being a nice person will get you places. You gotta pack the gear to win the assignment.

Many years later . . .

Personal Networking Story # 2

I received a phone call from the assistant to an assistant at a prominent Disney production company. I had befriended this young woman when I openly chastised her boss, a guy I was trying to sell a pitch to, for whacking her in the head when she pressed the wrong button on the computer. Not cool. A few months later she called me . . . out of the blue. I remembered her name. Jennifer said, "I was just wondering, do you know anything about seven-year-old girls?" I said, "Let me put my seven-year-old daughter on the line and let her answer that question for you." This "networking" ended up getting me my feature assignment from Warner Bros. to write *It Takes Two* for Mary-Kate and Ashley Olsen. Nuff said.

Sustaining Your Feature Film Writing Career

Congratulations! Your feature film writing career is officially *launched*! Now, like any newlywed, you will look at your new career/life partner, each and every morning, and either wonder, *What have I done?!* or realize that true commitment must be nurtured and reconfirmed on a daily basis. You must sustain what you have fought to achieve. Do you hear the theme music from *The Lion King* yet? Protect your spot in the sun, your baby career, with the fierce will of a majestic lion/lioness. Again, there are numerous tips and many pitfalls. Here are a few.

Read Writers Who Write a Whole Lot Better Than You Do

It's not that I don't think reading is important while launching—I just happen to believe it's more useful *after* you've found your unique voice. For instance: Now that you've been hired to write a film about an expatriate in pre–World War II Paris, if you don't have a pile of Henry Miller books on your bedside table, let me just say, you are nuts. Reading *exceptional* authors is number one on my to-do list. And I do actually mean exceptional.

Read the great writers who have come before you. If the theme of your film tries to answer the philosophical question "Is God dead?" stop watching reality television! Start reading Dostoyevsky, who is not just another dead Russian but is recognized by most critics as the best writer of all things psychological in world literature. You will also deepen your understanding of syntax, vocabulary, history, and theology. Read to find true inspiration, flawless character development, and the all-important, elusive, and critical mark that separates the beginner from the professional writer: subtext!

Those of you who have already logged on to your favorite website and ordered *Wuthering Heights* by Emily Brontë can stop reading this section right now. For the rest of you, I suggest the following: Spend half the time you waste procrastinating by reading a classic piece of literature. Knut Hamsun, Balzac, Thomas Mann, Joyce Carol Oates, Thoreau, Proust, Rousseau, Rimbaud, Gabriel García Márquez, Ralph Ellison, Lao-tzu, Jane Austen, Mark Twain, Lillian Hellman, Hermann Hesse, Goethe, Walt Whitman, Dorothy Parker! Even if what you pick up has no bearing on what you're working on—read, read, read. Then write, write, write.

Do Not Die of Alcoholism

So this is a strange subheading. And we do all need to die of something, right? It's just that during my sojourn in show business I have met many extremely talented humans. And some of them were drinkers. Accent on *were*. Writers are alone a lot of the time. Silence is our friend. Many writers prefer working late at night. We struggle, fail, and take it all too personally. Writers, purposely or not, paint themselves into corner after corner in the hopes that their story will be more surprising and exciting. And what about that writer's block?!

In short, the life of a professional screenwriter is not easy. And sometimes—I get it—the idea of having a glass of wine to relax seems medicinal. It *is* medicinal. The problem comes when what follows the bottle of Pinot are good pages, great pages, your *best* pages. Suddenly, alcohol is a necessary tool before every writing session, every new scene, every meeting, every morning, every hour. Then, long before you've said what you need to say, learned what you need to learn, entertained the world in a way only you can with your unique voice . . . it's over. Your career. Your marriage. Your life.

You Really Need to Take a Vacation

Almost every time I finished writing a one-hour television show, I would go to Europe. I wrote a lot of one-hour television shows. At one point, I remember feeling guilty that I would be in Bucharest during pilot season. I called my agent and had a long chat with her. I was ready to change my plans if she thought it was in my career's best interest. Devra Lieb of Hohman Maybank Lieb simply said, "No! Go! Have a great time! A writer's job is to experience life and then write about it." Devra is in good company with screenwriter Bo Goldman, who won Academy Awards for *One Flew over the Cuckoo's Nest* and *Melvin and Howard,* and also wrote *Meet Joe Black, Scent of a Woman,* and *The Flamingo Kid.* Mr. Goldman said, "Live life. Be in life. Try to tell the truth about it."

Every Day You Must Sit Down and . . . *Write*

Write every day. This is your life, your job, so stop thinking about it and start doing it. People ask me what to do about writer's block. The answer is: Write about your writer's block. You will, I swear, end up writing down the exact reason you're blocked. The late, great writer-director Preston Sturges said, "When the last dime is gone, I'll sit out on the curb with a pencil and a ten-cent notebook, and start the whole thing all over again."

I was down a few years ago and a talented producer, Bob Shapiro, took me out for sushi. I whined about how crappy I was feeling and how much I wanted to get back to work and Bob, who produced *Empire of the Sun* and *Confessions of a Teenage Drama Queen,* yelled at me. He said, "I wish I could get up in the morning and produce a motion picture, just because I want to. But I can't. I need a studio, a script, a crew, actors, a deal. Shame on you! All you need is piece of paper and a pencil. You want to split some sashimi?"

I went home and sat down at my desk. I actually looked at a blank sheet of paper for a few minutes. I sharpened a pencil. I love the way that smells. Then I started an original screenplay, which I later sold. Let me be less obtuse: If you don't write every day (like this is a real job), you probably aren't going to sustain much of anything but the lingering romantic urge to live the life of a feature film writer.

Live Beneath Your Means

Save your money . . . because this might be the last time you work. (Ha ha ha.) No, seriously, save your money because this might be the last time you work. Young people today say, "It's not like it was when you started in the business." And they speak the truth. To sustain your career, you need to be aware that there will be, more than likely, gaps between the sales that you make, and sometimes these gaps can last for years. Your yearly income can fluctuate more than Texas weather during tornado season. Given this reality, it would be so smart for you *not* to totally quit your day job. Just as struggling actors wait tables, struggling screenwriters do . . . something.

Once you are a firmly established screenwriter, don't believe your press! Your agent will tell you that the big sale you just made is going to make you the hottest writer in show business, that everyone is going to want to hire you, that you are going to be soooo wealthy! Listen to me: You need to wait until the checks clear your bank. Don't put in an offer on that Tuscan mansion in Malibu, not yet. Wait for the promise of all those magnificent job offers to turn into contracts and for the contracts to turn into screenplays and for the screenplays to turn into produced films. And now that you've mastered the patience of a bona fide feature film writer, you might as well wait for the first residuals from DVD sales. Wait.

A few sage colleagues I have met in my travels truly had this saving-their-money thing down. One left a writer-producer job on a major hit TV series, took his WGA pension early, bought a very expensive sailboat, and left for the South Pacific . . . he never came back. Another retired to a spacious ranch in Montana. Both of these gentlemen agreed on one thing: *Live beneath your means.* It worked for them and it will work for you.

Don't Be Overly Possessive with Your Ideas

It is not possible to sustain a screenwriting career without a vast well-spring of original ideas (this includes the original idea to adapt a book).

So how do you come up with all those many and varied ideas for all those possible films? How do you turn your favorite notion into a full-bodied story? How do you test your many themes, situations, characters, and/or high concepts on real people? I believe when a friendly waiter, butcher, banker, mechanic, or CPA asks, "What are you working on?" it is valuable to answer freely. Why not ask them if they would go to see a film about Einstein's Theory of Relativity being disproven by neutrinos? It is my experience that the more open you are with your ideas, the more you will have.

Conversely, writers who are afraid of discussing their work with anyone seem enthusiasm-challenged and sometimes fall short of actually bringing a good idea to fruition. Fear cannot be your middle name. I am a writer! I have a story! What's remarkable is that your story will grow, deepen, and change according to your audience's questions, reactions, and laughter, or, in some cases, their lack of laughter. Every writer is a giant eye making its way through the world, looking at things more closely than the average eye. So, if this feels right for you, go ahead and make your world your writing partner.

Again, my favorite guy, Henry Miller, says, "Writing, like life itself, is a voyage of discovery. The adventure is a metaphysical one: it is a way of approaching life indirectly, of acquiring a total rather than a partial view of the universe. The writer lives between the upper and lower worlds: he takes the path in order eventually to become that path himself."

Let's Talk Meetings!

The meeting is God . . . okay, maybe not God, exactly. But the meeting is the plasma that keeps our industry alive. Obviously, I'm talking about those rare chances when you are "invited" into a real, honest-to-goodness office at an iconic, world-famous studio to meet with a person who can say the magic word. And that word is—drum roll—*yes!* How does one get to that meeting? Frankly, the only way is through a series of other, far less glamorous meetings. The bottom line is this: Every exchange with every human might lead you into *the* meeting that will change your life and pay off your mortgage. There are lots and lots of things that will help make your meeting a success. Here are some of them.

Wear Clothing That Reflects Your Genre

Guys, you have it made. A pair of jeans, a white shirt (button-down or T-shirt), and a black jacket (wide range from designer cashmere to Gap zip-up) always works. Today, the sloppy writer is in. Sloppy isn't as easy as it looks. It takes finesse. The wardrobe department on the TV Series *House M.D.* washed, ironed, and stuffed clothing in a small drawer for days on end to achieve Dr. Gregory House's signature slept-in look. Please don't do that. But an old, clean, faded T-shirt that says Led Zeppelin on it could be the perfect touch if you're pitching a film with a retro feel. Thriller writers! Please do not wear brightly colored Hawaiian shirts to your meetings. Rom-com writers! Do not go in dressed like you just came from a funeral. This isn't brain surgery.

Don't Be Late

Forget that. Get there early. Professional athletes do not arrive at the stadium just as the whistle blows. The higher the stakes, the earlier they arrive. They stretch, they meditate, they team-build. You need to do all of this. Om. Pray. Center. Sing out as loudly as possible to your favorite music . . . all the way to the meeting. Open your throat. The meeting starts before you leave the house. Don't let your family intrude on your preparation. "I'm thinking!" seems to work at my house.

When the Receptionist Asks If You Want Something to Drink, Don't Be Wishy-Washy

You are on your way into a room to try to talk someone into paying you half a million dollars to write a screenplay that they'll have to invest another hundred million dollars in to actually make. You must know if you want bottled water or a can of soda!

And remember, the receptionist graduated from Columbia/Duke/

Brown/Berkeley. This brainiac who just asked if you want water is capable of real opinions and has an extraordinary memory. Also, he or she might be the first person to read your next spec script. Do I need to go on here?

Listen to the Person You Are Meeting With

Yes, you have been invited into this office to share your story, your vision. And this means you are going to be doing a lot of talking. But someone might interrupt you with a question. That's a terrific sign. And, if the exec is truly engaged, she might have a comment. *Listen to her. Let her talk as long as she wants,* then say, "Wow. I never thought of that. That's a great idea." This little bit of ass kissing shows the person you are meeting with that you're willing to collaborate. Execs will want to work with you more because of this.

And if this is a notes meeting . . . be sure to take seriously all of the notes you are given, even the beyond-general note to "make it better." This does *not* mean you must be *exact* in executing every little note (certainly not the truly bad ones). The secret of success here is just exactly like that annoying general note: Make your script better. Turn in a second draft with little or no "draft dust" (those loose ends that lazy writers forget to go back and adjust after making notated changes). Make it a boatload better than your original script and everyone will be thrilled! Even you.

Be Tough

No matter how badly a meeting goes, and sometimes they do . . . never tell the person you're meeting with to f*#k off and die. This, obviously, burns a bridge, and you should try as hard as possible to burn as few bridges as possible. Leave? Only if the building is on fire. Again, you are a writer. Be creative.

Laugh at Yourself

Have fun! Show the buyer that working with you will be fun. Show business may seem glamorous, but truth be told, there's day-in-and-day-out drudgery for those "suits" who have to go into the office every day and listen to weirdos pitch a script about a motorcycle gang that crashes a carnival starring Justin Bieber. ("The soundtrack would be awesome!") These poor development people can use a break, a moment of levity. And if said fun has something to do with you sharing with them that your iPhone just fell in the toilet in their restroom . . . so be it.

Don't Be Negative
Unless you're Larry David.

Argue Only for Your Writing . . .
. . . not about politics or any other off-topic issue. Don't be an idiot. That's what Thanksgiving dinner with the family is for.

Try Not to Accept Sexual Advances
It's fine to continue the meeting by going salsa dancing with a potential buyer to talk further about your fabulous idea, right? Wrong! Absolute suicide! Even if you're attracted to the buyer and the buyer is attracted to you and everyone is single, do not accept a ride in that new Porsche. Why? Because once you do, you have changed roles and now you are no longer in the writer's seat. You are now a crash dummy. How do you get out of it? Lie. Repeat after me: "Oh, I'd love to, but I have a huge meeting at Warner's to prepare for."

Know That You Will Fail More Than You Succeed
Sorry. Henry Miller said,

> In the ultimate sense, the world itself is pregnant with failure, is the perfect manifestation of imperfection, of the consciousness of failure. In the realization of this, failure is itself eliminated. Like the primal spirit of the universe, like the unshakable Absolute, the One, the All, the creator, i.e., the artist, expresses himself by and through imperfection. It is the stuff of life, the very sign of living-ness. One gets nearer to the heart of truth, which I suppose is the

ultimate aim of the writer, in the measure that he ceases to struggle, in the measure that he abandons the will. The great writer is the very symbol of life, of the non-perfect.

And know that there is no way for me to write a list of all of the things you need to do to make *all of your meetings successful.* Be aware and forewarned that winning an assignment in show business, in the current financial climate, is like hunting elk with a crossbow. You must be well rehearsed, confident, friendly, and in your personal zone.

Know What Your Personal Zone Is
(Note: This could require therapy.)

Tips for Taking the Lunch Meeting
Don't eat salad or any other food that might take up too much of your attention or end up in your teeth. Distraction is no good. So, *do not order your favorite food.* Stay focused on the sale, not the meal. And do not order exactly what the buyer orders. Have a mind of your own. Be nice to the waiter/waitress. This third party might like you and thereby make the buyer more apt to feel comfortable liking you as well.

One Tip for Taking the Phone Conference Meeting
Congratulations! You probably already got the job. I, personally, suck at these meetings, although a student at the last Writers' Program seminar I taught gave me a tip. Use the names of the people on the other end of the phone more than you would if you were in the room with them. This, she swears, makes phone conferencing more personal. I'm going to give it a try.

Tips for Taking the "Let's Grab a Cup of Coffee" Meeting
Be prepared with an exact location of a Starbucks, Peet's, or Coffee Bean near the studios and canyons (both Valley side and Westside) so you can offer a concrete place to meet for coffee. Be early. Buy your own coffee if you get there before the exec.

Tips for Taking the "Let's Grab a Drink" Meeting

Liquid courage, right?! If your enthusiasm is brightened and your tongue is loosened to the point of, finally, being able to spew your passion for your story and totally keep your wits about you . . . go for it!

But remember that every meeting is 100 percent about opportunity. And drinking too much is a sure way for you to miss yours. I'm just saying, club soda and lime comes to mind. Even if the buyer has had two Long Island iced teas and isn't really paying too much attention to you anyway, stay present and look for any possible way to make something good happen for yourself. This may be something human, like offering to drive the buyer home if he can't get a cab. Drinks meetings are about communication. This is business.

Meeting Preparation

When going into a meeting with your producer, your agent, talent, or even a writing partner you've known for twenty years, make sure you go over who will say what. It is horrifying when the person sitting next to you on the couch goes down in flames. She might say something like, "I told you that wouldn't work." He might blurt out who did it just seconds into a convoluted mystery pitch. In an effort to have a modicum of control, make a plan with the people on your team long before you're sitting in the outer office pretending you're not nervous.

Pitching: Practice Makes Perfect

During my Writers' Program seminar, I give students the experience of pitching in a real honest-to-goodness meeting atmosphere. I also find that they learn a lot when I share some of my *horror meetings from hell* because most of the time, once you get in an office, the meetings surprise the pants off of you. Meetings are with real people, and sometimes they have PMS, or a toothache, or just lost a ton of money playing poker the night before. I once pitched a romantic comedy to an executive at 20th Century Fox and when I spoke the words, "He's *not* Prince Charming," the executive burst into tears. How would you handle something like this?

Will weird things happen at every meeting? No! But that's just because not one single meeting is exactly like any other. And what constitutes weird, anyway? Is it weird for a producer to hand you a sunflower seed to put on your tongue so his pet African gray parrot can stick his head in your mouth to retrieve it? Yes! Very weird! And it happened. I swear.

So, *anything can happen,* and the truth of the matter is that if the only thing you are prepared for is benign meetings, you are at a terrible disadvantage. So, that said, here are some outlandish things that *really happened.* As you read these examples, ask yourself, "What would I do in a similar situation?" If running as fast as you can out of the meeting is high on your list of reactions, you need to rethink becoming a screenwriter.

- *What if . . .* all the producer wants to talk about is how good kale is for your colon and how being "regular" is of primary importance? And your pitch *isn't* about being a kale farmer?

- *What if . . .* the development executive has just received a toy remote-control helicopter and never stops buzzing it around your head throughout your pitch?

- *What if . . .* an award-winning producer, estranged from his father for more than twenty-five years, is so touched by your pitch that he tears up and telephones his dad, but is so overcome with emotion, he can't speak and hands the phone to you?

- *What if . . .* the president of the company stops you mid-pitch and asks if your movie could be made into a Happy Meal for McDonald's?

- *What if . . .* tomorrow is the distracted buyer's wedding anniversary and he asks you to go through the Tiffany catalog to pick out a present for his wife?

- *What if . . .* the person you've been waiting months to get a meeting with has taken some medication and finds it physically impossible to stop farting throughout the entire meeting?

Thinking on your feet, improvisation, staying focused, and being able to roll with the punches are skills actors learn but most screenwriters are never taught. That's a shame. Because the truth is, once you go into a meeting, you are still a writer, but you are also a salesperson. By the way, when you make anyone cry while telling your story, it's a good thing. You have moved someone with your well-thought-out words. After all is said and done, this is why we do what we do.

Know too that meetings can be successful even when you don't end up with a sale. And successful meetings beget more meetings. And more meetings increase your chances to score a big fat juicy sale. Persistence is the key. So, help the producer pick out a Tiffany bracelet for his wife. Then warmly wish him a happy anniversary! We are all human beings. It's okay to make friends. It takes some people years to get to the point where they are taken seriously enough to even set up a meeting; try not to blow your moment in the sun.

So what if the guy is farting! I mean, really. What did I do? I asked for a Diet Coke because when I drink it I'm a burping machine and those burps are nasty. I embarrassed myself so the farting producer wouldn't be the only one in the room who was embarrassed. Level the playing field whenever possible.

Writers Are Always at the Beginning

Five-four-three-two-one—*blast off*! Your career rockets across a powder-blue sky. The powerful g-force hits you when you deposit your first $90,000 residual check. The feeling of zero gravity is exhilarating when you lay your brilliant head down on your pillow the first night you go to sleep as a successful screenwriter—but remember you are always at the beginning.

Tomorrow you need to look out the window and dream up your next big idea. It's easier to tell people you're a writer now, but the action is still necessary because networking is still important. You need to leave even earlier for those meetings. People expect more from you now. You have a real job. Your mind has transmogrified into a voice that is no longer unheard in the proverbial forest. That, my darlings, makes you dangerous, valuable, and irreplaceable. Sustain your screenwriting career with respect for your craft, yourself, and others. Sustenance is quite simply . . . food. So be sure to remember to treasure and feed the fire of your calling.

There is no conclusion here. There is only the blank page. Fully embrace the lifestyle of a screenwriter, day to day, week to week . . . and the years will stack up like poker chips. Warning: Once you become a professional writer, know that you will never stop. You will write until the day you die. Your spirit will take on a different hue. And even when you fail . . . you will keep on writing. And if you never succeed in a monetary sense, I promise you this . . . you will find yourself. That is no small wonder, no small gift, no small achievement. All this is possible as long as you make your life your art.

Repeat after me: I am a writer!

ABOUT THE EDITOR AND CONTRIBUTORS

Editor

Linda Venis, PhD, is the director of the Department of the Arts at UCLA Extension, where for more than two decades she has guided the growth of the Writers' Program into the nation's largest screenwriting and creative program. Dr. Venis has taught at UCLA and USC and is the recipient of the UCLA Distinguished Teaching Award. She lives in Los Angeles, California, with her husband, Gary Berg, and daughter, Laura.

Editorial Board

Ellen Byron
Peter Dunne
Cindy Davis
Tom Lazarus
Steve Mazur
Billy Mernit
Linda Palmer

Ellen Sandler
Steve Sohmer
Victoria Wisdom

Contributing Authors

Chrysanthy Balis, WGA member; credits include the Paramount release *Asylum;* projects in development with CBS, USA Network, Flody Co. Productions.

Jon Bernstein, WGA member; credits include Disney's *Meet the Robinsons; Beautiful;* and *Ringmaster.* He has written for DreamWorks, Paramount, and Twentieth Century Fox.

Cindy Davis, WGA member; credits include the English-language screenplay for Hayao Miyazaki's Oscar-winning film *Spirited Away, My Neighbor Totoro,* and the Oscar-nominated *Howl's Moving Castle.* She has written for Pixar, Working Title, Miramax, and Disney.

Deborah Dean Davis, WGA member; credits include *It Takes Two, Little Rascals II,* and *Scorpio Rising.* Her film *Keeping House* is currently in development with Original Film and Sony Pictures.

Philip Eisner, WGA member; credits include *Event Horizon* and *Firestarter 2: Rekindled.* He has been a contract writer for Scott Rudin Productions, Robert De Niro's Tribeca Productions, Edward R. Pressman, TriStar, and Universal Pictures.

Juliet Aires Giglio, WGA member; credits include *Pizza My Heart, Noah,* and *Return to Halloweentown.* She was a story consultant on the Disney animated feature film *Tarzan* and has developed projects for Paramount, Warner Bros., and Universal Pictures.

Andy Guerdat, WGA member; has sold feature screenplays to 20th Century Fox, MGM, Walt Disney Studios, and Village Roadshow Pictures/Warner Bros. Credits include movies for Viacom Pictures/Showtime, the Disney Sunday Movie, and NBC.

Karl Iglesias, screenwriter and author of *Writing for Emotional*

Impact and *The 101 Habits of Highly Successful Screenwriters;* former development executive for Samson Entertainment whose feature film *America Reconquered* is in pre-production in France.

Steve Mazur, WGA member; credits include cowriting the feature films *Liar Liar, The Little Rascals,* and *Heartbreakers.* He wrote the teleplays *The Crooked E: The Unshredded Truth About Enron* for CBS and *Wedding Wars* for A&E.

Billy Mernit, WGA member; screenwriter, story analyst for Universal Pictures, and consultant. He is the author of *Writing the Romantic Comedy* (HarperCollins) and the novel *Imagine Me and You* (Shaye Areheart/Random House).

Quinton Peeples, WGA member; former writer/executive story editor for ABC's *FlashForward.* He directed the film *Joyride,* starring Tobey Maguire and Benicio Del Toro; TV credits include *The Moving of Sophia Myles, The Secret Path,* and *Heart Full of Rain.*

Laurence Rosenthal, WGA member; independent producer and development executive. At Woods Entertainment he supervised the development of *Scream, Beautiful Girls, Things to Do in Denver When You're Dead, Cop Land,* and *Citizen Ruth.*

Dan Vining, WGA member; screenwriter and novelist whose feature film credits include *Black Dog* for Universal Pictures and *Plain Clothes* for Paramount. He has written screenplays for Walt Disney Pictures, MGM, Paramount, and Showtime; his latest novel is *Among the Living.*

Michael Weiss, WGA member; former vice president of production for Miramax Films whose produced credits include *Journey to the Center of the Earth* and *I'll Always Know What You Did Last Summer.* He has written for Warner Bros., Sony, New Line, MGM, and Cartoon Network.

INDEX

INDEX

INDEX

INDEX

INDEX

INDEX